THE GHOST IN GENERAL PATTON'S THIRD ARMY

THE GHOST IN GENERAL PATTON'S THIRD ARMY

THE MEMOIRS OF EUGENE G. SCHULZ DURING HIS SERVICE IN THE UNITED STATES ARMY IN WORLD WAR II

To Alize,

Enjoy my stories and God Bless!

Eugene G. Schulz

Eugene G. Schulz

To order additional copies of this book, contact:
Xlibris Corporation
1-888-795-4274
www.Xlibris.com
Orders@Xlibris.com

THE AUTHOR

Eugene G. Schulz
Sergeant, XX Corps, United States Army
ASN: 36296972

My Mantra

I believed the promise of God that He would be with me during all the days that I served in the United States Army. When Joshua was ready to lead the Nation of Israel into Canaan, the Promised Land, the LORD gave him this command, which was my prayer.

Be strong and courageous. Do not be terrified; do not be discouraged, for the LORD your God will be with you wherever you go (Joshua 1:9).

TABLE OF CONTENTS

IMAGES

CHAPTER 1

The Desert Training Center

IT WAS A NORMAL SUNDAY in early winter in the small northern Wisconsin town of Clintonville, having a population of thirty-two hundred. I went to church with my parents in the morning. After eating a wonderful chicken dinner prepared by my mother, my dad took his customary spot on the couch in the living room for his Sunday afternoon nap. Mom sat in the soft easy chair reading a church magazine, and I sat at a card table working on my favorite hobby, building model airplanes from balsa wood. Most teenaged boys were involved in this kind of activity, and after I had built several American fighter planes, I decided to make a submarine. On this day, I was putting the finishing touches on my sub, and I was very proud of finishing this complicated project.

The Motorola radio in the corner of the living room was broadcasting a program that Mom was enjoying, when a news flash interrupted the normal programming. The announcer excitedly reported that Japanese aircraft had attacked the American Pacific Fleet anchored at Pearl Harbor in Honolulu, Hawaii. There was considerable damage and destruction of ships, including the sinking of the battleship *Arizona*, with the loss of many lives. President Franklin D. Roosevelt called this "a day that will live in infamy," and the United States found itself fully engaged in a war that was later called World War II.

This day was Sunday, December 7, 1941.

Mom and Dad were stunned when they heard this news, and no doubt their hearts were pierced because I was at the age of many young men who would now be eligible to be conscripted for military service. The tragic events of December 7 resulted in a major change of direction in my young life as I changed from a teenager to manhood, tempered by the hard knocks of war.

Clintonville is a small farmer's town located in the northeastern corner of Waupaca County, about forty miles west of Green Bay and forty miles northwest of Appleton. My dad, Gustave, who was born in Germany in 1876 in the province of Pommern, came to America with his parents and siblings when he was thirteen years old. It was always an amazing fact to me that the United States was only one hundred years old in the year of his birth. My mother, Minnie (the short form of Wilhelmina), was born on a farm in Wisconsin, the oldest of seven children.

Mom and Dad were married in 1902, and during the first winter of their marriage, they were hired by a big timber company to manage a logging camp in northern Wisconsin, near Rhinelander. Dad was in charge of maintaining the teams of horses, the sleds, and all the saws and logging machinery. (Trucks didn't exist.) Mom was the only cook at the camp, and as a new bride, her job was the endless feeding of hungry loggers every day. She got up at five o'clock every morning to bake the eight to ten loaves of bread, which were consumed daily. That's how she got her reputation of being the best bread baker around.

Charlie Folkman was a wealthy merchant in Clintonville, who owned the largest dry goods and grocery store in town, located next to the Pigeon River just below the dam. During every spring when the ice melted on the pond behind the dam, Charlie's store, called the Merc (from Mercantile Store), had a flooded basement. Charlie invested a chunk of his money in 120 acres of undeveloped and wooded land on the north side of Clintonville, about a mile from his store.

Charlie hired Dad to manage his new investment, and his first job was to clear the land of trees and dig out of the ground the many erratic stones and boulders that were left by the retreating glacier that sculpted much of Wisconsin's terrain millennia earlier. This was a back-breaking job. Next, Dad began to build a herd of Holstein cows because milk production was the main source of revenue for a dairy farmer. In order to feed the cattle and sustain them so they could produce milk, it was Dad's job to plant and harvest such crops as hay, corn, oats, and barley. There were also several "cash crops" to create extra income for Charlie, consisting of a seven-acre orchard with many varieties of apples as well as plums. Dad also tended a flock of thirty sheep that grazed in the orchard along with the lambs that were born every winter. He also raised a herd of twenty pigs, and each year's offspring was sold as fresh pork in Charlie's store.

After the winter of logging ended in the woods up north, Dad and Mom moved from the camp to the raw land that Charlie Folkman wanted to develop into a working farm in Clintonville. The years that followed were difficult times

Birthhome of the Author, Clintonville, Wisconsin (ca. 1923)

of very hard work, and Dad, along with two hired men who lived with them, developed the Folkman Farm into a successful enterprise. My two siblings, Gertrude and Amos, were born to my parents during their early years on the farm. I was born later in my mother's life, so my siblings were a generation older than I. Half of the land of the Folkman farm was within the city limits, and the other half was outside the town's border. Because of this fact, I was always proud to tell people that I was a "farm boy" and a "city boy" at the same time.

Folkman Farm, Clintonville, Wisconsin (ca. 1923)

My education began at St. Martin Lutheran Elementary School in downtown Clintonville. I graduated from Clintonville High School, Class of 1941, with a class of seventy-five students. During the summer of 1941 following graduation, Dad asked me to be his full-time "hired man" during the summer growing season and the fall harvesting months. I had applied for a factory job at the Four Wheel Drive Auto Company, which was the only manufacturing plant in town. "The Drive," or FWD as it was called by everybody in town, built heavy-duty four-wheel-drive trucks that were used by highway departments or off-highway in the oil fields to carry drilling derricks as well as fire trucks and utility trucks.

Since FWD Corp. didn't have a job opening for me, I did the normal work of a farm boy, and Dad and I were a two-man crew. The main chore was the milking of thirty-five dairy cows, morning and evening. With the team of two horses and a riding hay mower, I cut the fields of alfalfa hay, raked it into windrows for drying, and then hauled the hay into the barn with a large wagon pulled by the horses. When the oats and barley were ripe, I stacked the sheaves into shocks for later threshing. The final crop of the growing season was corn, and after it was cut by the corn cutting machine, the stalks were hauled to the concrete silo next to the barn where it was chopped by the silage cutter and blown up a pipe to the top of the fifty-foot-high concrete silo where it fell into the cavernous interior. The chopped corn stalks, called silage, were the favorite food of the cows—sweet, moist, and slightly fermented.

One day in October while I was working in the corn field, Mom came to see me with some good news. She said that I had received a telephone call from FWD that I should report to the company for a job interview. The next day I was offered a job in the office of the export department. The timing was good as the harvest season was almost over. After a month on the new job, the horrible news of the December 7 attack at Pearl Harbor would bring a major change in my life during the coming year.

On December 11, 1941, four days after the Pearl Harbor event, Adolf Hitler declared war on the United States, and suddenly America was involved in two theaters of war—in Europe and in the Pacific. In Europe, the German Wehrmacht occupied France, and British forces were pushed out of the Balkans and Greece, so "Fortress Europe" was now completely under Hitler's control. Meanwhile, German and Italian armies were fighting the British in Northern Africa in a desert war in the countries of Egypt, Libya, Tunisia, Algeria, and Morocco. The German Afrika Korps was commanded by General Erwin Rommel, one of the Wehrmacht's ablest generals, who had the nickname "The Desert Fox."

Two weeks after the disaster in Pearl Harbor, Britian's Prime Minister Winston Churchill went to Washington to meet with President Roosevelt to plan war strategy. They decided that the Allies should strike at the "underbelly" of the Nazi Empire in Europe, meaning that since Fortress Europe was impenetrable, the Allies should engage the German and Italian armies in the deserts of North Africa and in Sicily before striking them head-on in Europe through Italy and France. But there was one serious problem in this plan; the

United States had never experienced *desert* warfare in its entire history. Thus, it was imperative to establish a desert training program for the US Army and its air support units in preparation for possible combat in the Sahara Desert of Africa.

In Washington, Lt. Gen. Lesley J. McNair was the Chief of Staff of the US Army Ground Forces and Combat Training. On February 5, 1942, General McNair approved a comprehensive plan to establish a training area in a desert somewhere in the United States for the purpose of training men and operating machines to fight in the harsh and severe conditions found in the North African deserts. General McNair needed an able army general to find and establish this training ground. The man he selected was Maj. Gen. George S. Patton Jr., who at that time was the commander of the US Army's I Corps at Fort Benning, Georgia. Patton's order simply stated:

Locate, create, equip and command a training center for Army ground and air forces to be skilled in desert warfare.

General Patton was, no doubt, the best man available to tackle this job. He was a 1909 graduate of West Point and a tough and flamboyant ex-cavalry man who became a tank expert. McNair and the War Department had agreed that the general location of this desert training area should be in southeastern California, western Arizona, and southern Nevada. This vast land was geographically known as the Mojave Desert. General Patton and his personal staff arrived in southern California in March 1942, and he immediately surveyed the vast desert on foot, horseback, and by plane, which he often piloted himself.

The Mojave Desert is a vast inhospitable, remote, and bleak expanse of sand, cacti, scrub, jackrabbits, lizards, scorpions, and rattle snakes. There is very little water and vegetation. The elevation of this desert ranges from 227 feet below sea level at the Salton Sea to mountains reaching 7,000 feet in elevation. Temperatures range from below freezing to 120 degrees in the shade. Frankly, no human being would want to go to this forbidding wasteland.

After Patton had surveyed this huge area, he was ecstatic and went back to Washington with this report about the characteristics of the deserts of California, Arizona, and Nevada:

- Wide and empty spaces devoid of humanity.
- Numerous mountain chains that crisscrossed the desert.
- Dense vegetation present in many areas, suitable for all forms of combat exercises.
- Vast areas of sandy terrain including dry salt beds, wide valleys, rocks, and gorges.

- Weather that was varied and capricious, with temperatures ranging from extremely high in summer to below freezing in winter, and sudden arrivals of sandstorms, thunderstorms, and cloudbursts.
- Lots of rattlesnakes and scorpions.

After General McNair approved Patton's report, the general returned to California and set up his headquarters in the desert approximately thirty miles east of Indio at a place called Shaver's Summit. (Note: today its name is Chiriaco Summit, located at an off ramp on Interstate Highway I-10, where the General George Patton Memorial Museum is located.) This vast training area was named the "Desert Training Center," and Patton's new army camp was called "Camp Young," named in honor of Lt. Gen. S.M.B. Young, a nineteenth-century army officer who had fought the Native Americans in this area and later became US Army's first chief of staff.

The size and scope of the DTC was enormous, encompassing an area that was twice the size of the State of Maryland, ranging from Pomona, California east to Phoenix, Arizona, and from Yuma, Arizona north to Boulder City, Nevada. The APO address was Indio, California, a small town that consisted of sixteen hundred people set amidst the date palm orchards of the Coachella Valley.

On April 21, 1942, the *Los Angeles Times* reported a story of General Patton's arrival in the desert of California, with the following headline and descriptive paragraph:

Tank Army Turns Desert into Training Ground
Armored Soldiers Practice Warfare

"This huge arid country of the cactus, the ocotillo, the sagebrush, juniper and smoke tree, the lizard and the tiny desert rat has come alive in the last few days, its agelong desolation gone with a vengeance. The tankers are here. Under the command of Maj. Gen. George Smith Patton Jr., who bossed the American tanks in France in the other World War, the vanguard of a huge armored corps has established itself in the western end of a desert training area embracing 16,200 square miles. General Patton's rapidly expanding outfit is here to learn and perfect desert warfare under the toughest, most exacting conditions that can be found or devised."

The first troops arrived at the Desert Training Center in April 1942, and General Patton moved quickly to harden his troops by increasing their physical endurance for these primitive desert conditions. Within a month of arrival, every man had to be able to run a mile in ten minutes with a full backpack and carrying a rifle. The men were limited to one canteen of water per day, including Patton himself, and salt tablets were issued to prevent dehydration and heat prostration. Food was standard field rations. The early trainees called this harsh training area "The Land That God Forgot."

General Patton was the commander of the DTC for about four months when he was ordered back to Washington on July 30 and received a new assignment from the Army Chief of Staff, General George C. Marshall. His order was to organize and lead "Operation Torch" and be the commander of the Western Task Force in the allied invasion of North Africa. His experience in the DTC of California would now be tested in actual combat against the German Afrika Korps and the "Desert Fox," Rommel himself. It was an incredible fact that I would soon be following Patton to the DTC and later meet up with him in France!

The year of 1942 moved quickly for me, and I thoroughly enjoyed my job at the FWD Corp. I was the new intern in the Export Department which handled the shipments of trucks to the Federal Government and foreign customers. My job was to verify the documents for each truck that was ready for shipment, and I had to go to the assembly line in the factory to check the documents for each truck with government inspectors. FWD Corp. received a large order of hundreds of units as the sub-contractor for the Diamond T Truck Company. The truck was called the "Diamond T Transporter" and had an oversized cab sitting on top of a powerful engine with extra large tires that enabled it to maneuver off the roads on sandy, desert terrain. Its function was to pull low-bed trailers which carried fifty-ton tanks for the British Army in North Africa. When General Patton went to Morocco to lead "Operation Torch" in the African deserts, these FWD-built tank transporters supported his troops as well.

Now that the United States was fully engaged in war, the Federal Selective Service Department was actively recruiting men for the various services. Many of the young guys in town were enlisting, including some of my classmates from the Class of 1941. By enlisting in a specific branch, these guys could choose army, navy, air corps, marines, or coast guard, and I decided that I wanted to be drafted into the US Army. The first step in this process happened on June 30, 1942, when I reported to the Clintonville Armory to register for selective service. It was a very busy place that day.

I continued working at The Drive throughout the Summer and Fall, while I enjoyed my duties of processing the deliveries of military vehicles to the US Government. Finally, on November 23rd, I received my selective service questionnaire. I answered all the questions about my personal life and work skills and returned the form to the Draft Board in Waupaca, the county seat. On December 7 (one year after Pearl Harbor), the mail brought my "Notice to Registrant to Appear for Physical Examination." I walked downtown to Doctor Murphy's office on South Main Street for my physical examination. He was a very busy doctor those days, examining many boys who were being selected for military service. Dr. Murphy told me I was a healthy boy and wished me good luck as a soldier in the armed forces of the United States. I was excited and ready to perform my patriotic duty. My new draft classification was A-1.

Our family's Christmas celebration was subdued this year because of my impending call into military service. My parents were very patriotic citizens, but I sensed that deep in their hearts there was sadness and worry which was a natural feeling that all parents experienced during wartime. Even though I also felt some sadness that I would miss my family, I felt a great deal of excitement for the new life of being a soldier. Besides, many of my school and church friends were entering military service, and I wanted to be included. My family had strong Christian values and faith, and we put our future lives in the powerful hands of God. I chose as my mantra the words that the LORD God spoke to Joshua as he was about to lead the Nation of Israel into the Promised Land.

"Be strong and courageous. Do not be terrified; do not be discouraged,
for the LORD your God will be with you wherever you go."

The new year of 1943 entered quietly over the weekend for our family. On Monday, January 4, I walked home from my job at The Drive as was my custom. Mom was preparing supper at the big kitchen stove when she greeted me by handing me a letter. She looked distraught, and I thought she had been crying. I looked at the envelope—it was from the Selective Service Draft Board. The "Order to Report for Induction" was dated December 31, 1942, from the President of the United States to Eugene Gustave Schulz.

Order No. 12,420

GREETING:

"Having submitted yourself to a local draft board composed of your neighbors for the purpose of determining your availability for training and service in the armed forces of the United

States, you are hereby notified that you have now been selected for training and service in the Army.

You will, therefore, report to the local draft board named above at the Court House, Waupaca, Wisconsin, at 6:00 a.m. on the 12th day of January, 1943".

The inevitable event had occurred. Mom and Dad were sad and proud at the same time, while I was very excited that my new adventure in life was ready to begin. I was 19 ½, still a teenager. At four o'clock in the morning on January 12, Mom and Dad woke me up, and as usual, Mom prepared a big breakfast of fried eggs and potatoes and sausages, a real farmer's breakfast. It was hard to eat because of our emotions. My brother Amie drove Mom and me to Waupaca, and Dad went to the barn to do the morning chores.

The courthouse in Waupaca was crowded with boys and their relatives because it included all the selectees from the whole county. Three Greyhound buses transported us to the US Army Recruiting and Induction Station at 234 North Broadway, Milwaukee, Wisconsin. We received a very thorough physical examination for two hours, after which the Red Cross served us a big dinner. At 2:30 p.m., we were sworn into the United States Army by a recruiting officer. We were then released from active duty and transferred to the Enlisted Reserve Corps (ERC) for seven days, holding the ranking of "Civilian Soldiers." The buses returned all of us back to Waupaca.

On Monday evening, eleven of the inductees from Clintonville were honored by the Chamber of Commerce with a farewell banquet at the Marson Hotel. This was our final event as civilians because our induction into the armed forces came the next day.

Tuesday, January 19 was an extremely cold day in northern Wisconsin, and lots of snow covered the landscape. My sister-in-law, Leone, drove Mom, Dad, and me to Waupaca for the 1:45 p.m. roll call. Because of the extreme cold, the train was four hours late. When the time for good-bye came, there were many tears and big hugs for Mom, Dad, and Leone as I left my family behind, not knowing when I would see them again.

Sixty-seven men from Waupaca County were in this group of inductees, headed for the reception center at Fort Sheridan, Illinois. Since the train was late, we were taken to the Delavan Hotel in Waupaca for supper, after which we boarded the Soo Line train for the ride to Milwaukee. When we arrived there at midnight, we transferred to the North Shore Electric train to Highland Park, Illinois. Army trucks took us to the Receiving Building at Fort Sheridan, and during the early morning hours, we listened to lectures, received endless instructions, and were assigned to a barracks. It was 5:00 a.m. when we got to bed.

Reveille came quickly—at 6:00 a.m. A physical exam followed breakfast; then a walk to the warehouse to get my supply of army clothes. My new wardrobe included two woolen shirts and pants; two cotton shirts and pants; two sets of wool and cotton underwear; wool overcoat; raincoat; two overseas caps; four pairs of socks; two pairs of shoes; leggings; a field jacket; two pairs of fatigue suits and hats; a suit coat; and a helmet and helmet liner. In the afternoon, I wrote three classification or aptitude tests—on mechanics, on practical problems, and on radio telegraphy. After supper, we gathered in the lecture hall to hear the Articles of War, a lengthy document which detailed the duties and rights of a soldier in the US Army. My first day as a soldier ended with watching a movie about venereal diseases or sexually transmitted diseases (STD). This film graphically showed the horrors of the infections resulting from gonorrhea, syphilis, and genital herpes. Some of the new soldiers in the audience got sick, and my head was spinning as I also had the urge to vomit after viewing the body sores and results of these infections. I had lived a sheltered life in a devout Christian family, and these things were unknown to me and repulsive to my sense of decency.

I stayed at Fort Sheridan for ten days before shipping out. During these days, we had no formal basic training, so we had much free time. Some of the mundane jobs included "barracks fatigue" which meant sweeping and scrubbing the barracks and cleaning up the outside grounds. Since it was winter, we also shoveled snow. There were inspections, both physical and including footlockers and bunkbeds. We had inoculations for smallpox, typhoid, and yellow fever. Some of us took typing tests because I had taken the typing course in high school. Typing was not a popular course for boys, so I had a special skill that the army was interested in. We were interviewed by officers for the purpose of classifying us for the best job that used our skills and knowledge. Evenings were spent at the service center watching the latest movies from Hollywood.

On January 29, the order to "ship out" was announced, and at nine o'clock that evening, we boarded a troop train. We were assigned to a Pullman car, with berths, which meant that we were about to go on a long journey in a sleeping car. Our destination was secret. (All information was secret because it was war time!) I was very excited because I loved trains, and this would be my first time to sleep in a berth on a Pullman train. I wrote in my diary "we have a Negro porter," because I had not encountered any black people before, as there were none in my hometown of Clintonville.

Each morning after the porter made our beds, he pushed them into the wall above the nice seats that we occupied during daytime hours. We ate our meals in the dining car which was sandwiched within the long stretch of sleeping cars, and the meals were prepared by army cooks who had come onboard at Fort Sheridan. They had an enormous job of satisfying the young guys, who were always hungry. Our cross-country train ride went on day after day, and we eagerly watched the landscape changes and the names of each city that the train passed through because we tried to guess what our destination would be.

The first morning after leaving camp, we stopped briefly in the railroad station in St. Louis, then we followed the Mississippi River before turning southwest through the rolling hills which were part of the Ozark Mountains. My first view of the mighty Mississippi was exciting, and my thoughts turned to Mark Twain's characters who lived in these places. I even spotted a river steamer with a thick black plume of smoke rising out of the smokestack. During the next night, we passed through a corner of Arkansas and then arrived in east Texas at daylight. We all began to speculate whether our new camp would be in Texas, but all day long the troop train continued on its westerly course. Occasionally the train made a rest stop in larger cities where we detrained at the station platforms to stretch our legs, while the smokers enjoyed their cigarettes. We were happy with the mild climate, which was so much better than the cold and snow in the Midwest.

We still were traveling west on the third day, and we began to speculate whether we might go to California. I thoroughly enjoyed watching the changing landscape of our country, from the Ozarks of Missouri through the pine forests and oil fields of east Texas, the flat cattle country of west Texas, and the deserts and mountains of New Mexico and southern Arizona. We had passed through the big cities of St. Louis, Little Rock, Austin, San Antonio, El Paso, and Tucson.

On the morning of the fourth day, we found ourselves in Yuma, Arizona, where we crossed the bridge over the Colorado River. We had reached California, so we all concluded that this land had to be our new home because it was the westernmost state. Here we saw an irrigated desert with orange groves and cotton fields. The rail line now ran along a huge lake, and as we wondered what it was, the conductor told us it was the Salton Sea in the Mojave Desert. It was a strange sight for me to see such a large lake in the middle of the desert and dotted with a few scattered palm trees, because I was only familiar with Wisconsin lakes surrounded by beautiful pine trees and hardwoods. This trip across southern and western America was fascinating for me!

It was late morning on Tuesday, February 2, 1943, when our troop train arrived in the tiny town in southern California called Indio. Even though this town had few inhabitants, it was a large railhead, which I observed when I got off the Pullman car, carrying my duffle bag that I had lived out of during the past four days. The rail yard contained scores of flat cars, each one carrying a shiny new M4 medium army tank, fresh from the factory somewhere where it was built. The first thing that I noticed was the mild climate, because the sun was bright and warm—much more pleasant than the cold and cloudy winter of Wisconsin. Army 6×6 trucks were waiting to take us to our new home in the desert, which the welcoming officer told us was called Camp Young. Suddenly I had mixed emotions because I was excited to be in California; however, not really in the *desert*.

The convoy of trucks, carrying hundreds of new recruits, headed east out of Indio, driving on the only two-lane highway between Los Angeles and Phoenix. Indio lies in the Coachella Valley where the main activity is date growing. Past this agricultural valley, we entered a barren desert dotted with low shrubs and isolated Joshua trees and low mountains rising up from the desert floor. The thirty-mile, forty-five minute drive ended when the trucks turned off the main highway and stopped at a gate protected by a couple of MPs. The big sign said "Camp Young California, Desert Training Center, US Army." *Wow!* It was incredible that I now found myself in the same desert training camp that General Patton himself had established a mere ten months earlier.

The first thing I noticed about this camp was the large cluster of tents rather than individual barracks buildings. The tents were set in rows with a wooden sidewalk forming a street between them, and an offshoot entering each tent. The tents had wooden floors and accommodated five soldiers each. There was a small wood stove in the center with a tall smokestack protruding through a hole at the top of the tent. Each guy had a cot and three blankets because the nights in the desert got very cold, and the warmth from the stove helped to keep us warm before bedtime.

Tent City, Camp Young, California (1943)

The administrative buildings and mess hall were wood covered with tarpaper. They looked like sheds, and it was obvious that they were only temporary structures. The ground around the living areas of tents and the mess and office buildings was saturated with diesel oil to keep out such creatures as scorpions, tarantulas, and rattlesnakes which were daily happenings. The Camp Young Headquarters area was located part way up a long slope that stretched from the bottom of the valley where the main highway was located to the Cottonwood Mountain Range at the top of the slope. The view in all directions was spectacular.

On the first full day in camp, all of us new arrivals had a physical exam as the first order of the day. Immediately following the physical, I was put on KP (kitchen police) for the entire day, so I scrubbed pots and pans and washed dishes. I had developed a cold on the train trip, and it got lots worse, so I went on sick call. The medical officer sent me to the camp hospital for bed rest. This was a disappointing development that on my second day in camp, I was hospital-bound. I wrote a letter to my folks with this news, and I figured that this would be a big scare to Mom. But I thoroughly enjoyed the pampering from a male nurse and a ward boy in the ward, which was inside a huge tent with seventeen beds. Late each morning, after the sun had warmed up the desert, the south side of the hospital tent was rolled up to let in the wonderful spring air and warm sunshine. My meals were served in bed, and I enjoyed lots of fruit juice and milk—all I wanted. My ward got a radio from somewhere to pass the time, and during my recovery, I wrote letters and read magazines like *Life* and *Time*.

I was released from the hospital all healthy again after five days of confinement. During the next few days, I began to feel homesick because living in the desert, with its extremes of temperature, constant dust, the fact that I was two thousand miles from home, and missing my family during this period of my teen years all preyed on my mind. But my homesickness was short-lived because of developing events in camp which brought a new assignment and direction for me.

The Desert Training Center grew rapidly in size and scope after General Patton departed in July 1942 to lead the American forces in North Africa. More armored divisions were arriving at the DTC to receive their desert training, but there was no top administrative organization to coordinate and command all the individual divisions. Consequently, the Army Command in Washington, DC, decided to establish an Armored Corps Headquarters to oversee and administer several armored divisions under a single command. Thus, about five weeks after Patton's departure, the IV Armored Corps was activated at

Camp Young on September 5, 1942. I now found myself as a member of this army unit.

The command of the new IV Armored Corps was assigned to fifty-two-year-old Maj. Gen. Walton H. Walker, a Texan who graduated from West Point in 1912. The first personnel consisted of two officers and 186 enlisted men who arrived at corps headquarters from the 8th Armored Division in Fort Knox, Kentucky. Colonel William A. Collier arrived to become the Corps Chief of Staff. The Corps G-3 Section was headed by the newly arrived Colonel Welborn B. Griffith, another career soldier from Texas. He was a full colonel, aged forty-three, and was a teacher at the Command and General Staff School in Fort Leavenworth, Kansas. In his new capacity as the Corps G-3, Colonel Griffith would plan and execute all the planning operations during training exercises, and, later, in combat.

I was a member of the group of thirty-two new recruits from Fort Sheridan who were required to go through basic training. We formed the cadre of the new IV Armored Corps Headquarters, but the soldiers who had been the first arrivals here were sent deeper into the desert for maneuvers. While they were gone, our group of thirty-two guys was sent to the 4th Armored Signal Battalion to undergo four weeks of basic training. Sgt. Chet Phillips, who had taught us some marching maneuvers and the manual of arms and rifle commands, went with us to be our drill sergeant and instructor. We moved to another section of Camp Young and found it was a little more primitive. Our tent had no wooden floor, only desert sand. This detachment had six hundred new recruits, but my platoon had only sixty men with Sgt. Phillips in charge. We were happy with that arrangement because Chet was a nice guy.

Basic training started in earnest on Monday morning, February 15. We learned the fundamentals of marching, with all its commands and executions, and marched at any time of day at a moment's notice. In early morning or in the evening, marching was OK, but in late afternoon, when the sun was hot and temperatures were near 100 degrees, a six-mile hike was tough. We carried a cartridge belt and a canteen of water which had to last for the entire hike. Our column stirred up clouds of dust, and sometimes a few guys would pass out and were taken back to camp in a jeep.

There were endless inspections of our tent quarters and of our person. If the officer noticed that a soldier was unshaven, he got gigged and got extra duty, like doing KP or cleaning up the camp grounds. We had daily lectures on numerous subjects, such as learning the parts of the .45 caliber Thompson submachine gun and disassembling and reassembling it, the principles of driving a military vehicle like a tank, half-track or truck, how to throw a hand grenade, map reading, aircraft spotting, and how to scatter in the event of an air attack. We learned how to put on and remove a gas mask, and we smelled and learned to identify various poisonous gases used in chemical warfare. (The army expected the enemy to use chemical gas poisoning because mustard gas was a killer in World War I.)

Since we were attached to a Signal Battalion, we had classes in learning about the field telephone and how to repair telephones and string lines. This included climbing telephone poles, so I strapped spurs on my legs and learned how to climb the bare telephone poles that extended about twenty feet above the ground. This was very scary because I had to dig the spur into the pole at the proper angle so it would support my full weight. These perpendicular poles were smooth tree trunks with no horizontal spikes inserted like ladder rungs, and it was a strenuous job to lift my body weight each time I dug the spur into the pole to raise myself to a higher level. These exercises made my ankle, calf, and thigh muscles extremely sore for days. Aaron Schuster, who lived in my tent, had an unfortunate accident when he fell from the telephone pole, and his climbing spur penetrated his leg with a deep wound. He went to the field hospital for treatment. After several weeks, I passed the test of climbing the poles with spurs fifteen times in a row.

Sergeant Phillips was an excellent drill sergeant, and we practiced complicated maneuvers daily. One day I had the opportunity to drill our platoon of fifty-five men, and it was loads of fun to bark out snappy commands. I felt a great deal of authority as I watched these soldiers obey and execute my commands of attention, right face, left face, forward march, left right, left right, to the rear march, right oblique, left oblique, route step, company halt, parade rest, and fall out.

One afternoon, our platoon went on a ten-mile hike when the temperature hit ninety degrees. We didn't have to carry a full-field pack, only one canteen of water. We followed a desert trail up the north slope behind Camp Young along the Cottonwood Mountains. The view of the vast valley below was beautiful. We saw various creatures along the way, like jack rabbits, scorpions, lizards, and rattlesnakes. A small convoy of tanks passed by us and stirred up clouds of choking dust. We hiked for fifty minutes with a ten minute rest each hour. We tried to find meager shade under mesquite bushes, Joshua trees, or an occasional palo verde while keeping a sharp eye for desert creatures. We completed the ten miles in three and a quarter hours, very tired, sweaty, and dusty.

Our twenty-eight days of basic training with the Signal Battalion came to an end on March 11. It was also payday, and I received my monthly earnings of $62.17. At mail call, I received my camera that Dad had sent from home, and it stayed with me until the end of the war.

Later in the day, we marched in review past the officers and listened to a farewell speech. Following this event, we moved back to our IV Armored Corps Headquarters, and we were extremely happy for these better quarters and facilities. My accumulated mail included income tax blanks. I paid my federal income taxes of $97.00 and Wisconsin state taxes of $3.92, which was based on my salary in 1942 at the Four Wheel Drive Auto Company.

During my four weeks of basic training, many of the units attached to Corps Headquarters were deep in the desert on bivouacs and maneuvers. These units included infantry, artillery, tanks, and aircraft. During the war games, planes "bombed" the tanks with flour sacks; tanks and wheeled vehicles were tested in the extreme heat and dust of the desert. The art and application of camouflage was polished, and human endurance with limited water was tested. Other training included finding one's way back from being lost on unmarked desert trails, learning the battle tactics of "attack, destroy, and move on," engineers learning the methods of building pontoon bridges across the fast-moving Colorado River at Needles, California, and the ability to fry eggs on the steel hood of a tank that got as hot as a stove burner in the intense desert heat.

The IV Armored Corps troops became hardened soldiers with toughness and stamina as they learned to fight not only the enemy but also the desert itself. Speed and surprise were emphasized in their training, and these men perfected the surprise thrust that earned for it the title of "Ghost Corps" later on during combat when it confounded the German High Command in France and Germany by showing up where it was least expected.

With basic training and maneuvers ended, we all received three-day passes to Los Angeles. My buddies, Cliff Conahan and Eugene Heksel, and I hitch-hiked a ride on an army truck to Indio where we bought a round-trip Greyhound bus ticket for $3.20. I was excited about my first trip to Los Angeles and marveled at the numerous orange groves, vineyards, and palm trees on the way. We arrived in Pershing Square and walked to a hotel to get a room, but it looked pretty classy and expensive, and as we left, we discovered it was the world-famous Biltmore Hotel. The San Carlos hotel was across the street and the three of us got a room with one double bed and a single, on the top floor, with bath and shower, closet and radio (Wow—a radio). We noticed that Los Angeles was on a "dim-out" every night. The top half of each street light was painted black; neon signs were turned off, and all shades had to be drawn. Each block had an underground air-raid shelter. The West Coast of America was on alert for a Japanese attack.

The next day, we went to Hollywood on the streetcar, and it was thrilling to see the sites on Hollywood Boulevard. At Grauman's Chinese Theater, we looked at the footprints and handprints of movie stars in the concrete sidewalk.

Then, none other than Bob Hope drove past us in his cream-colored Chrysler convertible, and he waved to every soldier. He was my favorite celebrity, and I never missed his radio shows. We had an interesting dinner at a Chinese restaurant, which was my first experience of eating Chinese food, and it was delicious. After a full day, we went to the Greyhound Bus depot, but there were so many GIs waiting for buses that we didn't leave Los Angeles until 1:30 a.m., and finally arrived at Camp Young at 7:30 a.m. after reveille.

The new week was spent in the classroom with the thirty-two recruits who came to Camp Young from Fort Sheridan. We were instructed in subjects like army organization, the army clerk, how to type military reports and letters, and typing and clerical aptitude tests. At the end of the week, we wrote final exams, and my final grade was an "A." Job assignments were posted on the bulletin board, and I found that I had been assigned to the G-3 section.

On Monday morning, March 22nd, I reported for my new duties in G-3, the department which makes the plans for training and battle for all units under its command, including infantry, armor, artillery, cavalry, and air support. I was greeted and welcomed by my boss, Colonel Welborn B. Griffith, a Texan who was a graduate of West Point. He had a likeable personality, and I was intrigued to hear his "Texas drawl" when he spoke. He had difficulty pronouncing my German surname of *Schulz*, so it sounded more like "Private Schuss" when he spoke my name. He was a full colonel, and he wore his silver eagle insignia on his shirt collar and cap; sometimes referred to as the "bird." Colonel Griffith was also the deputy chief of staff of the IV Armored Corps, the number three officer in our corps hierarchy. The Assistant G-3 was Lt. Col. Melville I. Stark. It was an awesome feeling for me to be working with these officers who were the top brass of this Corps Headquarters. My first job was to type the final reports of the DTC maneuvers written by the officers who conducted the training exercises.

The next weekend, I got another pass to Los Angeles. Donald LeMoine, my buddy who was also a typist in G-3, went with me. This time we went to Beverly Hills to see the beautiful homes of the movie stars, then to the Hollywood Canteen, an electric train ride to Burbank and back, a radio program at NBC Studios, a movie at the Olympic Theater, shopping at the Army PX, and attendance at a church service at Trinity Lutheran Church in Los Angeles. On Sunday afternoon, we decided to hitch-hike back to camp, which required twelve separate rides.

For several weeks, there were rumors that the IV Armored Corps was destined to move to another camp out east. The desert war in North Africa was turning in favor of the British and American armies, and therefore attention now was given to engage Hitler's armies on the European continent. Armored units with tanks would still be important, but it would also require infantry to fight on mixed terrain that consisted of plains, forests, and mountains.

On March 29, General Walker received the order to move the IV Armored Corps to Camp Campbell, Kentucky. I received this news with mixed emotions as I had grown to love the desert and its environment, which was so different from Wisconsin. Now that it was spring, carpets of tiny flowers had sprung up after the rains came, and this beautiful desert became a "living" land. However, I would have changed my mind during the stifling summer heat in the desert. We packed all our office equipment and clothing, and at 5:00 a.m. on March 30, we loaded the trucks and drove to Indio. A train was waiting and we were happy to see that this troop train had Pullman sleeper cars.

The train departed at noon. We passed through Yuma, Phoenix, Tucson, and Douglas in Arizona. We crossed the Rio Grande River and made a rest stop in El Paso. We traversed the cattle ranges of western Texas and passed through San Antonio, Texarkana, Little Rock, and over the Mississippi River at Memphis. The trip across western Tennessee brought us to Clarksville, the nearest town to Camp Campbell, which was partially located in the two states of Tennessee and Kentucky. At four o'clock on the fourth day of travel from California, covering two thousand miles, we arrived at our new home. We were greeted by two military bands before we were assigned to our barracks, which contained bunks and inside toilets and wash rooms. Camp Campbell's facilities were considerably better than the California desert, and we knew we would be happy there.

Chapter 2

Camp Campbell, Kentucky

ON SATURDAY, APRIL 3, 1943, our first day in a new camp, we unloaded our office equipment and supplies from the troop train and moved into a new office building. Our new quarters were excellent compared with the tarpaper-sided sheds built on sand in the desert. Our living quarters were in two-story white barracks, with bunk style beds, a foot locker, and a coat rack for each guy. Paved streets connected clusters of buildings where there were self-standing mess halls, and day rooms with cushioned couches and chairs, writing tables, and reading materials. The Post Exchanges were huge with shelves stocked with lots of merchandise and plenty of beer and Coca Cola. The movie theaters were huge, and passes were readily available to the nearby towns of Hopkinsville, Clarksville, and Nashville. The biggest luxury was lots of water, especially hot water showers, which didn't exist in the California desert. We were elated to be training at this wonderful new camp.

Camp Campbell was established in 1942, just one year before our arrival. This reservation, with a size of over 102,000 acres, was located across the borders of the two states of Kentucky and Tennessee; ten miles south of Hopkinsville, Kentucky, and ten miles northwest of Clarksville, Tennessee. There were billets for 2,400 officers and 45,000 enlisted personnel, and we arrived as the first troops to occupy these brand new facilities. The camp was named after William Bowen Campbell, who was the last Whig Governor of Tennessee.

Don LeMoine and I were the two clerk typists in the G-3 section, and we organized our office with its typewriters, files, and supplies. Later in the week, the three G-3 officers arrived, with Colonel Griffith as our boss along with Major Stark and Lieutenant Lee. We were a closely knit crew that worked well together. General Walker issued a new order that all men in Corps Headquarters must undergo intense training, both physically and in battle knowledge of weapons, equipment, and fighting enemies. This meant that we would continue "basic training" for six weeks and later move into more battle hardening during the summer of 1943.

Schulz (left) and buddies on KP, Camp Campbell, Kentucky (1943)

During the month of April, we did lots of marching and drilling in formation on the parade grounds, as well as calisthenics and running obstacle courses. There were daily classes in many subjects including map and compass reading, first aid, reading aerial photographs, and identifying enemy aircraft. We learned how to field strip and re-assemble weapons, including the .30 caliber machine gun and the Thompson sub-machine gun. Some days we spent at the motor pool, learning to drive the jeep and the M2 half-track. The half-track was a very heavy armored vehicle with wheels in the front and tank tracks at the rear which propelled it. It was very difficult to steer because of its weight, and the shifting gears had four forward and one reverse. We practiced driving cross country and in convoys. I passed the driving test easily.

We visited the 20th Armored Division training area in another part of Camp Campbell to receive instruction about the army's new M4 medium tank. We climbed into the tank and squeezed through the front and turret hatches, which was a tight squeeze. The inside space was very small and compact, and we learned how to remove casualties from the tank. This was followed by a demonstration of the safety of being in a foxhole during combat.

In a nearby open field, each man dug a foxhole for himself that was three-feet wide and deep enough to reach one's chest when standing in it. After all the holes were dug in rows divided by the width of a tank, each man jumped into his own foxhole. I crouched deep in my foxhole wearing my steel helmet and waited for the roar of the tank's engine as it rode across the top of my hole and all the others. As the tank tracks rolled across the top of my hole, there was darkness and a shower of dirt covered me. And I heard the deafening roar of the engine. We all survived this demonstration, and it proved to us that a foxhole is a safe place to be.

Hiking became almost a daily routine as we went on long hikes wearing a full-field pack. These backpacks were full of various gear—sometimes only bricks to increase the weight that we had to carry. Many of the hikes were on hard roads, but sometimes we hiked cross-country through corn fields, pastures, and woods. In addition to all the physical training, classes, and visiting the firing ranges, I also spent many hours working in the G-3 office. I typed reports, kept files, graded test papers for other units, and often worked late into the evening, like ten or eleven o'clock.

Our frequent hikes became more intense as we moved toward goals of covering a prescribed distance in a limited amount of time. The first such test came on May 4, when we had to cover five miles in one hour, by walking for four minutes and double-time running for one minute. We carried two bricks in our backpack for extra weight. Two days later, we made a seven-mile hike, and on May 11, we had a surprise test of the "impossible." On this day, we were notified that the next test was to hike nine miles in two hours while wearing full-field pack and carrying the heavy Springfield rifle. All Headquarter Company's personnel, including the officers, were required to do this exercise. We starting hiking at two o'clock in the afternoon, and two hours later we were at the nine-mile mark. After a rest, we were told that this would actually be a twenty-five-mile hike; therefore, we would continue walking for another 3 ½ miles down this dirt road in the Kentucky countryside, and then turn around for the return walk of 12 ½ miles. By this time, motor pool trucks were following us with cans of water, and several guys dropped out and were taken back to camp in jeeps. Some soldiers just laid down in the ditch because their legs couldn't carry them. I kept going with a determination that I would complete this twenty-five-mile march in eight hours, so I wouldn't have to do it again. This test was one of the requirements for going overseas, and the guys who didn't complete it on this day had to try again; some even hiked two or three times before they were successful.

I trudged back to camp and arrived at my barracks at 9:30 p.m. thereby passing the test of walking twenty-five miles in 7 ½ hours. When I removed my backpack and rifle, it felt like a ton of weight came off my shoulders. I was extremely tired, and my muscles were terribly sore. And I was very hungry. I dragged myself to the mess hall for a 10 p.m. supper of chili and hot cocoa, which really hit the spot. All personnel were excused from reveille the next morning, and the officers gave us the day off. Everyone was stiff and limped like old men, but for those of us who finished this difficult test, it was a satisfying accomplishment.

Mustard gas was used in World War I, and it was a dreaded chemical that still might be used by the enemy in this war. So we visited the Chemical Warfare Battalion for a demonstration on mustard gas, and its dangerous effects on humans. Mustard gas is a poisonous and lethal gas that is yellow in color and smells like mustard. It comes in vapor, solid, or liquid form. It is a blister agent that kills tissue and mucous membranes inside the nose and throat by liquefying tissue. Mustard gas is not found in nature, but it's a compound developed by chemists.

At the demonstration, four drops of liquid mustard gas were put onto the inside area of my lower left arm. One of those drops was treated with preventative ointment, and one was washed with soap and water; another drop was dabbed with gasoline, and the fourth drop was not treated at all. There was no pain. The next day, there was no reaction on the drops that were treated with ointment and with soap and water, and the spots were invisible. The drop treated with gasoline was a red spot. However, the untreated spot reacted with a blister the size of a pea. Mustard gas was a dangerous "weapon" that the US Army believed was in the arsenal of the German Wehrmacht, and we learned how to operate the gas mask and filter kit which was one of our general issue items.

One day after a six-mile hike in the morning, we loaded our tents and equipment into trucks and half-tracks and went on a bivouac "somewhere in Tennessee." We camped in a thickly wooded area, set up the tents, ate supper, and went to bed. At ten o'clock, we were awakened and ordered to move out. So we broke camp, loaded everything on our vehicles, and departed, driving in total blackout in a convoy that was tightly spaced in order to follow the vehicle ahead of ours in the darkness. After two hours on the highway, we entered another woods, where we dispersed, parked, and set up the tents in total darkness. We slept on the ground that night. At 5:00 a.m., we got up, ate breakfast, loaded the vehicles, and moved out in a convoy again. After arriving at camp headquarters, we unloaded everything and washed the vehicles. It didn't make much sense but hey, this was the army.

I enjoyed the firing ranges, and the Thompson .45 caliber sub-machine gun was my favorite. I got an "expert" rating on the final test. We used bulls-eye targets for firing the .30 caliber carbine. The most difficult weapon to fire accurately was the .45 caliber pistol, but I qualified as a "marksman" by shooting at bulls-eye and silhouette targets at 15 and 25 yards. The most awesome weapon was the Browning .50 caliber machine gun. After having classes in the nomenclature and field stripping of this gun, we went to the firing range. With this heavy air-cooled gun mounted on a low tripod, I fired at moving targets at 400 yards. For the record test, I fired 106 rounds scoring 220 out of 256 points, which was a good score. This machine gun had an amazing amount of power, and it had a terrific muzzle blast in my face when I kept my finger on the trigger.

During another bivouac, we received a problem "to annihilate some paratroops who landed near our CP." Colonel Griffith picked me as one of the five enemy paratroopers, so the five of us laid mattress covers over bushes to simulate parachutes. We each carried a rifle with thirty rounds of blank ammunition and instructions "to advance, destroy, or capture the CP of the IV Armored Corps." I sneaked through the brush and fired blanks at officers and enlisted men, and I hid in the brush within sight of the CP. Suddenly, I was "captured" by a Corps MP. This was an interesting battle exercise.

The summer temperatures in July got very hot, and there was no air conditioning in camp buildings. On July 21, all officers and enlisted men of Corps Headquarters traveled to the "Assault Course" of the 20th Armored Division for a three-day training exercise. The course, which was ten miles from Camp Campbell, covered five hundred acres. There was no mess tent or cooking, so for supper, we ate "C Field Rations" consisting of vegetable stew, concentrated cookies, coffee, and candy. Nothing was planned for the evening, and each man went to bed in his pup tent by 10:00 p.m.

The next day was July 22, my twentieth birthday, and the most memorable day of intense activity. Reveille came early—at 0500. The day began with classes after which we learned the techniques of hand-to-hand combat, bayonet practice, and disarming a man carrying a bayonet, knife or pistol. The next activity was a mile-long obstacle course that contained the following obstacles: crossing a rushing creek on a log, jumping across, and crossing hand over hand on a rope. We went up and down rocky ravines and scaled an eight-foot wall and jumped fences. We had to climb up and over a swinging rope net that was twenty-six-feet high. This was a huge challenge. The final exercise of the afternoon was called the "Blitz Course" where anything could happen. There were surprises when dummies would fall out of trees, and we had to bayonet them. These activities ended at five o'clock, and we had an invigorating ice-cold shower with water that was pumped from a nearby creek and sprayed from a shower head tied to a tree branch. After a supper of C Rations, we had mail call, and I enjoyed the many birthday cards from my relatives. Before we went to bed at 10:00 p.m., we listened to a lecture and watched a demonstration about night scouting. I was very tired and had sore muscles at the end of the most rugged birthday I ever had.

We were up again at 5:00 a.m. the next morning, with a "K Ration" breakfast, which consisted of canned meat, eggs, and concentrated cookies. The first exercise was to learn the "close combat" firing of weapons, in which we fired the carbine, Tommy gun, pistol, and .30 caliber machine gun by holding them at the stomach level instead of from the shoulder. This was the kind of stuff that happened in gangster movies. The hardest weapon to control with my hands was the machine gun, which was heavy to hold and tended to move sideways and upward during the rapid firing of bullets. We redid the mile-long obstacle course, had more practice in unarmed combat, and watched demonstrations in demolition techniques. After a cold shower and supper, we watched training films on street fighting.

Saturday, the 24th, was our final day at the Assault Course, and it was the toughest one from a physical standpoint. It was called the "Infiltration Course" and consisted of a level field 100 yards long (the length of a football field), over which was strung barbed wire in a crisscross fashion about two feet above the ground. At the side of the field were a dozen .30 caliber machine guns, each manned by a gunner, with the gun muzzles pointed across the field. In this exercise, I laid flat on the ground on my belly, and I started to crawl on my stomach propelling myself by moving my legs forward and back like a scissors (or a frog), and using my elbows in the same way to crawl across the ground. During the crawl, I had to cradle my Springfield rifle across my elbows, so that it wouldn't touch the ground. Wearing a steel helmet on my head, I was sure to keep my head close to the ground, and I didn't dare to raise my body, or I would get caught on the barbed wire that was mere inches above me. During this crawl of a hundred yards, the machine gunners were firing continuous rounds of live bullets only thirty inches above my body. The tremendous speed of the traveling bullets over my head made loud cracking noises. These were tense minutes, very scary, and I prayed that the gunners had their sights set accurately. The heat of the day, the apprehension about my safety, and the difficulty of the crawl made me sweat profusely, which combined with the dust made me look like I had wallowed in the mud. I was very thankful that I finished this exercise safely, in spite of the sore arms and legs that plagued me for several days.

The next exercise was called "Village Street Fighting," which was set up as a "Nazi village" during which I carried a sub-machine gun with live ammunition. When I ran up to a house, dummy human targets appeared in the windows, and I had to shoot at them. In addition, I took a hand grenade from my pocket and pulled the pin to make it live, after which I had just a few seconds to throw it through the window. When it exploded, I hit the dirt fast to avoid getting sprayed by debris. Then I got up, crawled through the window, and fired at targets posted on the inside walls. After clearing the house, I repeated this procedure as I moved from house to house.

This exercise completed the rugged training of the three-day Assault Course, and I was tired, bruised, sore, skinned, black and blue, and hungry. The final "dinner" was the Field Ration "D," which was a highly concentrated chocolate bar of six hundred calories, but my hunger was not totally satisfied. We returned to Corps Headquarters at Camp Campbell in late afternoon. There were many birthday cards and packages waiting for me from family and relatives. Mom even sent a birthday cake which I shared with a couple of buddies, and this was a nice touch of home, which I greatly missed.

In one of my mom's letters, she wrote that my cousin, Ervin Graper, was stationed in Camp Campbell, so after a search around the camp, I found him living only thirteen blocks from my barracks. Ervin was the son of my Uncle Willie, who was my mother's brother. We got together many of the Sundays during our stay at Camp Campbell, and Ervin's sister, Norma, who worked in Evanston, Illinois, also visited us one weekend. We had much fun together in Hopkinsville.

One day, we noticed that German Prisoners of War were cutting grass and doing yard work around the camp buildings. They were paratroopers from the German Afrika Korps and wore blue coveralls with red patches of the letters *PW* sewed on their clothes. Headquarters MPs guarded them, and they received orders from an interpreter. Another day, Gen. Lesley J. McNair visited General Walker in our building. He was the Commander of the US Army Ground Forces in Washington, DC.

During the month of August, I began to work in the office in earnest, as we had finally completed the intense training we needed. Three of the Corps officers, along with Corporal Ball and myself, were a team selected to give final training tests to various battalions and companies in Camp Campbell. My job was to cut the stencils and mimeograph the test sheets. At division headquarters, I was an inspector, and I corrected the tests, graded them, and typed the test scores. We often worked as late as midnight.

The following table lists all the hikes and road marches that Corps Headquarters personnel took during the summer at Camp Campbell. Most of them included carrying a full-field backpack and a rifle.

Date	Miles	Date	Miles
April 20	10	May 27	8
21	4	June 1	10
22	10	4	4
27	10	8	9
29	10	11	5
May 4	5	15	8
6	7	22	4
11	25*	29	8
18	7	July 13	8
21	6	20	8
25	8		

*This twenty-five mile hike had to be completed in eight hours; my time was 7 ½ hours.

Thirty men from our company enjoyed a fun-filled weekend in August, when we went to a resort called Dunbar Cave, which was five miles east of Clarksville, Tennessee. There was a small lake with boating, a swimming pool, and a limestone cave. We set up our pup tents in a nearby field. The next day, we went into Dunbar Cave and were awed with the beautiful stalactites and stalagmites with droplets of water dripping from the icicles of stalactites hanging from the ceiling. Water oozed out of the limestone walls, and an underground stream flowed through the cave. This was my first visit into a cave.

On August 28, I received a document called Special Order No. 164, which stated that I was promoted to the rank of T/5, technician fifth grade. This was equivalent to the rank of Corporal. Private Denver Grigsby and I were the guys in G-3 who were promoted. I got a raise in pay of $16.00 per month.

As the summer of 1943 came to a close, the IV Armored Corps troops had completed a rigorous program of physical training and battle indoctrination. General Walker was pleased with our accomplishments, and he issued an order that the time had come to test our abilities and skills under simulated battle conditions. This order stated that all units under IV Armored Corps' command would engage in Tennessee Maneuvers for ten weeks of intense, simulated battle training.

CHAPTER 3

Tennessee Maneuvers

GENERAL WALKER ISSUED A GENERAL order that the entire Corps Headquarters' staff should move away from the comforts of Camp Campbell and move into the open country of central Tennessee where we would encamp in bivouacs and conduct simulated battles between two opposing armies. This ten-week period of war games, called Tennessee Maneuvers, began on Monday, August 30.

I was in the advance party of six men, two officers and four EMs whose assignment was to travel to the Maneuver Area near Lebanon, Tennessee, and set up the Corps' bivouac compound. This town was in the central part of the state, about ninety miles from Camp Campbell and forty miles east of Nashville. The mighty Cumberland River flowed through this area of the state. We had loaded the G-3 half-track with all or our department's equipment and arrived at the bivouac area in the darkness around midnight when we threw our bedrolls on the ground and went to sleep.

During the next two days, we lived on C rations for all our meals because the company mess crew remained back at Camp Campbell. We erected the big war tent and attached the G-2 and G-3 CP tents to opposite sides of the war tent. We staked out the spots for the other general staff departments and dug slit trenches in the woods which became our latrines. We were in woods four miles north of Lebanon, and we heard that the 310th Signal Battalion was a mile away and had a full mess unit in place, so we went to their CP and ate hot food with those guys. Smart move.

At eight o'clock on Thursday morning, September 2, we drove back to

Camp Campbell to participate in a big celebration of the first anniversary of the IV Armored Corps Organization Day. The IV Armored Corps was activated in the Desert Theater of Operations in California on September 5, 1942, but this first birthday was celebrated here in Camp Campbell three days early because the Corps was heading out for maneuvers.

It was a big day filled with lots of activities, food, and fun. There were softball and volleyball games between officers and enlisted men. Corps troops watched some ancient Kentucky sports including a "Turkey Shoot" that used live turkeys, so the men could practice their marksmanship and win prizes. There was a "Badger Fight" in which a bulldog named Sergeant from the Kentucky hills was pitted against a badger. Sergeant was the winner. At noon, we had a sumptuous chicken dinner served picnic style. A huge birthday cake was served later.

In the afternoon, General Walker conducted an award ceremony in which he presented each Corps Headquarters soldier a certificate for the completion of the five, nine, and twenty-five mile hikes and the many facets of the assault course during the summer. This was followed by the Corps Commander's reception in which the high brass from the Army Ground Forces in Washington participated. We thoroughly enjoyed this time of the day because there was plenty of beer and food available.

In the evening, the Organization Day Revue was presented on an outdoor stage. This production was created in New York by the USO (United Service Organization) and consisted of singers and dancers in a musical revue. The star performer was Conrad Teabo, the famous singer of the war years, and two comedians from the regular Eddie Cantor radio program.

But the highlight of the evening was the showing of the World Premier movie *Sahara* at the IV Armored Corps' open-air bowl theater. Columbia Pictures of Hollywood came to Camp Campbell on this anniversary day to show the new movie for the first time anywhere in front of our Corps troops. The main actor was Humphrey Bogart and his supporting "actor" was "Lulubelle," which was a twenty-eight-ton General Grant tank which was loaned to Columbia Pictures by our Corps. This action film takes place in Northern Africa during the desert campaign of the allies against the German Afrika Korps commanded by General Rommel in Tobruk, Libya. Bogart is an American sergeant who determines that his tank "Lulubelle" will not be captured by the Germans as it travels through enemy lines to a fort containing the only well with its precious water in this part of the desert. The tank protects the fort against Nazi attacks, and the enemy soldiers finally surrender in desperation for life-saving water.

During the filming at the DTC at Camp Young, General Walker as well as my boss, Colonel W. B. Griffith, assistant chief of staff of G-3, was featured in this movie. Over twenty-five thousand troops were packed into the field amphitheater to watch this film and the star-studded stage show that went with it. *Sahara* was a wonderful way to end the birthday celebration of the IV Armored Corps.

The morning after the big party, the entire Corps Headquarters moved to the Tennessee Maneuver Area to begin the war games. Each General Staff section set up its own command post consisting of a large, heavy canvas tent that served as its office. The CPs of G-2 and G-3 sections were attached to a large "war tent" which had doorways that permitted access to both CPs. The maneuvers took place around the clock, so our G-3 section was divided into two twelve-hour shifts. I was assigned to the night shift along with Sergeant Joe Messner, Sergeant Claude White, and Corporal John Massa, who was the draftsman. Our shift began daily at 7:00 p.m. and ended at 7:00 a.m. the next morning. We were the Blue Army, and our enemy was the Red Army. Joe Messner was the chief clerk of G-3; my job was to type the field orders and reports, and John Massa plotted all the pertinent information of all participating units on the acetate-covered war maps with grease pencils. The IV Armored Corps Command included the 26th, 30th, 75th, 83rd, and 98th Infantry Divisions and the 12th Armored Division.

Author Schulz (left) with Joe Messner, Tennessee Maneuvers (1943)

The maneuver area was in the bluegrass region of Tennessee where the terrain consisted of heavily wooded slopes that were slashed by deep gorges mixed with towering hills that were covered with thick stands of red cedar trees. The land was intersected by numerous rivers and small streams. During the first problem, the 12th Armored Division attacked the west flank of the Red Army and drove a spearhead into their territory, including the capture of the Red Army General. A couple of days of rain made for miserable living and fighting as our tents got soaked; there was mud everywhere, and it was hard to keep dry while sleeping.

For the next problems, we moved our command post fifty miles south to the city of Murfreesboro, a town that experienced many battles during the Civil War. We had to drop out of the convoy because our G-3 half-track had engine problems, so we hitched a ride with another vehicle. Whenever we moved to a new location, my first job was to dig my personal slit trench, required of each soldier. This was a putzy, miserable job because the Tennessee soil was very stony, and I usually encountered tree roots when digging in the woods. A slit trench was narrow, about two-feet wide and as long as my height, and about a foot and a half deep. This trench became a soldier's safety refuge during a time of danger.

Corps headquarters moved again, this time to a place north of Lebanon. At noon, two B-26 bombers from the Red Army made a simulated bombing of our bivouac area with bomb bays open. Since I was sleeping during the day, this bombing woke me up. Meanwhile the day shift moved out to a new CP, and my night shift stayed to work in the office until they had established the new CP. During this exercise, the new hours of our night shift crew were changed to 9:00 p.m. to 9:00 a.m. During tactical situations, smoking of cigarettes was prohibited during the hours of darkness, and this was tough for the habitual smokers.

During all the weeks that I was on the night shift, the mess tent was closed and no cooks were on duty. However, it was time for our "mid-day" lunch at about two or three o'clock in the morning, so we didn't get a hot meal like the daytime crew got. Instead, the cooks made peanut butter and jelly sandwiches for our lunch *every single night*! This got to be very monotonous, and a big joke—eventually I got extremely sick and tired of peanut butter. [Note: I couldn't stand the sight and smell of peanut butter for fifty years after Tennessee maneuvers. Eventually, I began to enjoy it again in later life.]

One night when it was extremely dark in dense woods, I had to carry a secret message to the G-4 CP. I knew where each staff CP tent was in daylight, but at night without a flashlight, I couldn't find it. Suddenly, a voice called out "Halt, who goes there?" A night guard stopped me, but I wasn't at the G-4 tent. So I wandered around in the woods completely lost for 1 ½ hours until I found the location and got back to my own G-3 tent.

Problem Number 3 ended when the Blue Forces pushed the Red Forces back across the Cumberland River and established a bridgehead near Hartsville, where the Red Troops were annihilated. We moved our CP to a nice area in lovely woods without any underbrush, and the officers gave us a few days of rest. It was a chance to wash my clothes and air-out my damp sleeping bag, clean my rifle and equipment, and above all, enjoy the hot and plentiful meals prepared by the cooks in a more permanent kitchen. At night we built huge campfires and sat around the fire drinking beer and eating sweet stuff that the guys got in their care packages from home. My family and my aunts always sent me cookies, cake, and candy. These evenings were loads of fun with guys singing and "batting the breeze" with conversation, jokes, and great camaraderie.

One day, Colonel Collier, Chief of Staff, gave all corps personnel a twelve-hour pass to Nashville, from noon to midnight. Transportation for the twenty-five-mile trip was provided by the motor pool, and we rode in a convoy of trucks. That was a fun excursion.

Problem Number 4 was scheduled to begin on October 4. On the day before, Corps Headquarters welcomed a group of distinguished, high-ranking foreign observers from thirteen allied and neutral nations. These men were sent by their governments to witness the field problems and battle maneuvers of our Tennessee maneuvers. This important news was reported in *The Nashville Banner*.

This group of men visited our offices where they were briefed about our maneuvers before they visited camp installations. It was fascinating to see the British, Free French, and Polish officers in their brightly colored and decorated uniforms while the Chinese general wore a gray cape. Later, fifteen observation airplanes were used to give the visitors an aerial reconnaissance of the terrain over which the Blue and Red forces would be engaging each other during the next field problem. The Nashville newspaper listed these military dignitaries:

- Maj. Gen. Ping Kung Whang; attaché China Air Forces
- Douglas L. Blackford; air attaché, Great Britain
- Col. Oldrich Spaniel; military air attaché, Czechoslovakia
- Lt. Col. Guy V. Gurney; military attaché, Canada
- Lt. Col. A. D. Dahl; assistant military attaché, Norway
- Maj. Cemal Aydinalp; military attaché, Turkey
- Maj. Jean A. Notz; military and air attaché, Switzerland
- Maj. M. R. Blagojevich; assistant military attaché, Yugoslavia
- Capt. John A. Ducq, acting military attaché, Belgium
- Capt. C. H. B. Nordenskiold; assistant military attaché, Sweden
- Capt. S. Zamoyski; assistant military attaché, Poland
- Flight Lt. W. J. Polny; assistant military attaché, Poland
- Lt. Col. Hansan Aktarzendi; military attaché, Iran

- First Lt. Ali Ghavam; assistant military attaché, Iran
- Maj. Dave Harrington; US Foreign Liaison Branch, Washington, DC.
- Maj. Robert N. Greathead, Jr.; US Foreign Liaison Branch, Washington, DC.

The battle plan for Problem Number 4 directed that the Blue Army should cross the Cumberland River in force, drive back the Red Army, and capture the high ground in the vicinity of Westmoreland. Corps Headquarters moved to a new CP five miles north of Lebanon, just a few miles from one of the meandering curves of the big river. Just before the exercise was to begin, Col. Stark told me to report to the 30th Infantry Division Headquarters and take part in the river crossing. My mission was to join the assault troops as an observer of the action and write a report for the senior officers of the corps.

Six enlisted men from Corps Headquarters traveled in two jeeps to the CP of the 117th Infantry Regiment, which were the "crack troops" of the 30th Infantry Division. I joined the 2nd Platoon of Company E. As the observer of this action, I wrote the following report of the river crossing which I later submitted to the Corps' staff officers.

* * * * * * *

Report of 30th Inf Div River Crossing
as observed by Cpl. Eugene Schulz
2100 5 Oct --1200 6 Oct 1943

Six EM from Corps Hq left the Corps CP on the night of 5 Oct for the 117 Inf Regt Hq. We found Col. Fuller, the Regtl Comdr, and he placed us in various platoons. I was with the 2d Plat Co E. At 2200 we came out of our positions in the woods and started walking toward the river. At the same time, the doughboys were bringing the rubber pontoon boats out of concealment in the woods and carrying them to the river, which was ½ mile away. Each pontoon boat was loaded with a platoon of infantry carrying packs and rifles. With this type of boat, the men straddle the inflated sides, the total capacity of each boat being 50 men. It is propelled by means of 8 paddles, 4 on each side; and 4 engineers go along to man the boat and secure it to the shore while the doughboys disembark.

We started to cross the CUMBERLAND RIVER at 2300 at a point straight south of BELOAT. When we were 50 feet from the N shore, a MG started firing on us. We kept going until we hit shore, disembarked, and started going up the steep bank. We were halted by the MG crew. The umpires declared that we were "knocked out of action." One .30 Cal MG and one BAR had destroyed our platoon of 50 men with rifles. My opinion is that we could have concentrated our rifles on the MG and thrown a grenade to destroy the nest. Some of the men could have escaped, and our whole platoon would not have been wiped out as the umpires had declared it. A criticism of our platoon was the men talked during the crossing and made unnecessary noise with the paddles. Another point is that the moon was shining brightly, and it was easy for the enemy to see us on the water.

Since we were "wiped out," the platoon laid down on the river bank and tried to sleep. The 1st and 3rd platoons of Co E landed without opposition. They heard the gunfire that got us, encircled the MG nest, and wiped it out. Then they mopped up the few remaining RED troops on the bank.

The two platoons then assembled into position and moved N and engaged the enemy about 500 yards from the river. They fought all night long with rifles, MG's and mortars and gradually drove the enemy back into the wooded hills about a mile N of the river.

At 0100, I saw our troop transports dropping paratroopers in the rear of enemy lines. Between 2400 and 0100, enemy artillery was in operation a number of miles N.

At 0400, I began to hear activity along the river but couldn't see anything because of the fog. At dawn, Co E came back to the river bank and consolidated their troops. The umpires declared that the 2d platoon could go back into action, but that the fire power of the entire Co would be reduced. After breakfast, the Co moved N again and "dug in" in a wooded area about ¼ mi N of the river.

Other Cos crossed the river at various points during the night. Co G reported that they captured one mortar, 4 MGs, 4–2 ½ ton trucks and 100 men.

At 1300, I came back across the river on a ferry. Three ferries were in operation, and the remaining elements of the 30 Div were crossing the river. AA guns were in firing position on both sides of the river. The 230 FA Bn was getting ready to cross.

The morale of the men was high, and their combat efficiency was excellent, especially when they were face-to-face with the enemy.

The 117th Inf Regt had made a successful crossing and had established a bridgehead N of the CUMBERLAND RIVER.

/s/ Cpl. Eugene G. Schulz

* * * * * * *

Problem Number 4 was declared finished by the umpires at noon on the second day. Private Bruce of G-2 and I began the trip back to our corps CP. We crossed the six-hundred-foot-wide Cumberland River on a ferry that the engineers had built during the night. This craft was constructed with five large pontoons lashed together with ropes, covered with planks, and propelled with an outboard motor. After the crossing, we hitchhiked back to Corps Headquarters with our bodies dragging and aching from fatigue, as well as extreme hunger, since our C-Rations were gone. This had been an exciting and unforgettable experience.

By the middle of October, the weather started to get colder, so a detail went back to Camp Campbell and brought back our duffle bags containing wool OD's, which were the new dress code. Problem Number 5 was a short one, which included the mission to capture rail facilities at Carthage Junction.

I was in the advance party to move the G-3 Command Post to a new location at Baird's Mill. At 9:30 p.m., Captain Overton asked me to return to our preceding CP to bring back the rest of our equipment. I used the G-3 half-track with a driver. We drove back in total blackout on back roads that were rough, narrow, and dangerous. We were delayed for a while because an overturned truck was being pulled out of a gully. In the darkness, the truck had run off the bridge and overturned with fifteen men riding in it. Fortunately, the men were not hurt. Another truck that was towing a 155mm field artillery gun was in the ditch as well. It was a scary night, and after an hour and three quarters, my driver and I arrived safely at our CP. This three-day problem ended with the annihilation of the Red Forces.

We usually had weekends off during Tennessee maneuvers, and I went on four passes to visit Nashville, which was never far from our various bivouacs. It was on one of these passes that Don LeMoine and I ate at one of the famous restaurants in Nashville, the "Brass Rail in Jackson's Stable." This building belonged to former President Andrew Jackson, and it was the place where he kept his horses and carriages. The décor included many antiques displayed throughout the restaurant, including pistols, rifles, harnesses, carriages, and chinaware. We ate southern fried chicken with potatoes, beans, warm bread, and coffee. It was a delicious and memorable meal, which we enjoyed in a historical place.

Joe Messner went to Nashville with me on another pass, but we couldn't find a hotel room, so we went to the YMCA and got a bed for fifty cents. We ate at the Brass Rail again and later visited the Tennessee State Capitol Building, which was located on the top of a hill. The beautiful interior contained many relics from the civil war. We saw an outstanding MGM movie called *The Phantom of the Opera*. It was in color and featured Hollywood actors Susanna

Foster and Nelson Eddie. Movies in color were not very common in those days.

Between October 25 and 30, there were two short problems back at camp, Numbers 7 and 8. The location was near the Kentucky border at a place called "Payne's Store." The mission was to cross the Cumberland River and capture the high ground on the other side. The infantry established a bridgehead which enabled half of the 12th Armored Division to cross the river during the night. During these exercises, the Blue Forces annihilated the Red Forces.

At 5:30 p.m. on Wednesday November 3, the news came from the Corps Commander, General Walker, that the Tennessee Maneuvers were over! There was an immediate outbreak of whooping, yelling, and cheering from all headquarters' personnel. That evening we built a huge bonfire by the CP tent and celebrated with lots of food and drink that we raided from the kitchen tent. Bill Kramer, a sergeant in G-1 who had a beautiful voice, sang songs for entertainment, and our party lasted until midnight.

Two days later, the siren on the General's half-track woke us up at 4:00 a.m. It was time to move back to our permanent garrison at Camp Campbell. I rode in the G-3 half-track as our convoy headed for Clarksville. In Nashville, we passed by the home of Andrew Jackson, called "The Hermitage" and crossed the Cumberland River on the "Old Hickory Bridge," which used President Jackson's own nickname of "Old Hickory." Upon arrival at Camp Campbell, we moved into brand new barracks that were built after we left the camp in early September. It felt good to be back in garrison again after ten weeks of living in the woods and the constant movement of our command posts. We didn't have to endure the rain, mud, and cold anymore, as well as my perpetual menu of peanut butter and jelly sandwiches and the ever-present biting from chiggers and wood ticks.

The Corps Commander and his staff concluded that the Tennessee maneuvers were a great training exercise for the troops, and the experience gained from these war games was invaluable for the various units involved. The lessons learned included the following:

- Engineers learned how to throw pontoon bridges across rivers under combat conditions, while infantry made assault crossings in rubber boats.
- Establishing bridgehead operations where supply forces learned the techniques of keeping the flow of materials to combat troops.
- Learning communication via telephone and radio.
- Learning traffic control along the roads, in convoys, and in congested areas.

- Establishing road blocks and road nets that are necessary in armored warfare.
- The envelopment and "capture" of Tennessee towns in the strong jaws of a pincer movement.

The daring and aggressive battle techniques practiced during Tennessee maneuvers welded the techniques of the combined infantry, artillery, armor, and cavalry into a complete and well-honed battle team.

While we were away from Camp Campbell on maneuvers, the IV Armored Corps received a new name and designation from the War Department. On October 9, 1943, we became the *XX Corps*. The mode of war in Europe was much different from the nature of fighting in the deserts of North Africa where armored tanks were the major method of fighting. Armor was still important, but it was to be used in support of infantry. This was evident in our training during Tennessee Maneuvers.

IV Armored Corps Insignia

XX Corps Insignia

The new shoulder sleeve insignia for the XX Corps (using Roman numerals for 20), consisted of a blue shield upon which were four crampons crossed and interlaced salterwise within an orle in yellow, with a border of red, three inches long and 2 5/8 inches wide. The three colors of red, yellow, and blue representing the artillery, cavalry, and infantry, respectively, were carried over from the Armored Command insignia. The crampons denote the "gripping and tenacious hold" that the XX Corps was proud to be known for during its history of combat in the future.

[Note: A crampon is a grappling iron with hooked ends used for raising heavy objects. An orle is a border that surrounds a shield. Saltire refers to the shape of the crampons, which are bent like a St. Andrew's cross, i.e., an X-shaped cross "X."]

In Camp Campbell a new chapel, theater, and PX (Post Exchange) had been constructed across the street from our barracks. I went to church for the first time since maneuvers began at the beginning of September. The first two weeks of November were easygoing with very little work to do in the office. We spent our time cleaning all equipment and clothing, painting the boxes containing files and drafting materials, pulling guard duty, and preparing our personal clothing and equipment for inspection. There were frequent physical inspections too.

A general order was issued that all Corps personnel would receive furloughs, and we were urged to go home and enjoy our families and settle our private affairs. This news was ominous and it sounded like we were destined to go overseas to a war zone very soon. Whether it would be Europe or the Pacific was unknown at this time. The time for our deployment was at hand because we were well-trained, tempered, and ready to enter combat.

Chapter 4

Furlough

MY APPLICATION FOR A FIFTEEN-DAY furlough was signed by Colonel Griffith and became effective on Sunday, November 14. My buddy, Don LeMoine, who was from Upper Michigan, also got his furlough, so we took the camp bus to Hopkinsville, Kentucky, where we boarded the overnight train to Chicago. At eight o'clock Monday morning, we arrived at the Dearborn Station where Don and I separated because he took a different train to his hometown. I took a cab to the Northwestern Railroad Station and boarded the fast Chicago and Northwestern "400" train whose route to Minneapolis passed through Milwaukee.

At the Milwaukee stop, I changed trains, and within a couple of hours I arrived in Appleton, where Dad and Leone, my sister-in-law, were waiting for me. We drove the forty miles to Clintonville where Mom and brother, Amie, welcomed me home. It was a wonderful homecoming, and since that day was Mom's birthday, we had a big birthday party that included several of my aunts, uncles, and cousins. It was a great feeling to be home again.

The following days of my furlough were filled with sleeping late, leisure, seeing relatives, and visiting old friends. However, many of my male friends were in military service, so I didn't see

Author Schulz at home
on furlough (1943)

39

them. I visited often with my best friend, Kenny Johannes, because the army rejected him due to his failing the physical exam. He was engaged to Lorna Thiel from Weyauwega, and both of them lived in Clintonville, where they worked at The Drive.

My brother was a game-bird hunter, and he successfully shot some pheasants because it was hunting season, so Leone prepared a pheasant dinner for me, which was a delicacy. I went bowling with friends, went to movies, and chatted with people on the street and in downtown stores, because in our small town everyone knew each other. I had several dates with Bettie Marquardt, who was the younger sister of my high-school friend, Orvil Marquardt. Amie let me use his car to drive to Appleton for an evening of fun because there was lots more to do there than in small-town Clintonville.

I spent one day at FWD where I visited with my former boss, Peg Stockland, who was Manager of the Export Department, and with other colleagues that I had worked with before I left for the service. One night, the Clintonville Rotary Club invited me to a dinner at the Marson Hotel. After a delicious turkey dinner, I was asked to say a few words about my experiences in the army.

I had a pleasant surprise during these furlough days when my sister, Gertrude, arrived for a visit to see me and the folks. She had traveled on the Greyhound bus from her home in northern Minnesota. Gertrude and I made many visits to our relatives as well as relatives on her husband's side of the family. Mom and Dad decided that they needed a family portrait since our family was all together at this time, which was a rare event. Mom, Dad, Gertrude, Amie, and I went to Dekarske's photo studio for this photo shoot.

Schulz Family, l. to r. Amos, Minnie (Mother),
Gertrude, Gustave (Father), Eugene (1943)

The Walther League, which was the young people's organization of St. Martin Lutheran Church, invited me to the Thanksgiving party. I was a member of this group before I left for the service, so it was great to be with many of my friends from earlier days, and they were curious about my experiences in the army.

Thursday, November 25, was Thanksgiving Day. After church, we went to Amie and Leone's house for a wild duck dinner. Amie was a skilled hunter, and he had shot these ducks a few days earlier. Later in the day, we drove to Tigerton, twenty-one miles from Clintonville, to visit my uncle and aunt, Emil and Olga Schulz, and my "double cousins" Bernice, Cordella, and Ruby. We always considered ourselves to be very "special" cousins, because our parents were brothers and sisters who married each other. Mom and Olga were sisters, and Dad and Emil were brothers. This really was a special relationship, and we cousins always touted this special kinship.

The next day, we took Gertrude to the train station for her return trip to Minnesota. I had a date with Betty Hornburg, and later I got together with Kenny and Lorna for a farewell visit as my furlough was drawing to a close. On the Sunday after Thanksgiving, Mom had a big dinner with some of the relatives around the table. This was the last wonderful home-cooked meal that I would enjoy for an unknown length of time before I'd be home again. Even though this was a festive gathering of my family, we all had heavy hearts and a tinge of sadness concerning my impending departure to a war zone.

On Monday, November 29, Mom made a big breakfast, but it was hard to eat because it was my last meal at home for a long time to come. There was a big lump in my throat, as well as tears when I said "good-bye" to Dad. He stayed home to milk the cows, while Leone and Mom drove me to Appleton to the train station. There were more tears and hugs as well as unspoken thoughts concerning whether we would see each other again on this earth.

The train left Appleton at 8:00 a.m., and it traveled through Milwaukee arriving in Chicago at noon. I took a cab to the Dearborn Station and found my train loaded with servicemen. At eight o'clock, we stopped in Evansville, Indiana, for a free meal at the Red Cross Canteen next to the station. I had not eaten all day, so this stop for food and rest was most welcome.

I arrived in Hopkinsville at midnight, took a bus to camp, and went straight to bed. My furlough was a wonderful respite from the rigors of Army life, and I felt refreshed and happy.

CHAPTER 5

POM—Preparation for Overseas Movement

TUESDAY, NOVEMBER 30, 1943 WAS the first day back in camp after my fifteen day furlough. I had a wonderful time at home with my family and friends, and I wondered how long it would be before I saw them again. It was hard to say good-bye to Mom and Dad because we all knew deep in our hearts that I was headed for combat soon.

During the following days in December, XX Corps personnel continued the routine of physical training and conditioning according to the procedures listed in the POM requirements. We attended lectures on the Articles of War and classes in first aid taught by Captain Norall, the Corps' physician. We watched films about wounds and fractures. There were classes in compass and map reading which included a walk through the woods using a prismatic compass to find various points.

We attended a class in chemical warfare which included going through a gas chamber containing tear gas. I entered with the gas mask covering my face, then removing it, and running outside. There was an out-flowing of tears. Next, I entered a room filled with poisonous chlorine gas without wearing the gas mask, and when I got the first whiff, I covered my face with the mask. It had a terribly disagreeable odor.

We spent the day on the firing range to use the M1 Garand rifle, which was a new weapon that none of us had fired before. It was a nice weapon with excellent accuracy and hardly any recoil. We fired at bobbing targets which were silhouettes of men at two hundred, three hundred, and five hundred yards.

We were given the following rugged physical fitness and agility tests which I was able to pass with high scores:

- Ten burpees in twenty seconds
- Thirty-four push-ups
- Run seventy yards in thirty seconds or less (my score: twenty-seven seconds)
- Run ten yards; crawl ten yards; run ten yards; creep ten yards; run ten yards; jump ten yards; run ten yards
- Three hundred yard dash in fifty seconds or less (my score: forty-seven seconds)
- Seventy-five yard piggy-back run in twenty-five seconds or less (my score: twenty seconds).
  (I carried a 160 pound man on my back, i.e., my weight)

This grueling test left me pretty sore and stiff for a day or two.

On another day, we went on a four-mile hike, during which I carried a new thirty-five pound infantry backpack and a heavy rifle. We had to complete the hike in fifty minutes, and I finished in the record time of forty-four minutes, an average of one mile in eleven minutes with a heavy load. I had to run much of the way and was completely exhausted when I crossed the finish line. My legs ached for days.

We had personal time off from all these physical fitness tests, and there were personal preparations for Christmas, which was only a few days away. I received a Class A Pass, which meant I could leave Camp anytime I wished, provided that I was off duty. The pass was limited to sixty miles from Camp, and I merely had to sign out in the orderly room. I went to Clarksville, Tennessee, with Don LeMoine to do a little shopping, eat at a restaurant, and attend a show. We always had fun.

I was CQ (charge of quarters) one weekend before Christmas which gave me a chance to address Christmas cards and wrap presents to send home. On the Sunday before Christmas, I went to church in which the Lutheran Chaplain conducted the service. The Clarksville State Teachers College a cappella choir was present and sang Christmas carols. They were wonderful. In the evening, a dramatization of the Christmas Story was given in the chapel.

On Christmas Eve, I went to the Lutheran church service at the chapel, and later I returned to the barracks to open my presents. Most of the guys had gone to other places, so I celebrated Christmas alone. Mom and Dad sent me a tiny spruce tree about two feet high with a couple of ornaments and icicles, and I set my Christmas tree on my foot locker while I opened my presents. Gifts were sent from my parents, siblings, aunts, and uncles, and even from my former employer—the FWD Company. This was a different kind of Christmas Eve for me and I felt homesick, but I didn't go to bed because I had to serve guard duty from 2:00 a.m. to 6:00 a.m.

I went to bed at 6:00 a.m. and slept until ten o'clock when a guard woke me up so I could get to the Lutheran worship service. I was quite lonely celebrating Christmas without my family, and my thoughts turned to home for most of the day. Mess Sergeant Kelly had prepared a sumptuous Christmas dinner at one o'clock, consisting of turkey with celery dressing, mashed potatoes, tomatoes, olives, cream peas, salad, buns, mince meat and pumpkin pie, fruit cake, oranges, apples, tangerines, grapes, milk, coffee, and chocolate candy. I pulled guard duty again from 2:00 to 6:00 p.m. I needed sleep and went to bed early.

After Christmas, Sergeant Joe Messner and I received new orders to go on a detached service for two weeks to Fort Leonard Wood in Missouri. Our assignment was to conduct and umpire training tests for the 75th Infantry Division. Three officers, along with Joe and I from XX Corps Headquarters, were chosen to perform the training exercises.

On Tuesday, December 28, Joe and I took the train to St. Louis, where we arrived at 6:00 p.m. and spent the night at the downtown Mayfair Hotel on the sixteenth floor. We enjoyed a T-bone steak at the New Yorker Restaurant. (We were on the army's expense account, so we were permitted to buy "rations" while we were off base). It was difficult to get to sleep that night because the hotel's beds were too soft with their inner-spring mattresses. We were used to sleeping on hard bunk bed mattresses or on cots.

The next morning, we took the Frisco train (St. Louis-San Francisco Railroad) at 8:30 a.m. Our destination was the small town of Newburg, Missouri, the nearest town to Fort Leonard Wood. When we arrived at noon, a camp bus transported us to the headquarters twenty-seven miles away. Fort Leonard Wood covers a large area of the Ozark Mountains, and it is covered with thick stands of oak forests. The brown and dried oak leaves were still hanging on the branches and presented a pretty sight under a blanket of snow.

Upon arrival at the camp's administrative building, we found the three Corps officers who were on the testing team. They were Colonel Nelson, who was in charge, Major Kirkbride, and Captain Herman. We started working immediately. Joe did the drafting work on the maps, and I was assigned to do all the typing. We worked until 11:00 p.m. on the first day. During the last two days of 1943, Joe prepared many overlays, and I typed the orders for the exercises that were scheduled to begin after New Year's Day. On New Year's Eve, Joe and I went to a movie, and at midnight, we wished each other "Happy New Year" and went to bed. We worked at the office the next two days preparing the plans for the upcoming field exercises while a wet snow fell, causing a very muddy mess on the ground.

Monday morning, January 3, began with some exciting news. Major Kirkbride received a telephone call from XX Corps Headquarters at Camp Campbell informing him that a Special Order was issued on the first which stated that I was promoted to the rank of Sergeant, or T/4 (Technician fourth class). The title of "Sergeant Schulz" had a nice ring to it, and I immediately changed the patches on my sleeves to three stripes. My raise was $12 per month, giving me a new salary of $71.00 monthly.

We moved from the Fort's main headquarters to the Fort Wood Reservation, where our Umpire Headquarters was set up in the Bloodland School House. We used one of the rooms in this old rural two-room school house as an office with desks, typewriter, files, and field telephones. A large "war map" showed the locations of the various infantry units involved in the exercises, and Joe's job was to keep track of the movement of the units during the exercises, while my job was to type the results as dictated by our umpire officers. We worked around the clock, while I worked Joe slept and vice versa. We had cots in a large canvas tent which had a pot-bellied coal-burning stove in the center. The smoke was carried up through a tall stove pipe which stuck out of the top of the pyramidal tent. Its meager heat was much appreciated in the cold Ozarks.

After forty-eight hours of round-the-clock exercises in the field, we returned to the main camp headquarters. During the next few days, I typed endless reports, and Joe supplied the overlays to accompany the reports. The XX Corps Field Artillery Battalion was in training at Fort Wood, and it was now their turn to move into the field for exercises. Joe and I ate supper at their Headquarters Battery, after which everybody moved out to the Bloodland School. The weather turned ugly, with a heavy snowfall and a strong wind that turned the storm into a blizzard. That night we slept in a small range house or shack in the oak forest. The stove had a good fire going all night long as we crawled deeply into our sleeping bags.

The next morning, the blizzard had ended, but the temperature dropped to 10 degrees above zero. The exercises assigned to the artillery guys went on for most of the day, and they had a tough time maneuvering in the deep snows. Late in the day, when the problem was finished, everybody returned to Fort Wood headquarters. The following day was Sunday, and it was a welcome day off. Joe attended Catholic church services, and I went to the Protestant service.

I spent the rest of the day at the Service Club writing letters and relaxing. At the mess hall, the cooks served a delicious chicken dinner, and after the meal, I watched a movie.

The second week of exercises began Monday morning as we headed to the southern boundary of the reservation. This problem covered a period of two days, and Joe and I again took shifts of working and sleeping. The weather turned warm and sunny, a major improvement from the preceding week.

We completed our special assignment of detached service at Fort Leonard Wood on Tuesday, so after supper, Joe and I got on the Frisco train at Newburg for our return trip to Camp Campbell. When we arrived at St. Louis at 12:30 a.m., we took a cab to the Mark Twain Hotel. At 2:15 p.m. the next day, we boarded the Louisville and Nashville train to Camp Campbell. I had my first experience of eating in the diner of a moving train. The turkey dinner was a big treat. At 11:00 p.m., we arrived in Hopkinsville where a staff car met us, and we returned to camp. I found a huge stack of mail waiting for me as well as a box from Mom filled with cookies, cake, and nuts. Wow!

On January 19, 1944, I noted that it was one year since I entered the army. I had many great experiences and changes in my life, and I was humbled to think that I was now a sergeant in the United States Army. Later that day I finally got the airplane ride that I was promised from a sergeant who I met during Tennessee Maneuvers. He was a pilot of a light plane. I went to the Campbell Air Base where I strapped on a parachute on which I sat while riding in a Stinson L-5 light liaison aircraft. We flew over the air base at 2,500 feet, and I saw all of the training sites on the reservation where we spent two months of maneuvers. Then the pilot gave me some thrills as he did a couple of loops and several other tricks like stalls, dives, and vertical banks. There was ringing in my ears, and the blood rushed from my head and back into it. This was more fun than riding on a roller coaster.

In the next few days, we had more training exercises, including throwing hand grenades at dummy targets, firing our carbines on the firing range, and attending lectures about identifying enemy and friendly aircraft, censorship, and the dreaded disease of malaria and its control.

I learned that Delbert Johannes, who was the brother of Kenny, my best friend from home, was stationed at Camp Campbell after he had finished Tennessee Maneuvers. So I surprised him with a visit at his 14th Armored Division headquarters. We had a good visit.

On January 24, the XXII Army Corps assumed all the duties of our XX Corps at Camp Campbell because our Headquarters was alerted for movement to an *active* theater of operations. Col. William A. Collier, the Corps Chief of Staff, took an advance party of corps personnel to an overseas destination that was a secret.

This was exciting news for us, and I immediately wrote a letter home to tell my parents that we had received our orders to go to a war zone somewhere overseas. I was sure that this news would hit Mom and Dad pretty hard, but they were not alone as many parents in and around Clintonville received letters like mine with news that their sons were off to battle. There would be a steady stream of prayers for my safety in the days and months to come.

On Friday, January 28, 1944, corps personnel marched to General Walker's office to hear his speech about our departure to an active theater of combat. Afterward, he awarded honorary medals to all of us. I received "Expert" medals for shooting the .30 caliber and .50 caliber machine guns, and a "Marksman" medal for shooting the automatic pistol. I also received the "Good Conduct Medal" which was awarded after a year of military service.

Monday, January 31, 1944, was our last day in Camp Campbell. After a general clothing inspection, I packed my duffle bag with the required equipment and all my worldly possessions. I sent home my diary after I made this final entry: "Everything is packed and ready to go!"

CHAPTER 6

The XX Corps Goes to War

ON FEBRUARY 1, 1944, OUR XX Corps Headquarters Company departed from Camp Campbell for an unknown destination. We were leaving Kentucky for overseas. Our long period of military training and physical conditioning was completed, and we were ready to meet the enemy on the battlefield, wherever that engagement would occur. We didn't know whether we were headed for the European or Pacific Theaters of Operation, but the only thing we were told was that our first destination was a US port of embarkation for overseas movement.

Reveille came early, and we followed the Class A uniform dress code that was ordered by General Walker. That meant the olive dress uniform with leggings, steel helmet, field pack, and carbine. After breakfast, I tossed my fully packed duffle bag onto a huge pile of bags in the back end of a 6x6 truck. My name and serial number were stenciled on my bag in large black letters: *EUGENE G. SCHULZ 36296972.* It contained all my worldly possessions: olive drab and khaki shirts and pants, dress uniform including a jacket, soft dress caps, underwear, socks, toilet kit, leggings, shoe laces, and web belt. My backpack contained my aluminum mess kit including a canteen with aluminum cup and eating utensils, flashlight, and gas mask.

We piled into the back of the truck and headed for the Hopkinsville train station. I was awed when I saw the long troop train with many coaches. I then realized that there were many units from Camp Campbell that were also heading for overseas, such as armored and infantry divisions and support groups, including artillery and quartermasters.

After several thousand troops had boarded the train, we pulled out of the station. As we passed through several cities, we recognized that they were in Pennsylvania. That meant we were heading for the East Coast—maybe New York, Boston, or Baltimore. Occasionally, the train stopped at a station for a thirty-minute rest stop, so we got off the train to stretch our legs. Smokers had a chance to light up a cigarette. When the train moved slowly through some stations, local people waved at us and cheered.

The mess car was manned by our own corps cooks, so at meal time we took our mess kits to the mess car, got our food, and returned to our seats to eat. It was hard to sleep in the seats, which didn't recline. Each time the train stopped and started, there was a big, noisy jerk, which nearly gave us a whiplash because of the looseness of the couplings that connected the cars together. The jolt caused coffee spills from our canteen cups along with expletives from the soldiers. To keep from getting bored during the long hours, the guys spent their time reading, talking, eating, and sleeping.

On the third day, February 3, we realized that we were in the state of New York, and we began to speculate whether our port of embarkation might be New York City or maybe Boston.

Eventually we arrived at a train station which displayed the name: *New Rochelle, New York*. This was our final destination, but we wondered why we would detrain in a northern suburb of New York City.

Army trucks transported us from the train to a dock at the waterfront where we boarded a ferry. A short ride took us to an island in Long Island Sound, called David's Island. An old army camp, called Fort Slocum, became our temporary quarters for the next week. David's Island is a very small island which is only a short distance from the mainland near New Rochelle. Fort Slocum is a seacoast fort that was established in the mid-nineteenth century to defend the approaches to New York City. In the 1900s, Fort Slocum served as the headquarters for various military commands. During World War II, Fort Slocum was a marshalling camp for army units that were headed overseas, and this was the reason for the XX Corps Headquarters Company to be stationed here for a few days. The XX Corps Artillery Battalion was permanently attached to us at this camp. This was the unit that was training at Fort Leonard Wood, when Joe Messner and I observed their training exercises in early January.

We lived in barracks at Fort Slocum, and our daily routine was extremely busy. There were constant inspections, both physical and of our equipment and personal effects, as well as attending lectures and orientations and receiving inoculations. We got vaccinations and shots for numerous diseases, including

TB, diphtheria, tetanus, hepatitis, meningitis, and others. Some of these gave us extremely sore and lame arms and butts.

The corps doctor who was in charge of our Medical Detachment was Maj. Victor D. Norall, who frequently ordered the much-dreaded "short arm" inspection, in which he searched for infections from the venereal diseases of gonorrhea and syphilis. There were many "groans" and remarks like "not again" whenever we heard the horrible announcement to prepare for it. Everybody hated it because it was very embarrassing to wait in a long line of naked GIs and stand in front of the doctor sitting on a low stool with his trusty flashlight pointed at one's genitals.

One day, there was a complete field inspection of our equipment. The whole company marched to the parade ground where we lined up in rows with wide spaces between us. Each man erected his personal pup tent and spread a tarp on the ground. Then we neatly placed all of our newly issued equipment on the top: pants and shirts (both OD and khaki); underwear, socks, dress uniform jacket, shoe laces, mess kit and eating utensils, canteen, cup and web canteen holder, web belt, leggings, gas mask, and flashlight. The OD (officer of the day) walked past each man's display to make sure every GI was completely equipped. After the inspection, we had to repack everything into our duffle bags.

Our stay on David's Island did not only include lectures, inoculations, and inspections. Evenings were free, and movies were shown daily. Passes were easy to get for trips to New Rochelle, or even more exciting, to New York City. (The city had not yet received the nickname of "The Big Apple.") Most soldiers opted for the big city, and I did too, along with a couple of my buddies from northern Wisconsin. We were a little scared to go to this huge city by ourselves as we were Midwestern farm boys used to wide-open fields and pastures.

But after getting enough nerve, we took the ferry from David's Island to the dock on the mainland and boarded a commuter train at the New Rochelle station. In no time, we were in Grand Central Station in mid-town Manhattan. I was amazed at seeing the large number of people on the sidewalks, and looking up at the cloud-tickling skyscrapers. I gawked at the tall buildings, silently and in awe, with barely a word except—*Wow!*

I walked up and down the streets, looking in store windows, watching people and enjoying the sights. The Empire State Building was the tallest building in New York in 1944 with 102 stories, and the elevator ride to the top floor was very fast and exciting. The observation deck on the eighty-sixth floor was a big room surrounded with a continuous wall of floor to ceiling windows. I pressed my face against the glass and looked down on a canyon of streets set between tall buildings. It was a spectacular sight, and I was mesmerized with my birds-eye view of this exciting city.

We all enjoyed an exciting evening in New York, but we had to get back to camp because the last ferry to David's Island departed at 12:30 a.m. We got back to bed in Fort Slocum about one o'clock. However, two master sergeants in our Corps Headquarters, who went to New York City together, probably lost track of time. They returned to the ferry dock after the 12:30 deadline and therefore missed its last trip of the night. After spending the night on the dock, they took the first ferry back to camp at 6:30 a.m. When they reported to the commanding officer, he "busted" them on the spot because they were AWOL. Being "absent without leave" during these days just before shipping out was a very serious and major infraction of the rules. This punishment was devastating to these two men. They were master sergeants with six stripes, the top rank for NCOs (non-commissioned officers), and now they were demoted to buck privates. Their supervisory positions were lost, and they had to start over at the bottom, which was an extremely embarrassing and demoralizing blow to them. They had to remove their stripes from all of their shirts and jackets. I wondered what their thoughts were when they wrote letters home and substituted the word "private" for "sergeant" in their addresses. The rest of us in corps headquarters were stunned by these events, and the lessons learned from their dilemma stayed in our minds for a long time.

We got our official orders on February 10, 1944, which said "We're shipping out—tomorrow." Our long wait was over as we were finally leaving for overseas. The next morning, there was a final complete inspection of our equipment; then we repacked our military gear and personal effects back into the duffle bag. It was really stuffed, and it was very heavy!

After dinner that night, we all assembled in the large meeting hall for roll call. Our group was "all present and accounted for." At 10:00 p.m., the OD shouted "everybody move out," and I slung my duffle bag over one shoulder, and my carbine over the other shoulder and marched across the parade field to the dock.

A ferry operated by the US Navy was waiting for us. After all corps personnel had boarded the vessel; we sat on the floor, as there were no benches or seats. The area was large enough for each of us to stretch out into a prone position, and my duffle bag became a headrest—hardly a pillow. The navy ferry steamed through Long Island Sound and into the East River. We rounded the tip of Manhattan at Battery Park where we entered the Hudson River and headed north. I didn't see any of the skyscrapers along the river because I was on the bottom deck, which didn't have windows. Neither could I sleep.

After sailing for four hours from David's Island, we docked at Pier 88 at 49th Street on the Hudson River. It was dawn on Friday, February 11. We had not received any information about the troop transport we would sail on, and the only stories we heard were about troop ships that carried maybe a couple of thousand military personnel and moved in large convoys of ships, crossing the ocean at slow speeds, which meant many days at sea.

When we disembarked from the ferry we saw a gray ship that was berthed at the pier next to us. My gaze moved from eye level upward, and upward, and upward until my neck was bent completely back. This was awesome! The hull of this ship was as high as a skyscraper! What was this behemoth? Nobody could answer this question at this moment. We boarded the ship through a wide door in the side of the hull, and we walked through long corridors and up wide stairways from deck to deck. Finally, we arrived at one of the top decks where we were told that this would be our "home" for the voyage to come soon.

Our Corps' Master Sergeant called our names from the roster and assigned our cabins. Joe Messner and I had decided to "room together," and fifteen names were read. Then our little "family group" was escorted into a large room, actually a stateroom, and I was surprised to see hammocks from floor to ceiling attached to three of the four walls. Each wall contained five hammocks that were anchored to the floor and ceiling with steel rods. It was a "tight squeeze" between each hammock, but I picked one that was second from the top. It required a climb up the framework, but I was agile and I figured it would be worth it because I heard that when the seas are rough and a GI gets seasick, it's safer being higher up so you don't get vomited on. I was confident that I would not get seasick!

It was now 6:00 a.m., and we had not slept all night, but we got the order to assemble in one of the public rooms for a briefing. A captain, who identified himself as an Army Information Officer, arrived to tell us about our upcoming voyage. His first announcement was that the name of this large ship was the *Queen Mary. Wow!* This news gave me goose bumps as I had read about this great British passenger ship which had been converted to a troop ship. Now I was going to sail on this magnificent queen of the seas, and it was unbelievable that it could happen to me, a farm boy from northern Wisconsin. I wished that I could tell my parents, siblings, and friends about this exciting news, but that was impossible due to censorship rules.

The briefing continued. The officer said that we would be traveling with 16,000 troops on this ship—an astounding number! As the voyage unfolded, we learned that many rules and regulations would come into play, which will be disclosed in the next chapter.

The next statement made by the army captain was shocking. He said: "*Queen Mary* will cross the Atlantic Ocean *alone*, that is, without escort and not in a convoy." All of us gasped out loud and in unison with the same thought. We knew that all ships that traveled in convoys during the Battle of the Atlantic were protected by US Navy cruisers and destroyers. We would certainly be sitting ducks if the *Queen Mary* sailed solo. The Captain quickly allayed our fears when he said, "Don't worry guys, the *Queen Mary* can outrun any German U-boat. This ship also has added to its speed because its horizontal stabilizers were removed, thus increasing its speed to over thirty knots, (about 34.5 miles per hour), and it can maintain this speed for thousands of miles. However, without these stabilizers, the ship will roll more because its original purpose was to make sailing smoother. These stabilizers are fin-like arms that move out from the part of the hull that is under the water line and operate much like airplane wings."

The officer continued his talk. "Also, as we cross the Atlantic Ocean, the ship will zigzag continuously, because an erratically moving target is harder to hit with a torpedo from a submarine." We didn't understand what he meant until we were at sea. The Captain had more to say in his briefing. "When this ship leaves its berth at Pier 88, no one is permitted to go to the top deck to get a last view of New York City and the Statue of Liberty. Everybody, and I mean everybody, will be restricted to their quarters." This announcement came as a big disappointment as I wanted so badly to get a final look at this great city. I couldn't even look out of the windows and port holes because they were painted black. When sailing alone on the high seas, the *Queen Mary* was totally blacked-out, as all running lights and deck lights were turned off.

"And one more thing" the officer added, "you will get only two meals per day during this voyage. Your appointed time for chow will be announced later on the bulletin board. That's all for now. Enjoy your trip."

This news was troubling, as I wondered how I could survive on only two meals per day, but as a practical matter, the logistics of feeding sixteen thousand troops in a confined vessel was daunting. I noted in my mind that this huge number of people was four times the number of people who lived in my home town of Clintonville. This new perspective was difficult for this small town boy to comprehend.

[Note: an interesting fact is that *Queen Mary's* berth on the Hudson River was Pier 88. The adjacent pier was Pier 90 where *Queen Elizabeth* had its berth. Pier 90 was used by the first *Queen Elizabeth* and later by *Queen Elizabeth 2* until that ship retired in 2008.]

During the early morning hours of February 11, it began to snow and soon the storm grew into a raging blizzard that continued during the day. The *Queen Mary* stayed in its berth because it wasn't safe to navigate down the Hudson River, especially with this 80,800 ton liner fully loaded with thousands of people plus tons of gear, supplies, and food. The blizzard subsided during the evening hours, and finally ended by the next morning, which delayed our sailing by twenty-four hours. Soon we heard the purring sounds of the ship's engines, and we felt the throbbing vibrations of the propellers. We knew that the *Queen Mary* was moving through the water.

Our voyage to an unknown destination had begun...!

Chapter 7

My Life Aboard a Troopship— The Gray Ghost

THE *QUEEN MARY* LEFT ITS Hudson River berth at Pier 88 on February 12, 1944. The ship headed south toward the mouth of the Hudson River, then around the tip of Manhattan and out to sea. Before our departure, we had received orders that all personnel were confined to their assigned quarters until we were at sea. Of course, being below the top deck, we could not look out of the portholes at New York City as we sailed past the impressive skyscrapers because the windows were covered with black paint. We soon learned the reasons for what seemed like a harsh and strictly enforced rule.

Several years earlier, when the *Queen Mary* was converted from peacetime use to troopship use, its capacity increased to be able to carry as many as fifteen to sixteen thousand troops, and the engineers made calculations about how the added weight of this many men, along with their equipment and supplies, would change the draft of the ship.

Queen Mary, Retired in Long Beach, California

The normal draft of the *Queen Mary* was twenty-nine feet, six inches; however, with sixteen thousand troops aboard, the draft would increase to something like forty-four feet. At this draft, the over-weighted ship would barely clear the Holland Tunnel and the Lincoln Tunnel, which run under the Hudson. As the ship sailed in this area of the river, engineers imagined that many soldiers would be on deck and would probably crowd to one side of the ship to get a last glimpse of New York's skyline as they left for the open sea. Thus their combined weight toward one side would cause the ship to list considerably. Even a five degree list would cause the *Queen Mary* to scrape or hit the Holland Tunnel. Obviously, this would cause great damage to the ship, as well as to the tunnel and those inside of it. Therefore, the engineers suggested that the only way the ship could cross over the tunnels without hitting them was to require all troops on board to remain in their assigned quarters and keep completely still until the ship had safely passed over the tunnels.

There was an enormous amount of preparation involved when both *Queen Mary* and *Queen Elizabeth* shuttled troops between New York and the U.K. Every troop movement, including every convoy that crossed the Atlantic, had to be coordinated with every other allied troop movement and with all other allied shipping of war materiel and supplies. This prevented bottlenecks and minimized confusion at both the port of departure and the port of arrival. The British Admiralty had the overall responsibility for this job. The Admiralty's Trade Division had ultimate charge over all British-flagged merchantmen, regardless of which country exercised local control. This included both the *Queen Mary* and *Queen Elizabeth*, which were British ships but carried American troops and supplies.

Alongside the Trade Division was the Operational Intelligence Center, which kept track of German U-boat movements and surface ships, and the naval control service, which kept track of all non-British shipping. Escort assignments had to be determined for both sides of the Atlantic; when in British waters, the assignments were given by the British Home Fleet and the Western Approaches Command; and when in American waters, the coordination was done by the US Navy's Atlantic Fleet and the Royal Canadian Navy.

These details included setting courses and speeds for the ships and convoys and rendezvous points for all the ships in a convoy. Also, on both sides of the Atlantic, there needed to be coordination of road transport services, airlines, railways, docks, and shipyards. All of these things were required to enable both Queens to keep their tight schedules.

For an eastbound crossing of the Queens, an elaborate procedure that involved many officials and organizations was put into play. It all began in the allied combined shipping operations' office which was located, ironically, in the German Consulate in New York. The other center for controlling the allied convoys on the North Atlantic was in the Admiralty Building in Whitehall, in

London. At these offices, the Queen's captains were briefed on all the details of troop loading and escort procedures for each convoy. However, the *Queen Mary* and *Queen Elizabeth* were each considered a complete convoy by themselves.

People present at these captain meetings included representatives for the British Ministry of Transport and the US Army Transportation Corps, as well as liaison officers from the Royal Navy, Royal Canadian Navy, and the US Navy. An intelligence officer informed the group about the estimated locations of German U-boats and surface raiders in the Atlantic. After the briefing ended, each ship's Captain was given a set of sealed orders, which he could not open until his ship was out to sea. These orders would reveal the course, speed, and the zigzag pattern he was to follow. The captain then informed the navigating officer and helmsman of this information. Each Queen ship never followed the same course twice.

It took several hours for the *Queen Mary* to sail down the Hudson River and over the Holland Tunnel, past Lower Manhattan and the Statue of Liberty, then through the Verrazano Narrows, where Staten Island is on the west and Brooklyn is on the east side of the river. The narrows open up into Lower New York Bay, where the Atlantic Ocean begins. At the tip of a spit of land called Sandy Hook is the famous Ambrose Light. This famous marker was built in 1823 and was the gateway, faithful guide, and warning light for all ships entering and leaving New York harbor. The Ambrose Light, together with Bishop's Rock in England, were also the markers used by the great transatlantic ships in their races across the ocean between 1907 and 1936. In August 1936, the *Queen Mary* captured the Blue Riband prize from the *Normandie* by completing the Atlantic crossing in three days, twenty-three hours, and fifty-seven minutes from Ambrose Lightship to Bishop's Rock. The *Queen Mary's* average speed was 30.63 knots (over 35 MPH) for the three thousand mile crossing, an impressive speed considering its weight of eighty thousand gross tons.

After the *Queen Mary* had passed the Ambrose Light, the captain was able to open the sealed orders he had received earlier. Meanwhile, the troops on board could now move about the ship to a limited extent and get acquainted with the daily routines that everyone would live by for the next six days. At this point, the *Queen Mary* was joined by its escort of five US Navy destroyers, which surrounded the ship fore and aft and on either side. The escort ships turned back to New York when the Queen was approximately 150 miles at sea. However, there was additional protection from navy patrol planes and blimps which patrolled above the ship for some distance further in the ocean. After the last escort planes had turned back to the mainland, the *Queen Mary* was all *alone* on the North Atlantic Ocean. We were "on our own!" This was always a very risky time for the ship, and scary as well. Occasionally the ship passed other convoys.

Adolf Hitler knew the Queen's strategic importance very well, and his government had placed a bounty of one million reichs-marks, or the equivalent of $250,000 (in World War II dollars) to the U-boat skipper who would be successful in sinking either of the Queens. If Hitler had been successful in these schemes, he would have gained tremendous prestige in his war effort, and the morale of the allies would have been devastated. The sinking of a Queen would have meant a loss of the equivalent of more than a whole army division, a tremendous tragedy.

Not only did the *Queen Mary* carry troops, but Prime Minister Winston Churchill made three trips to North America on it to attend war conferences in the United States and Canada in May 1943, August 1943, and September 1944. He always traveled under the pseudonym Colonel Warden, a code name to confuse enemy agents. The *Queen Mary* was his seaborne office, and it was on this ship when he first reviewed the plans for the D-Day invasion and signed off on them.

A U-boat attack on the *Queen Mary* in the North Atlantic was claimed by Captain-Lieutenant Ernst-Ulrich Bruller, who commanded U-407 of the German navy. He said he fired four torpedoes at the *Queen Mary* when it was about one thousand miles west of the British Isles. Fortunately, they all missed! The date was October 1, 1942.

When the *Queen Mary* was drafted into war service as a troop carrier, she underwent many changes and alterations. The horizontal stabilizers that provided stability and smooth sailing for peacetime passengers were removed in order to gain speed through the water. Also, the ship received a coat of gray paint on the hull to camouflage her, and her name, which was painted in large 2 ½ foot high letters, was removed. Thus the *Queen Mary* soon became known with the unique *nom de guerre* of "The Gray Ghost." It was an apt title because with her speed and quiet sailing, she could slip in and out of a fog, and if perchance a Nazi U-boat spotted her, she seemed to magically disappear from their periscopes.

There was an enormous concern for the safety of the *Queen Mary* when crossing the ocean because there was always the chance of U-boats lying in wait. Therefore, the British and American officials in the Allied Commands of the fleets devised a plan for the two Queens to follow when each one sailed without escort. It was called a "zigzag course." The zigzag was a seemingly random series of course changes that would prevent the ship from staying on any one bearing long enough for a submarine to target it and fire its torpedoes.

In reality, it was not random at all because it was imperative that the ship make steady and constant progress to its destination. The zigzags were arranged in such a way that the cumulative effect kept the ship traveling on its base course at a constant relative speed. The zigzag pattern most commonly used by the Queens was the Number 8 Zigzag. It began with the ship steaming along her base course for four minutes, then altering course 25 degrees to port and maintaining that new course for eight minutes. Then the ship swung to starboard 50 degrees, held that for eight minutes, and turned 25 degrees to port again, which would bring her back on her base course, holding that for four minutes.

Then the ship made another 25 degree turn, this time to starboard, followed eight minutes later by a 50 degree turn to port, and eight minutes after that a 25 degree turn to starboard, which brought her back on her base course again. This cycle was repeated every forty minutes all the way across the Atlantic Ocean. A special clock in the wheelhouse chimed when another course change was due. During these maneuvers, the ship maintained a steady speed of twenty-eight to thirty knots, which was sufficient to easily outrun any submarine in the German fleet. Thus it would be nearly impossible for a German U-boat captain to calculate a torpedo-firing timing with his plotting chart and torpedo officer, trying to hit a zigzagging moving target traveling at a speed of 30 knots.

[Note: "Port" is the left-hand side of the ship facing forward, and "Starboard" is the right-hand side facing forward.]

The ship was divided into thirds, with the sections labeled from bow to stern into "Red," "White," and "Blue." Each person received a button in one of these three colors which had to be worn constantly. Mine was Red because my unit was billeted in the front part of the ship. Each color group was restricted to their colored section of the ship. When moving about the ship and its many corridors and stairs between decks, the military police were responsible for controlling traffic. Therefore, to prevent men from getting lost, all starboard passageways were used only for forward movement, and all port-side passageways were used only for moving aft. There were continuous traffic jams as the guys would invariably get mixed up, and the MPs had to untangle the mess.

Our XX Corps Headquarters unit consisted of about one hundred enlisted men, so we were like family and knew each other very well, as we had trained together for approximately a year. We had "lucked out" in regard to our sleeping quarters because we occupied several staterooms which were located on the upper deck of the ship. I was in a group of twenty guys who shared one stateroom. The bunks were five deep, one above the other from the floor to the ceiling. The bunk had a canvas bottom like a hammock. The space between each vertical bunk was only a few inches, so it could easily lead to claustrophobia when lying in one's own bunk. This room was very crowded when each guy was in his bunk because each GI had his huge duffle bag stacked in the corner or in front of the bunks. Each person's personal carbine was hung by its strap on the corner of his bunk.

During a couple nights, the seas were very heavy, and the big swells made the ship roll and pitch. We felt these effects in our stateroom because it caused the carbines to fall to the floor, and the guns along with duffle bags slid back and forth across the floor with each roll of the ship. These were restless and noisy nights.

The *Queen Mary* had a total of 12,500 permanently fixed bunks. However, when it carried an entire division of 15,000 thousand or more troops there were not enough beds to accommodate everyone. This dilemma was solved by using a rotation system, used only in the summer months when the weather was warm. Thus, some men slept on the open upper decks for two nights, twenty-five hundred men at a time. Then they rotated with another group. Also, the large below deck swimming pool was used by some troops who slept on cots. Obviously, the pool was not used during wartime. One of the strict rules in place during the voyage was the requirement that all GIs had to wear their life jackets at all times, and to wear their steel helmet whenever they were out in the open on the top decks.

Probably the most important aspect of life on a troopship was food. Soldiers were always hungry and had enormous appetites. After all, these young men led very active lives and expended a great deal of energy, and all the guys wondered how they could live on only two meals per day. But the ship had a feeding procedure that turned out to be quite efficient, and nobody went hungry.

The logistics of feeding fifteen thousand or more people in the close quarters of the ship meant that only breakfast and dinner could be served. Breakfast began at six o'clock in the morning and ran until eleven o'clock. Dinner was served from 3:00 p.m. until 7:30 p.m. The officer's mess was in the Tourist Class Lounge, and their meals were served by stewards. No queuing up! Enlisted men had their meals in the very large first class dining room which was converted to a cafeteria-style mess hall and seated twenty-five hundred men at one time.

The men ate in shifts determined by the section of the ship where they were billeted. Each person had only forty-five minutes in which to get his food, sit down and eat it, clean his mess kit, and get out of the dining room. As the slower eaters were leaving, a new chow line had already arrived and made a queue. I found myself gobbling down my food quickly, which was pretty hard to do given that I was always a slow eater because I loved to "savor the flavor."

When it was time for our unit to eat, we filed into the cavernous diving room of the *Queen Mary* and moved quickly to the steam tables. We brought our own mess kit and eating utensils because there were no dishes or utensils available. If you forgot to bring your mess kit, you got nothing to eat. Each of us were given two lengths of wire about a foot long, and we looped one wire through the D-ring of the aluminum mess kit and the other through holes in the handles of our knife, fork, and spoon. This was important when the time came to wash these items.

When we arrived at the steam tables, we didn't have to make a decision about what we wanted. It was an automatic system of plopping the potatoes, meat, and vegetables onto the bottom section of the mess kit, all mixed together real nice by the kitchen patrols (a.k.a. KPs). The top lid of the mess kit was divided into two sections, and we tried to keep that clear for desert and bread so they wouldn't get soaked in the gravy. However, the KPs couldn't have cared less as they slammed the cake or pie onto the cover of the kit. The most difficult part was when they put a ladle of canned peaches together with its juice into the kit, and it ran over everything. Of course, there was a lot of bitching about that, but it got you nowhere. Then one had to juggle all of this while walking to the table. It was a real challenge when the ship was in rough seas, so there was plenty of spillage. Besides, we hated the obnoxious sergeant from the kitchen who stood at the end of the steam table who constantly yelled "All right you guys, get the lead out of your rear and keep moving. Chop! Chop!"

The cavernous first-class dining room, which during peacetime voyages contained a number of tables which seated two, four, six, or eight persons, was now fitted with long tables that each seated between twelve to sixteen soldiers. These tables and their benches were bolted to the floor. The perimeter of each table had a one-inch rim of wood running along the edges to stop dishes and food from sliding off the table to the floor below. There were numerous times when the ship was in heavy seas that the mess kit or aluminum cup of the guy across the table from you slid across and banged into your own kit or hit the ridge at the edge of the table. At these times, the spillage remained mostly on top of the table, but when a giant wave or swell hit the ship, the food crashed over the ridge onto the floor.

The food was generally pretty good with generous helpings, army style. But, being on a British ship, there were two foods that definitely were not palatable to me, nor did any other American GI rave about them. One was kidney soup, and the other was English mutton; they usually went into the garbage. I didn't like the taste or smell, especially when the ship was pitching and rolling, and my stomach was churning and feeling like throwing up.

In the *Queen Mary's* main dining room, the upper half of one wall showed a huge map of the North Atlantic Ocean. It was a stylistic drawing showing the outline of the east coast of the United States on the left and on the right the west coast of Europe and the British Isles. Each day the approximate position of our ship was plotted on it, and I could follow our progress each time I ate in this hall. This was fascinating to me, and it will always live in my memory as I marveled at my great privilege of being somewhere in that great ocean sailing into a new adventure in my young life.

When we finished eating, we took our mess kits to another area for cleaning. We discovered that the reason why we had attached a length of wire to the mess kits and utensils was so we wouldn't burn our hands. Four large vats, like garbage cans, stood in a row. We dipped and swirled our kits, utensils, and cup in the first vat, which contained hot soapy water. The second can contained boiling fresh water to rinse off the soap. The third can held boiling disinfectant, and the fourth contained a salt water rinse. This was a great system which thoroughly cleaned our kits and was good hygiene.

On the way out of the mess hall, there were tables laden with all kinds of sandwiches made with ham, cheese, and roast beef. We were invited to help ourselves, which we did, and it turned out to be a God-send which helped allay our later hunger pangs until the next meal that was many hours away.

There was an enormous amount of stores which were needed to feed everyone for a six-day crossing of the ocean. These are the statistics for a typical crossing:

155,000 pounds of meat
124,000 pounds of potatoes
76,000 pounds of flour
53,000 pounds of eggs, butter, and powdered milk
31,000 pounds of canned fruit
31,000 pounds of coffee, tea, and sugar
29,000 pounds of fresh fruit
20,000 pounds of ham and bacon
20,000 pounds of jams and jellies
4,000 pounds of cheese

The *Queen Mary* carried sixty-five hundred tons of fresh water, but water usage for such a large number of passengers was strictly rationed.

One of the most popular venues for the GIs was the canteen, with nine of them scattered around the ship. These canteens were stocked with fifty thousand bottles of soft drinks, five thousand cartons of cigarettes, four hundred pounds of candy, and miscellaneous supplies of soap, shampoo, shaving cream, razor blades, and other toiletries. The one item that was conspicuously missing was chewing gum. Why? Because gum-chewing people usually parked the spent gum onto railings, seats, and other spots on the ship, and these places had to be kept free of this nuisance.

Food and eating were probably the most important concern of the troops during a long voyage, but there were many other activities and events that kept us occupied. The most important safety procedure was the fire drill which took place the first day at sea. It was a scary thought of how to evacuate fifteen thousand or more people in the event of a fire or, even worse, a torpedo hit. It was tough for the guys who smoked because smoking was only permitted on the outside decks. Each unit on board was assigned a specific time of day to be on the outside decks, and that was the only time they could smoke, so the heavy smokers got pretty desperate.

It was late on the first day at sea when I was outside on the top deck that I noticed how mild the air felt even though it was February when the North Atlantic is usually a cold and stormy place. The reason for the balmy weather was that we had entered the Gulf Stream, which is the long river of water that flows from the southern part of the United States across the North Atlantic Ocean to Europe, where it bathes the countries of England, Iceland, and Norway with a mild maritime climate during the winter months.

For the thousands of GIs aboard this ship, the prospect of being bored during the tedious six-day crossing was certainly daunting. The officers knew that this would be a major challenge, so a number of work details were arranged for the troops. Each unit had to clean their own quarters, sweep and mop the floors, and clean the latrines. Sometimes a person would have a job in another section of the ship far away from the quarters of their own unit. I received an interesting assignment to pull guard duty for four hours on one of the lower decks. My guard post was at the base of a stairway which led to the galley for the ship's British crew. This place was in the bow of the ship, and my job was to stop any wandering or lost soldiers from entering this restricted area.

During my time at this post, no GI ever appeared, but it was fascinating to watch the Limeys at work in their kitchen and the movements of British sailors in and out of this area as they picked up snacks and tea during their work details. These guys usually stopped to chat with me, and this was my first exposure to English people, so I had a hard time understanding them. They did a lot of joking, razing, and laughing with each other, and I was thrilled to have this unique opportunity. Then, to my surprise and delight, a sailor asked me if I would like a cup of tea, and I accepted his offer. I was introduced to my very first cup of English tea as the sailor added sugar and milk to the cup.

I expected only straight tea, but it was an enjoyable part of my four hours of guard duty.

There were many activities going on during days and evenings to keep the guys occupied and busy. This included numerous lectures on topics like military tactics, equipment, personal hygiene, and venereal diseases. The guys wrote letters and read books, and we received a booklet entitled "A Short Guide to Britain" which listed the dos and donts of living in the British Isles.

The ship's film library showed movies every day, and whatever was shown made little difference to the troops.

Gambling was strictly forbidden, but this was definitely the most popular event all over the ship. Poker and blackjack were the hottest card games, but craps were also very popular. Makeshift gaming tables popped up in all kinds of locations, but most likely in the space between bunks where one guy would take an army blanket and stretch it tightly across a box so it looked like a real table in a casino. The two, three, or four players were surrounded by GIs all pressing against each other to watch the action while other guys hung from the bunks above the game. Each player had his own cheering section so it got noisy. In addition, some guys devised side bets as to whether a certain card would be played or whether a particular player would win or lose. Some of these card games went on and on, not even stopping for the entire length of the voyage. If a player lost, he would leave the game, and he would be replaced by a new player.

The *Queen Mary* was not a naval warship, but it had some anti-aircraft batteries mounted in strategic locations on the upper deck. Another small six-inch gun was anchored at the stern. This armament would be ineffective against a massive attack from enemy submarines, warships, or aircraft, but it would be useful against small vessels or observer aircraft. One of the memorable activities on board was the daily gunnery drills and firing of the Queen's anti-aircraft batteries. These drills were held to keep the skills of the gun crews honed. The gun crews consisted of both British and American troops, and they received their orders from the firing director who was located at the aft end of the Boat Deck.

These daily drills helped the morale of the troops too. It was deafening to our ears to hear the staccato barks from the 20mm and 40mm anti-aircraft guns and machine guns, as well as the bursts from the three-inch guns and the tremendous thunder from the six-inch gun at the ship's stern. It was a reassuring and impressive event for the troops on board as we listened to these shells speeding out into an empty sea. It was a good feeling.

On the morning of the fifth day at sea, when I went to the top deck to get my daily dose of fresh air, I noticed a very distinct change in the climate. It was very cold and blustery and not pleasant to be outside. There was a rumor that our ship had been spied by a German U-boat, and our captain had changed course by going farther north into much colder waters of the North Atlantic Ocean. We never learned if this rumor was true. In reality, we were about one day out from our destination in Scotland, and in order to navigate into the Firth of Clyde, we had to sail around the northern part of Ireland, so we were in the colder northern waters, and it was still February.

Our transatlantic voyage was nearing its end with one more day at sea. Everyone was ready for its completion, and the first sight of land became the most anticipated event. The time had arrived for the *Queen Mary's* rendezvous with British escorts for the final hours before we entered the safe port in Scotland. Everyone experienced an overwhelming feeling of joy, tears, and anticipation, with goose bumps running up and down our spines, when we spotted the first Royal Air Force aircraft that came to greet us and welcome our ship. The feelings of loneliness, isolation, and worry during the long ocean voyage of the last five days were quickly dissipated when the British bomber suddenly appeared and circled the ship. This aircraft was the Sunderland "flying boat," which was the main patrol plane of the Coastal Command of the RAF. It was a big four-engine bomber that carried many guns, and it was described as a "humpback whale with wings." It was greatly feared by the German Luftwaffe and U-boats. There were also other Coastal Command aircraft used for escorts of the two Queens, including these American bombers: the B-17 Flying Fortress, the B-24 Liberator, and the Catalina PBY.

The Sunderland bomber greeted the *Queen Mary* when she was about six hundred miles from land. About twelve hours later, we approached the Irish coast at a headland known as Bloody Foreland where a half-dozen destroyers of the Royal Navy and an anti-aircraft cruiser arrived to take up their protective positions. The destroyers went ahead of the ship using their sonar to sweep the sea for mines and to listen for enemy submarines, while the light cruiser stayed close to our ship like a mother hen protecting her chicks. This was an indescribable sight to witness, and it seemed like too much for my mind to fathom as I thought about such things as duty, honor, awe, and thankfulness that made my heart beat a little faster and gave me tingles over my whole body.

From my viewpoint on the upper deck, I saw the various islands of Scotland in the distance off the portside, and from the starboard side, I saw the rugged headlands of Northern Ireland. We had sailed from the open ocean of the North Atlantic into the more sheltered waters of the North Channel of the Irish sea. I was struck by the different color of the Irish sea because it was light green instead of the dismal gray of the ocean that I gazed at for the last five days.

Our flotilla sailed around the southern tip of the Western Isles, with the main one being Kintyre, and next to it, the Island of Arran. Between Arran and the mainland is a body of water called the Firth of Clyde. "Firth" is a Scottish term for a narrow inlet of the sea, or a fjord, and the *Queen Mary* was shepherded through the firth and into the River Clyde toward the port, which was our final destination. In this area, the River Clyde is quite broad, and the sights were awesome. The river was crowded with ships of all kinds, including various vessels of the British Royal Navy, as well as merchant ships carrying war materiels and troops. Several tugs attached themselves to the *Queen Mary* and gently pushed her through the maze of ships to her pier in the city of Gourock, Scotland. The port of Gourock was the first location in the river that could accommodate the huge *Queen Mary*, but other cities upstream had docking facilities such as piers and wharves too, including Greenock and Port Glasgow, the latter being about twenty-five miles upstream from Gourock.

The Firth of Clyde, from Gourock to Glasgow was a reasonably safe haven for shipping because of its long distance north from the English Channel and the continent, and thus beyond the reach of the German Luftwaffe. The longer distance between the French coast and the Clyde also gave the RAF more time to scramble and intercept any enemy aircraft that might get through the anti-aircraft defenses of England itself.

The banks on both sides of the River Clyde contained numerous docks, piers, and wharves as well as eighty shipyards that could handle every size and type of ship that needed attention for repairs, from battleships and aircraft carriers to cruisers and destroyers and small corvettes. Among all the ships that were scattered in the river, I noticed a British cruiser at anchor only a few hundred yards away. It was painted in camouflaged shades of gray, but I was stunned to see a huge gaping hole in the bow of this warship. It had obviously been in a fight at sea, and it was awesome to see the result of war up close. Suddenly I began to realize that I was now in a war zone. This prompted me to think more seriously about my new life and my safety for the duration of my service for my country.

Meanwhile, the tugs had gently guided the *Queen Mary* into its pier at Gourock. The date was February 18, 1944. It was mid-morning of the sixth day after we left New York, and we had safely completed a remarkable voyage of this ship across the North Atlantic Ocean. *Thanks be to God!*

Before too long, our ship was securely tied to the dock. Gangways were attached to the A, B, and D decks in each of the "Red," "White," and "Blue" sections of the ship. Since it took a long time to disembark 16,000 troops, we had to wait until the next day. We were surprised that morning when our XX Corps Chief of Staff, Colonel William Collier, came on board to welcome us to the United Kingdom. The colonel and a few aides had secretly sailed to the UK on the *Queen Elizabeth*, which had departed from the States a few weeks before our departure in order to make preparations for our camp facilities and living quarters.

The streets that ran along the many docks in Gourock were buzzing with activity. Thousands of troops were disgorged from the ship into the streets where rows and rows of army trucks were parked, waiting to carry them away. The local citizens were gathered in large groups, waving flags and cheering the troops.

Our turn to disembark had arrived. I donned my steel helmet, put on my backpack, put my carbine on my right shoulder and my fully packed duffle bag over my left one. I proceeded down the "Red" gangplank and stepped onto the soil of a foreign country. I just entered a new phase in my young life, and I silently sent a prayer of thanks to God for his protection and great goodness during my perilous voyage across the sea.

CHAPTER 8

Sojourn in England

THE WELCOME RECEPTION THAT WE received when we disembarked from the *Queen Mary* was unexpected. Large groups of British citizens lined the streets by the docks, cheering and waving flags, both the Union Jack and the Stars and Stripes. Since we were in Scotland, it was quite appropriate that a group of bagpipers serenaded us, although the shrill music was strange to our ears. We mingled with the folks while we waited for the trucks to take us to the train station. One of the first things I noticed was the strange architecture of the buildings which was so different from what I was accustomed to back home. It was quite unusual to see the numerous chimneys on the roofs of each building and the thick black smoke oozing forth from coal-burning stoves. These centuries-old structures were blackened from many layers of carbon soot that had covered them year after year.

As I was taking in all these new and strange sights in a country so foreign to me, I encountered a pleasant surprise. To my delight, a group of American Red Cross girls greeted us and distributed hot coffee and doughnuts. This really hit the spot as it was a bit of home with actual American girls who had volunteered for duty in a foreign land to provide a little cheer for all the American boys they met. All of the GIs savored this encounter with the Red Cross girls and the small conversations we had with them.

We gradually worked our way along the street in Gourock, still carrying our own gear, until we arrived at a long line of 6x6 trucks that were parked there. These were our own US Army trucks that were already stockpiled in England. We jumped into the rear of a truck which held twelve guys including all our gear. Our convoy left Gourock and drove on a road next to the River Clyde, leading to the city of Glasgow and to our destination, which was the train station. It was now obvious that we were not staying in Scotland but were heading for a camp "Somewhere in England." (We had orders that on the letters which we wrote home, we should not disclose our location as an actual place, but instead write the address as "Somewhere in England.")

The British trains were very strange. The passenger cars were small and had doors along the side instead of a door at each end of the car as in the States. These were small compartments that held about six people, and the car didn't have seats from front to rear as American train cars. I also noticed that the freight trains consisted of miniature box cars which the English called "goods wagons."

When all boarding was completed, our express train left Glasgow. There was a lot of excitement and joking among our corpsmen, and we were a happy group thoroughly enjoying our new adventure. We slowly realized that this funny train we were on was no joke, but the steam engine pulling us was pretty efficient as we sped over the narrow gauge rails at a very fast clip. We had no idea where we were heading, but we enjoyed the view of the countryside which was so different from America. As we traveled south, we passed through several large industrial cities, and I was shocked by the sights of destruction done by German bombers. There were destroyed factories, burned-out homes, cratered streets, and guardian barrage balloons floating above important installations. These were sobering sights.

Soon darkness came upon us as we continued our journey through northern England. I began to realize a new meaning for darkness, because all of England was "blacked out." This was the law of the land during the entire period of the German Luftwaffe air raids. Cities were totally dark; no street lights; no lights in buildings and houses; no headlights on cars and trucks. It was truly eerie! The lights in our train car were dimmed and completely out in some cases. I enjoyed looking out of the window because I was curious about what was going on. Suddenly I was "rewarded" with a sight that still remains in my mind today. As the train approached the outskirts of an industrial city, I saw batteries of anti-aircraft guns and huge searchlights that were piercing the darkness of the night sky with their powerful rays of lights moving from side to side and in circles. Then I saw the scattered lights of tracer bullets that were mixed in with the live bullets from these big guns. This was a common occurrence in most British cities, especially those with industrial plants, during the years of the "Battle of Britain." These were sobering reminders that I was now in a war zone and that my life would change.

Our journey continued through the night, and as daylight arrived, we also arrived at our destination—the city of Marlborough, a town that I had never heard of before. Our long, hard train ride from Scotland to southern England was over, to our great relief, as we were dead tired. The XX Corps Command Post was established in Marlborough, in County Wiltshire. This camp was built on a hillside at the edge of town called Marlborough Commons, and it was only about a ten-minute walk to High Street, which was the main drag. Our arrival date was February 20, 1944.

The various buildings in camp were called "Quonset Huts." The quonset hut was a prefabricated, portable building which had a semicircular roof of corrugated metal that curved down to form walls. The English called them Nissen huts. We learned that this temporary camp was built to serve as an evacuation hospital for use after the invasion of the continent. It was close to the city of Swindon where there was a mammoth air base to which the wounded soldiers would be evacuated from the battlefields.

Our headquarters offices were set up in several of the Quonsets, where the rooms were configured into what later would be operating rooms, clinics, and examining rooms for doctors and nurses. They were not yet outfitted for use as a hospital, but that would happen when it got closer to D-Day. Our new living quarters were in self-standing wooden barracks for the enlisted men in our unit. The officers were billeted at the Ailesbury Arms Hotel on High Street in Marlborough, while our commanding general and the chief of staff lived in an elegant house called Ogbourne Maizey Manor.

Marlborough was a small town in County Wiltshire, shortened to Wilts, in southern England. It was about eighty miles west of London and thirty-five miles east of Bath. The city took its name from the vast hillsides of marl which were just west of town. The white cliffs of marl were a loam consisting of a mixture of clay, calcium, magnesium, and marine shell fragments of organic matter. This area had been mined through the years, but mining had stopped for the duration of the war.

Marlborough is situated at the northern fringe of the Salisbury Plain, a rather flat area of land that includes the famous city of Salisbury at its south end. The most important historical site on the Salisbury Plain is Stonehenge, only twenty miles south of Marlborough. Stonehenge is a prehistoric ceremonial ruin consisting of a circular formation of huge stone slabs standing upright and having horizontal slabs, or beams, also called lintels, of huge stones lying across the upright ones. This structure, it is believed, was constructed during the megalithic period. We got intimately acquainted with this site later during our stay in England.

There were other prehistoric sites even closer to Marlborough than Stonehenge. Only seven miles west of town was the prehistoric ruin at Avebury, called the Stone Circle, which was a large area of huge stones that were also arranged in a circular shape similar to Stonehenge. About a mile from the Avebury ruins was a huge mound called Silbury Hill, which seemed out of place on the flat Salisbury Plain. These strange places would become new and exciting discoveries later as we got settled in to our new home in England.

At the far end of High Street in Marlborough stood a stone building with Grecian columns gracing the architecture on its front side. The beautiful landscaped ground that surrounded this building was the campus of Marlborough College. The British were extremely proud of this school because one of its most famous graduates was Sir Winston Churchill, the war-time Prime Minister of England. So you could say that Winston Churchill and I had one thing in common—we both lived for a time in the same town!

As new residents of England, we gradually adjusted to new expressions, customs, and foods. The American GIs were known as "Yanks in the ETO" (European Theater of Operations). The English people said "petrol for the lorries," and we said "gas for the trucks"; they said "you cawn't miss it." But invariably the most common question we were asked, especially by the children, was "any gum chum?" because the Yanks always had gum—it was part of our weekly rations from home. Yanks didn't care much for the beer they drank in the pubs—it was *warm*, not good cold beer as they had enjoyed at home. Our corps cooks began serving us dehydrated vegetables and the awful *powdered* milk and eggs. There was constant bitching about the powdered quality and the unpalatable taste, but this was to be our lot for the duration of the war while we were in Europe. Fresh milk and eggs were not available.

We also were introduced to the strange names of British currency and coins and their denominations and values. We were paid in British currency, so we had to learn the confusing values of pence, shillings, half-crowns, crowns, ten shilling notes, and pounds. The paper money was made in different sizes, wider than US bills, so it didn't fit in our American wallets unless it was folded.

All of these first impressions and experiences in a land and culture that was strange to us soon were placed in the back of our minds. We were in England for only one reason, to destroy the tyrant Adolf Hitler, who with his Wehrmacht was destroying the people and lands and cities of Europe. His "Festung Europa" was across the English Channel not too many miles from where we were stationed. It was time to get down to the business of war.

Gen. Walton H. Walker was the Commanding General of our XX Corps Headquarters and Col. William A. Collier was his Chief of Staff. They promptly set into motion an intensive training and conditioning program for all Corps personnel, including instruction both in the classroom and in the field. We attended classes in camouflaging, waterproofing vehicles, recognition of allied and enemy aircraft, maintenance of fire arms, and many other topics.

The XX Corps Artillery Battalion was attached to our headquarters, and they also set up their camp near Marlborough. This was one of the combat units that Joe Messner and I had observed and tested when we went to Fort Leonard Wood in Missouri for two weeks of detached service in December, 1943. This heavy artillery battalion with long-range firing ability would be traveling side by side with our Corps Headquarters until the war's end.

Training exercises increased in intensity as more and more combat units arrived in England along with vehicles and support groups and the materials of war. The crack 4th and 6th Armored Divisions were attached to our Corps, and together with the XX Corps Artillery, they conducted field exercises with vigor. Frequently, the Corps Commander would alert us to move out into field exercises without prior warning. This included simulated attacks by our tank and infantry troops against pillboxes, accompanied by the rolling barrage of the artillery batteries. This training was very thorough and intense, and high-ranking US Army observers watched the exercises. One of these visitors was Gen. George S. Patton! General Patton had arrived in England from the campaigns in Africa and Sicily, but his whereabouts were deliberately kept secret from the German High Command.

Savernake Forest was just three miles south of Marlborough. Its stately trees consisted of beeches and oaks that had grown there for hundreds of years, so they were ancient and beautiful. There was no underbrush, so the forest was like a huge park covered with a canopy of high branches, but at this time the forest contained the second largest ammunition dump in Britain. It was an awesome sight when we drove through this forest to see rows upon rows of shells of all calibers neatly stacked like piles of bricks. They were arranged by size from small arms ammunition to shells for machine guns, anti-aircraft guns, mortars, howitzers, and the gigantic four thousand pound blockbusters. During our stay in Marlborough, this huge storage area grew in size almost daily, as the British Isles became a mammoth storage ground of war materiel for the coming invasion of Europe.

Physical conditioning of Corps Headquarters personnel was a high priority for Colonel Collier. Morning calisthenics and drills were routine events, but the frequent road marches were the high points which were thoroughly enjoyed by all of us. These marches occurred two or three times per week, announced at a moment's notice, and included full-field equipment. That meant carrying a full backpack containing all the gear necessary for survival under battle conditions, including a pup tent and tarp, rain coat, small shovel, mess kit, socks, and underwear. We wore our heavy steel helmet, carried a canteen full of water on our web belt, and carried a carbine over our shoulder. These marches were at least four miles and up to six miles in length, and we marched in all types of weather conditions.

All Corpsmen participated in these road marches, and we were a happy bunch as we bonded with each other in our common mission of becoming the best physically fit fighting men in the US Army. These marches were not marching-in-step as the word suggests, but they were more like hiking. There was no drill sergeant barking out orders like "forward march," "column left," "column right," "left foot left," "to reverse, march," or "platoon stop." We really enjoyed walking along the lovely English roads and lanes that radiated out from our barracks at Marlborough Commons. We walked beside the quiet meandering River Kennet and through villages with names like Mildenhall, Axford, and Ramsbury. On another day, we hiked through other towns with the names of Fyfield, West Overton, and East Kennet. These places were very charming with typical English cottages covered with thatched roofs and tiny front yards showing the early spring roses and other flowers. English barges used the River Kennet to carry goods and people, and we often marched across a lock where a waiting barge was either raised or lowered to another height, so it could proceed on its trip. I had seen pictures of scenes like this in geography books, and now it was a thrill to actually see these quaint English scenes with my own eyes.

Hiking through this peaceful English countryside was a pleasure, but the highlight of each march was our singing—beautiful singing, because our guys always broke out into songs. We were like a men's glee club singing in harmony because there were many excellent voices. We sang familiar American songs: from the west like "Home on the Range," or from the south like "Suwannee River," and many campfire songs like "White Choral Bells." If a song was new to you, it was learned quickly, so with everybody's input of new songs our repertoire grew. But the all-time favorite was an English ditty that had this line (the only words that I remember): "Roll me over in the Clover." Our singing was beautiful, in harmony, and rendered with gusto. As we walked past a meadow, the grazing cows looked up at us in awe as we marched past their pasture, and also in the villages, the women and children came out of their houses and gathered in the lanes where they waved and thanked us as we passed by. These wonderful days in England still live in my memory.

The British people celebrated a wartime feature called "Salute to the Soldier" week during our stay in Marlborough. This was a colorful time of pageantry and patriotism during which the citizenry paid tribute to the British soldiers. On one of the days during this week, the City of Marlborough hosted the event with all the troops of the XX Corps invited to participate. We wore our dress uniforms and carried our carbines as we stood in review by a General of the British Army, the mayor of Marlborough, and our own General Walker. This occurred in front of the Castle and Ball Hotel, the biggest one in town.

The mayor and some of the prominent political leaders and citizens of the town were on the reviewing stand. The mayor looked regal, dressed in a long robe, wearing a felt hat, and holding a long scepter. A large pendant hung around his neck. After the formal ceremonies, there was a parade on High Street, the main drag. Our Corps Headquarters personnel and troops of the XX Corps Artillery, numbering perhaps 500 or more soldiers, proudly marched in honor of our Allies of the British Empire. High Street was lined with the townsfolk along with their children, cheering us and waving British flags. This was a day off for us and a new and exciting experience.

Our sojourn in England was not "all work and no play." The Corps Commander signed an order that gave us a few days for sightseeing during the first week of April, 1944. The motor pool provided a 6x6 truck for ten of us guys who chummed around with each other. The body of this big truck was covered with a big tarpaulin and had benches around its perimeter. We often traveled to various historic sights and to English cities using this form of transportation. It was a rough ride, but it was free.

The Salisbury Plain in County Wiltshire contains three of the world's most intriguing Neolithic structures, dating back to prehistoric times circa 3,000 BC. They even predate the Great Pyramid of Cheops at Gaza in Egypt by three hundred years. These huge stone structures are known as Avebury and Stonehenge, together with Silbury Hill. We visited these places during our first day of sightseeing, but at the time I was unaware of the awesome significance of the places I was seeing.

Avebury is a mere five miles west of Marlborough. Here on the chalky downs of Wiltshire, an ancient people built a huge stone structure enclosed by an enormous earthwork. The Neolithic builders dug a circular ditch into the earth, probably using picks made from deer antlers. They dug a large circle of ground and piled the excavated earth into a six-foot high bank which surrounded the circle. The area inside the circle was approximately twenty-five acres and 330 feet in diameter, larger than a football field. The original ditch was more than twenty-five feet deep, and the height of the bank made from the excavated chalk rubble averaged about twenty feet. Along the inner edge of the original ditch, the builders erected a ring of one hundred sarsen stones that weighed approximately fifteen tons on average, with some stones weighing as much as three times that much. These hard sandstone boulders were probably dragged on sledges and log rollers from the chalk downs located about two miles to the east, near Marlborough. The stones were then erected to an upright position at the site, where most of them still stand today.

Barely one mile from Avebury is another ancient Neolithic enigma called Silbury Hill. It is an enormous mound of earth in the shape of a cone that is

130 feet tall and 500 feet in diameter. It seems out of place on the flatness of the Salisbury Plain. The mound is made up of over three hundred thousand cubic yards of chalk blocks and is the largest man-made prehistoric mound in Europe. No one knows why this dirt mound was built, but it probably was a monument erected for a certain event.

We continued our sightseeing trip by driving south twenty miles to the most important Bronze Age monument found anywhere in Europe. Experts place a date of initial construction at approximately 3,000 BC. and it is believed that its construction continued over a period of fifteen hundred years. This site is called Stonehenge—"henge" means "outdoor sanctuary." At our first sight of it, we saw the circular arrangement of huge vertically placed, rough-hewn stones, some erect and some toppled, with some of them capped with horizontal stone beams called lintels. The circular area was 350 feet in diameter, surrounded with a trench that was dug around its perimeter.

Within the circular area, the builders placed a ring of huge sandstone slabs standing upright, and capped with a continuous ring of thirty lintels or horizontal beams. Originally, there were thirty of these upright slabs that were about eighteen feet long and set four feet below ground level. Each upright slab weighed about twenty-five tons, and each lintel weighed about seven tons. These slabs of gray sandstone were quarried at Marlborough Downs, twenty miles north. The builders then dragged, pushed, or rolled them on large logs to the building site. Inside this continuous ring was a horseshoe-shaped arrangement of Bluestone slabs, but what is remarkable is that these Bluestones were quarried in the Prescelly Mountains in southwest Wales, 135 miles away!

The stone workers fitted the upright slabs and the horizontal lintels with tongue and groove joints, all accomplished with crude tools of very hard stones used as hammers. The slabs were also curved and smooth. A pair of vertical slabs formed a portal at the outside of the circle, and further away aligned with this portal was a single large slab called the Heel Stone. The placement of these particular stones probably had astronomical significance because the rising sun on June 21st, the summer solstice, cast its beams through the line of axis of the gap in the embankment, the portal of slabs, and onto the Heel Stone on the avenue outside the gap. So, Stonehenge may have been an astronomical observatory and time clock as a method of determining a calendar based on the longest day of the year.

The big question is, "who were these people that built this fantastic stone monument so many centuries ago?" Archaeologists have argued about this question for many years. The most likely theory is that the builders of Stonehenge were the Druids, who were described as a powerful, priestly, religious order within the ancient cultures of Celts and Gauls from Ireland and Wales. They perhaps practiced their pagan rites in this temple of stones for hundreds of years before they disappeared from history, but they left us with this enigma of Stonehenge as a leftover of prehistory.

I, together with my buddies, were a group of ten American soldiers who romped around on these huge monoliths, and we climbed the fallen slabs and played "hide and seek" with the many vertical upright slabs. We took pictures of each other on and by the boulders on this cold, blustery day in England. At the time of our visit, Stonehenge was an abandoned site consisting of all these boulders lying on the Salisbury Plain, and there was no official authority or tourist office that sold tickets to view it. Our small group of GIs had this "sacred place" all to ourselves, and we had no knowledge of its history and significance. Some years

XX Corps soldiers at Stonehenge, England (1944)

after the end of World War II, archaeologists and the British government took notice of preserving this Neolithic site, and they cleaned it up, developed it, and designated it as a monument of the British Heritage National Trust. It is also listed as a UNESCO World Heritage Site.

On April 3, 1944, two days after our travels over the Salisbury Plain, we left camp for another sightseeing trip. Heading north this time, we passed through the cities of Newcastle-Under-Lyme, and Birmingham, a very large industrial city, which had sustained considerable damage from German bombs. We observed the many commercial and manufacturing buildings that lay in ruins. This was another grim reminder that we were in a war zone.

Our final destination on this day was a stop in the famous city of Stratford-upon-Avon, the home of William Shakespeare. We walked on the streets of this small town, looking at the many sites relating to Shakespeare, including his home and Ann Hathaway's cottage. There were no tourists, only soldiers, visiting here because all activities concerning this famous dramatist and poet were shut down for the duration of the war.

It was awesome as I walked along the River Avon and saw a dozen beautiful white swans swimming lazily, while other swans were preening themselves on the river bank. I was surprised to see that the Avon is merely a small meandering stream, with hardly a moving current as it flows through the city. I thought how lucky I was to walk on the banks of the same river that William Shakespeare walked on during his lifetime about four hundred years ago, between 1564 and 1616. Another thought came to my mind when I remembered my English class at Clintonville High School, a mere three years earlier. I had read and studied Shakespeare's play, *The Merchant of Venice*, and I recalled the famous speech in that play that Portia, a rich heiress, made about mercy. Our class had to memorize this speech from Act IV, Scene 1, in the Venice Court of Justice.

The quality of mercy is not strained,
It droppeth, as the gentle rain from heaven
Upon the place beneath: it is twice blessed;
It blesses him that gives, and him that takes:
'Tis mightiest in the mightiest; it becomes
The throned monarch better than his crown;
His scepter shows the force of temporal power,
The attribute to awe and majesty,
Wherein doth sit the dread and fear of kings;
But mercy is above this sceptored sway,
It is enthroned in the hearts of kings.
It is an attribute to God himself;
And earthly power doth then show likest God's,
When mercy seasons justice.

Wow! This day I had walked on hallowed ground where the author of this play had lived his life. I was on an emotional high during the ride back to camp as I stored these memories into the back of my brain.

The Corps Commander gave us some additional time off during the first two weeks of April, 1944. We had two separate passes to visit the sights of Stonehenge, Avebury, and Stratford, but the most exciting trip was announced on April 6—a visit to London. A bunch of us guys boarded a train which whisked us there, only 80 miles away.

London was exciting as I walked around the city and saw the famous sites in person that I only had read about before. Cars and trucks drove on the "wrong" side of the street, so it was confusing which way to look when crossing them. The old English taxis looked strange because of their odd and different designs. And the double-decker red buses were fascinating. I always got a seat on the top deck because it was so cool to see the sights while sitting so high. These buses had two entrances, one in the front by the driver and one in the back, each with a conductor who collected the fare. Here is where I nearly suffered a serious injury. At a bus stop, many people were boarding the rear platform, and my buddies had stepped onto it in front of me. I was the last person in our group, and my hands were holding the steel pole at the back of the platform, ready to step on board. But before I was able to get my feet onto the platform, the bus drove off with a jack-rabbit burst of speed, and to my horror, my legs were flying in the air behind me while I frantically hung on to the pole. I was very scared and didn't know if I should let go with my hands and fall off, or just hang on for dear life. Fortunately, my buddies grabbed my swinging body even while they also had to hang on to the pole. It seemed like an eternity, but my buddies got me solidly onto the platform and pulled me to safety. We all were shaken.

We continued our exploration of London. A walk across London Bridge was pretty cool as I remembered the nursery rhyme that we chanted during recess games on my elementary school playground: "London Bridge is falling down, falling down, falling down; London Bridge is falling down, my fair lady." Fortunately, German bombs had not destroyed this bridge, and I was surprised to see that it was just an ordinary bridge across the Thames River, which merely had a low railing without any ornamentation.

From the middle of the London Bridge, I looked toward the next bridge crossing the river, the Tower Bridge, which I remember seeing in my grade school geography book. Its two towers anchored the roadway which opened up for river traffic. The bus passed under the ornate towers, and I looked up in awe because so much English history was involved with this bridge that led to the Tower of London. This is the castle with a tower on each of its four corners, where the British Crown Jewels are stored in a huge vault deep in the bowels of the castle.

The beautiful boulevard called Pall Mall leads directly to Buckingham Palace. In front of the palace, there is a huge granite pedestal on which is the high statue of Queen Victoria. A big brass gate is part of the high fence of tall vertical bars that surround the pavement in front of the building. We were lucky to see a company of royal palace guards march through the gate to take up their guard duties at the palace. The showy changing of the guard was suspended during the war years.

Big Ben, the tall clock tower, was still standing without any damage from bombs, and the Houses of Parliament lined the Thames River next to it. Nearby was Number 10 Downing Street where we were kept away at a good distance by barricades, because this was the home of Churchill. The London fish market along the Thames was a fascinating and busy place, and the smell was overpowering. Teams of horses were hitched to big four-wheeled wagons which were stacked perhaps ten feet high with boxes of fish to be delivered to London restaurants. Bobbies with their tall black police hats held with a chin strap, carrying night sticks, were slowly walking among the wagons, horses, and people.

London Fish Market (1944)

A short walk took us to St. Paul's Cathedral, the architectural gem built by Christopher Wren between 1675 and 1710. The granite stones and pillars of the structure were blackened from centuries of smoke and soot that had emerged from the many chimneys in the city. Two elegant clock towers graced the front of the cathedral, one on each end of the front façade. But the real beauty was the huge dome that covered the nave of the church. St. Paul's received a direct hit by a German bomb that was dropped on September 12, 1940, during the London Blitz. The bomb blasted a huge hole in the dome and landed on the floor of the nave, but miraculously it did not explode. We entered the nave and looked around, but the interior was stark. All paintings and works of art, fixtures, and ornaments were removed and placed in secret storage somewhere in the UK outside of London. The beautiful stained glass windows were replaced by clear glass. We looked up into the dome which now was patched and boarded up with scaffolding and temporary repairs. The damage was horrible, but it could have been worse, even with the possible total destruction of this edifice.

Our day in London turned into night, and we had visited many of the main sights as we darted around the city. Nights in London meant total blackout, and this was a weird experience, as there were no street lights or lights on buildings, only dim lights visible at ground level. The headlights on buses and taxis were covered with black screens that had a narrow slit which let dim beams of light shine onto the street. This light was not visible from the air and enemy aircraft.

Our final activity was a visit to Piccadilly Circus, which is the famous square on the West End of central London. This is the theater district, and Piccadilly Circus is the most popular spot for visitors and locals alike. Several streets converge at this wide intersection surrounded by restaurants and night clubs. In the center of the Circle is a huge granite monument with statues at its base and several ledges on which people can sit. There was a large crowd of people, servicemen, native Londoners, and the ever-present prostitutes milling around in the dim light of the night. The latter is what gave Piccadilly Circus its dubious reputation, and this image is the one that instantly popped into people's minds when its name was mentioned. The big USO Center (United Service Organization) and dance hall, called Rainbow Corner, was also located here. The big bands from the States, like Glen Miller, played at this club, and the place was always jammed with American GIs and English women for dances. It was extremely popular.

It was time to go back to camp as the evening was getting late, so we made our way to the train station for the ride back to Marlborough. Even though I was dead tired, I was on a "high" and chatted and laughed with my companions about our wonderful day in London.

On April 9, 1944, three days after our London trip, General Walker gave us one more day off, so a truck from the motor pool took us to the city of Bath. This is a very old city built by the Romans when they had a colony in the British Isles. The commercial part of the city lies in a valley alongside the Avon River. This is where the ancient Romans discovered natural hot springs, so they built elaborate bath houses which still exist. I stood beside the pool and watched the steam rising from the hot mineral water. A promenade surrounded the pool, and elegant marble pillars held up a ceiling with elaborate designs carved into the stones. There was no roof directly covering the pool, only open sky. This was awesome when I thought about the Roman citizens, perhaps only the upper class as well as soldiers, who lived in this outpost nearly two thousand years ago, enjoying their leisure time here. How appropriate that the name of the city was "Bath."

Only a few feet beyond these baths stood a beautiful cathedral called "Bath Abbey," built around 1500. Its design was in Gothic architecture with a square-shaped tower at the front façade, with numerous arches. The windows were very tall, and the main portal was a huge wooden doorway with big, bold carvings and triple arches and statues of saints on each side. It so impressed me that my buddy took my picture standing at the door. I entered the Abbey and stayed a while as there was a worship service in progress. The residential sections of Bath are built on hillsides surrounding the river valley. The long streets of row houses and the countless chimneys were very striking. This was a lovely city.

The XX Corps personnel had thoroughly enjoyed two weeks of travel and sightseeing of places that we had only read or heard about, but now we had seen them with our own eyes. It was thrilling and educational for me, and I felt fortunate to enjoy this experience as a twenty-year-old farm boy from northern Wisconsin. Wow!

US Army band concert, Ramsbury, England (1944)

Jay Ottoson, Journalist with
XX Corps, (1943-1945)

CHAPTER 9

The Enemy We Faced

AS THE MONTH OF APRIL 1944 was coming to a close, we noticed that more and more activities were happening in England for the preparation of the invasion of the European continent. There was a feeling of anxiousness and tenseness observed in the top brass at Corps Headquarters. The days of "fun and games" had turned very serious.

There were a number of significant events in past European history that led to the huge military buildup that was now occurring in this country. A review of these events is a grim reminder of the reasons why I was in the UK, along with millions of servicemen who made up the Allied Expeditionary Force, whose mission was to invade Hitler's "Festung Europa," or "Fortress Europe," and defeat this enemy—Germany!

World War I ended with the signing of the Treaty of Versailles on June 28, 1919. Germany was defeated and its monarchy ended with the establishment of the Weimar Republic. However, Germany was required to pay for all civilian damages caused by the war, and she also lost her colonies and a large portion of her territory. The terms of the Treaty were extremely humiliating to the German people. Resentment of these harsh terms provoked widespread condemnation, undermined the new Weimar government, and served as a rallying cry to the unhappy people who thought Germany was ultimately destined for greatness.

In the midst of this turmoil, a new voice arose in Germany. It came from a young man who was a charismatic orator, and he spoke to numerous crowds of unhappy people around the country who eagerly listened to his eloquent rhetoric. He was born in the small town of Braunau, Austria, situated on the Inn River which formed the border between Austria and Germany. *This man was Adolf Hitler!*

Hitler's birthhome, Braunau, Austria

Hitler was born on April 20, 1889, the fourth child of six children born to Alois Schickelgruber and Klara Hitler. His father was a customs official and moved to several different places during Adolf's childhood, so his schooling was sporadic and he quit school at the age of sixteen. His parents both died when he was a teenager. During World War I, when Hitler was in his mid-twenties, he was caught up in the patriotism of the time, and his passions against foreigners, especially Jews and Slavs, were inflamed. He got involved in the German Workers' Party, which became his platform for displaying his masterful demagoguery and diatribes denouncing the Jews and blaming them for hyperinflation, political instability, and unemployment. Along with anti-Semitism, Hitler also was anti-Marxist and blamed the Jews as being the leaders in certain forms of Socialism and Bolshevism.

The German Workers' Party was disorganized and had no useful platform when Hitler got involved, but its members held a right-wing doctrine that Hitler liked. He felt that he could use this party as a vehicle to reach his political goals. The name of the party was changed to the National Socialist German Worker's Party, or *Nazi* Party. Its infamous logo was adopted in 1935, and consisted of a red flag with a swastika. The swastika was an ancient religious symbol in the form of a Greek cross with the ends of the arms bent at right angles in either a clockwise or counterclockwise direction. When Adolf Hitler was a young boy, the family lived across the street from a large Benedictine Monastery, and he was intrigued with the Monastery's coat of arms, whose main salient feature was a swastika!

Swastika on Nazi flag

On November 8, 1923, Hitler held a rally at a Munich beer hall where he proclaimed a revolution against the

Weimar Republic, and where he announced that he was ready to march to Berlin to rid the government of Jews and Communists. This plan failed as Hitler was arrested and imprisoned in Landsberg. This event became known as the Munich Putsch (revolt). Hitler served only nine months of his five-year term, but while he was in jail he wrote the first volume of his book called *Mein Kampf*. The title means "My Struggle," and it became the standard textbook of Nazi political doctrine. The book was crudely written and filled with glorified inaccuracies and self-serving half-truths.

[Note: I found and brought home a copy of *Mein Kampf* when we were camped in a school house later in our sweep across Germany.]

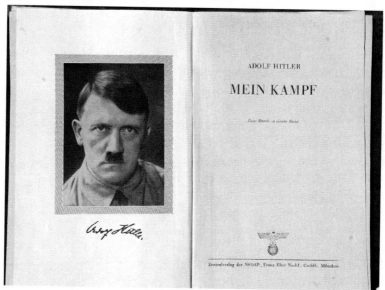

Hitler's book Mein Kampf

In his book, Hitler targeted political groups such as democrats, communists, and internationalists with his vicious diatribes, but he particularly labeled the Jews as the true enemy, especially the enemy of the Aryan race, which in Nazi ideology meant a Caucasian gentile, especially of a Nordic type. These enemies needed to be eliminated because the future of the German people needed something called Lebensraum, or "living space" without which the superior German culture would decay. In order to obtain this living space, Hitler would have to conquer Russia and the Slavic countries, and he would become the leader of this plan.

After Hitler was released from jail, he began to make speeches to mass audiences calling on the Aryan race to create a new empire—The Third Reich, which would last for a thousand years. In 1932, Hitler ran for president against Paul von Hindenburg, an election that Hitler lost, but in a political deal in 1933, Hitler was appointed Chancellor. In the following year, Hindenburg died and Hitler became the Fuehrer, or supreme dictator.

The 1936 Summer Olympics, the XI Olympiad, brought some international attention to Nazi Germany, as Berlin was the host for the Olympic games held from August 1 to August 16. Berlin won the bid to host the games over Barcelona in 1931, which was before the Nazi Party gained power; however, Hitler seized this opportunity to promote Nazi ideology and racial supremacy and to use it as a propaganda tool. Only "Aryan" Germans were allowed to compete, and Jewish athletes were ousted. Signs and slogans such as "Jews not Wanted" were removed from tourist attractions, and the city was cleaned up.

In the United States, there was considerable debate whether or not American athletes should compete in Berlin. In the end, President Roosevelt and others decided that the US Olympic team should attend. America's most notable athlete was Jesse Owens, who was African American. Interestingly, he received better treatment in Germany than in America where segregation and discrimination was still rampant against black people. Owens won four gold medals in the sprint and long jump events, and he became a national hero in America long before he and black people would get equal status and rights with whites. Adolf Hitler did attend many of the events in Olympic Stadium, but he did not congratulate or shake the hands of Jesse Owens or any other winning athlete.

Adolf Hitler and Hermann Goering, (Photo found by Author in a German school)

In 1937, Hitler outlined his plans for world domination by Germany. He began his plan by launching a vast construction program of civil structures, including autobahns, railroads, dams, bridges, and other civil works. He also began a huge expansion of industrial production and the rearmament of the German military war machine, called the Wehrmacht. He increased the size of the German navy (Kriegsmarine), and he introduced an air force (Luftwaffe). Hitler prepared his new war machine to enable him to reach his goal of gaining Lebensraum for the German people.

Hitler's first move to obtain lebensraum came in March 1938 when the German government annexed Austria, called the Anschluss. Several months later, on September 29, the Prime Minister of Britain, Neville Chamberlain, the French Premier Edouard Daladier, and Benito Mussolini, the dictator of Italy, met with Hitler in Munich. This summit resulted in the Munich Agreement in which the Allied leaders gave in to Hitler's military demands. After that meeting, Prime Minister Chamberlain spoke these immortal words predicting "peace for our time," that are forever etched into history books. Ironically, *Time Magazine* named Adolf Hitler as their "Man of the Year for 1938."

On March 15, 1939, the German army entered Prague, Czechoslovakia, and Hitler proclaimed Bohemia and Moravia a German protectorate. His timetable to overrun and conquer the countries of Europe had begun.

Next, on September 1, 1939, Nazi tanks and infantry invaded western Poland in a swift conquest that coined a new word, called "blitzkrieg," or "lightning war." Britain and France then declared war on Germany on September 3. Meanwhile, the Nazis and Soviets had decided to carve up Poland between them, so on September 17, Soviet forces invaded eastern Poland. Hitler then turned to Germany's northern frontier in April 1940 when he marched his armies into Denmark and Norway. In the following month, Germany also conquered the Netherlands, Luxembourg, and Belgium, and on June 22, the Nazi forces entered Paris, since France had surrendered! Fortunately, General Charles de Gaulle escaped to London, where he set up an organization called the Free French, to continue to fight for the French people. Now, Hitler had achieved his goal with his armies overrunning all the countries of Europe. The British Isles were now isolated from the rest of Europe. The British nation stood alone! A German propaganda picture showed Hitler's Luftwaffe flying over the waves of the English Channel and a quote from him stating: "England ist keine insel mere", which means "England is no longer an island."

During the summer of 1940, after the surrender of France, Hitler added a new development in his plans to conquer the world. His ally, Benito Mussolini, the fascist dictator of Italy, decided to join the war on the German side. Italy declared war on the Allies on June 10, 1940. This shifted Hitler's attention to the Mediterranean region and specifically to North Africa where Italy held some colonies that needed to be defended.

The British had a modest military presence in Egypt, commanded by General Bernard Montgomery (Monty), primarily to protect the Suez Canal. Libya, just west of Egypt, was a colony of Italy, and Mussolini was anxious to link it with its other African colony, called Italian East Africa (Ethiopia and Eritrea). He also wanted to capture the Suez Canal and the Arabian oil fields beyond the canal.

Italian infantry and tank divisions invaded Egypt on September 13, 1940. There were continuous back-and-forth battles between the Italian and

Commonwealth forces, and eventually the Italian forces retreated to Libya. Because of this disaster, Hitler deployed reinforcements to North Africa with fresh German troops and equipment. This was the Deutsches Afrika Korps under the command of a very charismatic and able general, Erwin Rommel, who later obtained the nickname "The Desert Fox." The Desert War continued with various battles of losing ground in retreats and then retaliations and the regaining of lost ground. This occurred in Egypt and Libya during the period of June 1940 to February 1943, at which time the Axis armies were driven out of Libya into Tunisia. The Allied forces consisted of British, French, and American troops.

The Tunisia Campaign, or the Battle of Tunisia, covered the period from November 1942 to May 1943 and resulted in an Allied victory. In the meantime, the "Desert Fox," Rommel, had been defeated and crushed by General Montgomery, and in February 1943, Rommel was recalled to Germany. General Eisenhower was named the commanding general of the ETO and went to London. During 1942–1943, Gen. George S. Patton was at the Desert Training Center in the Mohave Desert of California, the founding of which was the brain child of Patton. The results of the grueling training in the harsh desert conditions were for eventual deployment to the deserts of North Africa. That was the reason why I was sent to Camp Young in California when I entered the army in January 1943. Our unit, the IV Armored Corps, was in training to eventually be sent to North Africa. Patton received orders to leave Indio before I arrived there, and he took his troops to North Africa where he would lead one of the task forces, which later captured French Morocco and Algeria. It had the code name "Operation Torch."

In March 1943, General Patton took over command of the US II Corps at Casablanca, Morocco. It was after the successes of the Allies in defeating Rommel's armies in Morocco, Algeria, and Tunisia, that my IV Armored Corps was relocated to Camp Campbell, Kentucky. The reason was that our training for desert warfare was no longer necessary because the North African campaigns were over. This move to Kentucky occurred in April, 1943.

In the summer of 1940, after the German Wehrmacht had achieved many victories and had overrun most of Europe, Hitler stood on a cliff on the French coast next to a concrete bunker containing a huge coastal gun. He looked across the English Channel and dreamed about his forthcoming plan to invade Britain. The cross-channel invasion had the code name "Seeloewe" ("Sea Lion").

The surrender of France meant that England now stood alone, with a serious shortage of guns and aircraft. Winston Churchill now occupied Number 10 Downing Street as Prime Minister. The British people were demoralized after the retreat of their troops and the subsequent disastrous evacuation from Dunkirk, as well as the loss of their French ally. It was imperative that the British people needed encouragement to stay in the frightful fight that lay before them, so Churchill made a speech in the British House of Commons on June 18, 1940. These were his eloquent words:

"I expect that the Battle of Britain is about to begin. Upon this battle depends the survival of Christian civilization. Upon it depends our own British life, and the long continuity of our institutions and our Empire. Hitler knows that he will have to break us in this island or lose the war. Let us therefore brace ourselves to our duties, and so bear ourselves that, if the British Empire and its Commonwealth last for a thousand years men will still say, 'This was their finest hour'".

German General Wilhelm Keitel signed a significant directive on July 2, 1940, which stated: "The Fuehrer and Supreme Commander has decided that a landing in England is possible, provided that air superiority can be attained." The key words were "air superiority" which was Hitler's main goal at this time, so a new phase of the war was at hand. The words of Prime Minister Churchill—"the Battle of Britain is about to begin" were prophetic, as Hitler's Luftwaffe began strategic bombing of RAF bases with regularity. During one of these raids in August 1940, German bombers accidently bombed part of the city of London. RAF long-range bombers retaliated by making a raid on Berlin. This event infuriated Hitler, so he ordered his air force to drop their bombs on London itself.

It was five o'clock in the afternoon of September 7, 1940 that the first wave of 364 German bombers escorted by 515 fighters flew up the River Thames to London in a surprise attack. Another wave of 133 Heinkel He 111 bombers attacked later that night. The fighter escorts were Messerschmitt BF 109 aircraft. During the disastrous raid, many tons of high explosive and incendiary bombs were dropped on the eastern section of London, where the Royal Arsenal, power stations, gasworks, warehouses, and homes were destroyed. In the London Docklands, some five ships were moored, with over half a million tons of food and other vital supplies in their holds. They were set on fire and sank in the river. The incendiary bombs set London ablaze so returning waves of Nazi bomber pilots were able to see their targets easier. The destruction that night was immense, and the death toll was high.

The night of September 7 was the beginning of the London Blitz. During these nightly raids, London was subjected to 57 *consecutive* nights of bombing. Many of London's landmarks were hit with bombs or destroyed. On the night of October 10, 1940, a five hundred pound bomb penetrated the roof of St. Paul's Cathedral, demolishing the High Altar, which I saw later.

The London Blitz continued for a period of eight months, or 246 days, from

September 7, 1940 to May 10, 1941. Each night during the Blitz, some sixty thousand Londoners bedded down in the city's underground rail stations. The last night of the Blitz was May 10–11, 1941 when during a full moon some 515 German bombers penetrated the anti-aircraft defenses and caused a very high death toll, including 1,364 killed plus 1,616 injured. The British Museum, Houses of Parliament, and St. James Palace were damaged, among others.

Suddenly, however, Hitler changed his plans and abandoned his mission to invade Britain. Instead, he turned his efforts to the invasion of the Soviet Union, which required the movement of German air power to the east. A non-aggression pact that Hitler had signed with the Soviet Union in August 1939 was ignored, so on June 22, 1941, three million of his troops attacked the Soviet Union over a two thousand mile front. During the invasion, named Operation Barbarossa, the German armies gained a great deal of success by overrunning the Baltic States as well as Belarus and Ukraine. But when the Nazi forces got to Moscow, they were stopped at the outskirts of the city in December 1941. The Russian winter was very fierce, and the Soviet resistance stopped Hitler cold. It was a crushing defeat, and Hitler's invasion of Russia failed!

Sunday, December 7, 1941 was "a day that will live in infamy." These were the words spoken by President Franklin D. Roosevelt when the United States received the news of the Japanese attack on Pearl Harbor, Hawaii. Four days later, on December 11, Hitler declared war on the United States, and this was six days after the Nazi's closest approach to Moscow on December 5. Now Hitler was facing some formidable opponents: the world's largest Empire (British Empire), the world's greatest industrial and financial power (USA), and the world's largest army (USSR). The United States was now engaged in a war that encompassed two theaters—Europe and the Pacific. Prime Minister Churchill went to Washington, DC, to meet with President Roosevelt just before Christmas to plan strategy. Their ideas were to strike at the "underbelly" of the Nazi empire in the Mediterranean, North Africa, and Sicily, and later to strike the German army head-on in Europe—in Italy and France.

These two dictators, Hitler and Mussolini, and their henchmen, had committed gruesome crimes against humanity by exterminating millions of people. These horrible mass killings were unknown to the outside world at this time, but they would be discovered later when our troops would overrun German concentration camps that contained countless numbers of emaciated, starving inmates who were still alive, and also the cremation ovens and mass burial pits of the people who had died. The time had come to engage Hitler and Nazi Germany in battle and rid the world of this brutal tyrant.

D-Day and the invasion of Europe was inevitable!

CHAPTER 10

Hitler's Defenses of Western Europe

ADOLF HITLER BEGAN TO REALIZE that an allied invasion of Europe was inevitable, and he knew about the enormous buildup of military troops and equipment in the United Kingdom. However, Hitler was unsure where it would take place because there were about seventeen hundred miles of coastline to protect from the North Cape of Norway to the French border with Spain. Because of the enormous length of these borders, it was feasible to only fortify and protect the most valuable places, especially the French coast between Calais and Cherbourg. As a consequence, Hitler finally ordered the building of a defense line, an "impregnable front," to protect Germany and all of Europe from an "Anglo-Saxon invasion in the west." It was called "The Atlantic Wall."

This defense system was to consist of concrete, steel, mounted guns, and would be manned by one million men. This building project began in 1942, using 250,000 workers, including conscripts, prisoners, and slave laborers. Some ten thousand strongpoints were constructed consisting of casemate coastal guns, blockhouses, artillery batteries, mortar positions, machine gun pits, ammunition bunkers, and observation posts. One million tons of steel and twenty million yards of concrete were used.

German intelligence indicated that the most probable place for an Allied invasion would be along the Pas-de-Calais, France (the Strait of Dover), where the English Channel is at its narrowest width—only twenty miles. This was the most direct route straight into the heart of Germany, so it was where Hitler decided to build his strongest defenses. There were more than one hundred coastal guns up to sixteen inches in size placed inside twenty-foot-thick concrete walls. The port of Cherbourg became a citadel, and along the cliffs and beaches of Normandy, they built interconnected bunkers containing eight-inch up to fifteen-inch guns. They were designed with overlapping fields of fire to cover the sea along the Normandy beaches.

Hitler picked one of his greatest generals to oversee the defense of the coasts of France, Belgium, and Holland. He was Field Marshall Gerd von Rundstedt, the Commander in Chief West. Rundstedt was a Prussian who was a tank commander on the Russian front. His plan for the defense of the Atlantic Wall was to have his Panzer tank forces ready to attack any beach landings, and in addition, he would have armored divisions further inland in reserve.

However, Hitler was nervous about these defenses so he appointed another general to aid in the protection of the Norway coast when he recruited Gen. Erwin Rommel, the "Desert Fox" of the North African campaigns, to help in the defense of the Norway coastline. Rommel had recently been relieved of his command in Africa and was recalled to Germany in February 1943 when Hitler picked him to take a new post for the defense of the Atlantic Wall.

General Rommel's defense plan was to stop the invading enemy troops while they were *still in the water* before they could land on the beaches and climb the cliffs. To supplement the completed fixed defenses of coastal guns, casemates, bunkers, and tunnels, workers started to build many kinds of beachfront obstacles and laid some four million land mines. These obstacles were quite ingenious. They were built along the beaches between high- and low-water marks of the tides, and were designed to rip apart landing craft and tanks.

- Set into the sand farthest from shore were iron frames, with dimensions of 7 × 10 feet loaded with explosives. These anti-tank obstacles were dubbed "Belgian gates."
- Floating rafts were armed with mines, and posts were set into the sand at a slant with mines and shells on top.
- Closer to shore were obstacles called "Czech hedgehogs" made of bars of iron welded together in criss-cross fashion, and more obstacles called "tetrahedrons," draped with barbed wire.
- At the high tide marks of the beach, concrete "dragon tooth blocks" were built, and barbed wire and mines were placed at the land's edge.

By May of 1944, a half million of these obstacles had been built. They were not visible during high tide, but at low tide, they were prominent in the wet sand of the beach. Rommel called them "the devil's garden."

Czech Hedgehog, a German beach obstacle   Tetrahedron, a German beach obstacle

Time was running out for Hitler, and he kept changing his mind about which general's plan should be used, i.e., Rommel's plan to stop the enemy in the water or Rundstedt's plan to smash them with armor after landing on the beaches. He finally compromised, giving Rommel three Panzer divisions and Rundstedt four divisions in reserve. So on June 5, the day before D-Day, the Germans had fifty-three infantry divisions poised along the Atlantic Wall in France, but Rommel still had reservations about these defenses. He protested to Hitler with written memos which Hitler ignored, and finally Rommel decided to speak to Hitler face-to-face. He decided to go to Berchtesgaden to meet Hitler in early June. Ironically, Rommel was not even near the Normandy Beaches on the morning of June 6, D-Day!

The construction of the Atlantic Wall was carefully watched and plotted on maps during all its construction phases. At Oxford University in England, a secret group of intelligence experts, geographers, geologists, and photographers were busy preparing maps of the projected invasion sites. Aerial photos were taken by high-flying B-17 Flying Fortresses that showed details of the tidal currents, beaches, and defenses that the Germans were constructing. In addition, low-flying fighter planes like the P-38 Lightning and the RAF Spitfire photographed shore lines, giving them very detailed pictures of enemy defenses.

During the darkness of night, US Navy frogmen landed on the beaches and checked the sand, probing with instruments to see if the sand was firm enough to support tanks. In France, fighters of the French Underground and the Free French group secretly drew sketches of coastal fortifications which were then sent to the London planners. All of this information obtained in secret fashion was eventually printed into very detailed maps of each possible landing site, and on D-Day, the coxswain of each landing craft used a map showing the detail of his assigned beaching point.

The enormous construction activities surrounding the building of the Atlantic Wall along the coastline of France were not a big secret to the Allied Command in England. In the months leading up to D-Day, the Allies as well as Germany played high-stakes games of intelligence, intrigue, deception, and illusion. Prime Minister Winston Churchill said that "In wartime, truth is so precious that she should always be attended by a bodyguard of lies." Interestingly, the word "Bodyguard" became the code name for a huge scenario of events sent to the German enemy during the several months just preceding D-Day in 1944.

One of the most important discoveries by the Allies before D-Day was the deciphering of the German "Enigma Machine," a cipher machine used to encrypt and decrypt secret messages. The Enigma Machine was a combination of mechanical and electrical systems with a keyboard and rotating rotors. Keystrokes activated electrical currents which in turn triggered

The German Enigma Machine

the rotors to encipher the letters. The Enigma was already used commercially in the early 1920s, and later Nazi Germany adapted it for military use before and during World War II.

Bletchley Park, England (Where the German Enigma code was broken)

At Bletchley Park, north of London, Allied cryptologists and intelligence experts developed a decryption machine which had the codename "Ultra," which was able to read German messages that had been encoded by the Enigma Machine. By using Ultra, these analysts were able to read and decipher hundreds of German military messages daily. It was estimated that because of the ability to decrypt German ciphers and obtain secret intelligence, the Ultra hastened the end of the war in Europe by probably two years.

The main dilemma for the German High Command was to determine *when* and *where* D-Day would happen. In order to keep them wondering, Allied secret agents used all kinds of spy and counterspy methods. These included lies, false documents, wiretaps, disguises, mail drops, disappearing ink, betrayals, counterfeit passports, fake radio transmissions, and others. There were underground agents working in Europe using rumors, feints, and guerrilla actions.

The Allies created a fictitious scheme called "Fortitude," divided into two plans. One was named "Fortitude North" which called for an Allied invasion of Norway. Fake radio transmissions described a mythical British 4th Army of 250,000 men who were training in Scotland with descriptions of "ski training" or "climbing rock faces." The Germans strongly believed that this army would cross the North Sea and invade Norway, and as a consequence, they held seventeen divisions in this region.

The other plan, called "Fortitude South," was built around Gen. George Patton. The Germans had high respect for Patton because of his military genius and victories in North Africa and Sicily, and they were quite sure that he would spearhead an invasion of the continent. The Allies built on this concern and created radio chatter that leaked false information about Patton's "First US Army Group," which contained fifty divisions totaling five hundred thousand troops. This fake army was in a marshaling area near Dover in southeast England where the English Channel is only twenty miles wide to Pas de Calais. The harbors around Dover actually held some four hundred sham landing craft which were built on the sets of film studios. There were hundreds of tanks made of inflatable rubber mockups that were parked in fields. Patton was even seen from time to time in this area, so the German leaders believed this invasion plan as the most feasible.

There were a few close calls where Operation Bodyguard was nearly discovered. For example, a GI postal clerk on the D-Day staff inadvertently sent invasion documents to his sister in Chicago, but they were safely recovered. At a party in London, a US general blurted out that the invasion would occur by mid-June. He was court-marshaled! A British general forgot his briefcase which contained some "Overlord" documents in a taxi, but the driver turned them over to Scotland Yard.

As a result of all of these intelligence operations, secrecy, and intrigue, the German High Command was completely bewildered as shown by a meeting that Hitler had with the Japanese ambassador to Germany. It happened on May 27, 1944, just ten days before D-Day, when Hitler told the ambassador that the Allies had assembled eighty divisions (which was twice the actual number). Germany expected that the Allies would make diversionary attacks in Norway, Denmark, and southern France, and maybe a beachhead in Normandy. Hitler, however, expected the most likely location to be at Calais. "Operation Bodyguard" was very successful!

CHAPTER 11

Countdown to the Invasion

THE BIG BUILDUP FOR D-DAY in the British Isles had the codename "Operation Bolero." During the two years preceding the spring of 1944, England had become the world's largest camp and supply depot. America's industrial might produced most of the military equipment, arms, and food, while Britain gave its land, labor, railroads, and seaports. Each month over one hundred Liberty ships arrived in the ports of Liverpool, Glasgow, Bristol, and others, and delivered over six million tons of war supplies, including one thousand locomotives, one-half of a million tons of munitions, fifty thousand vehicles, and uncounted cartons, cases, and carloads of items, including combat boots, rifles, helmets, hospital beds, coffins, and so on.

By the spring of 1944, England was occupied by some 3.5 million combat and support personnel of soldiers, sailors, and airmen. There were 1.5 million Americans stationed mostly in the westernmost part of southern England because they were scheduled to go ashore on Normandy's western beaches. British troops numbered 1.7 million and were deployed in England's southeastern coastal region because they were headed for Normandy's eastern beaches. Other combat forces numbering three hundred thousand consisted of Canadians, Australians, New Zealanders, and various exiled men from Poland, Belgium, Czech, and Dutch countries.

There was a considerable increase of traffic through Marlborough because this town was on one of the main routes leading directly to Southampton, Portsmouth, and other ports on England's southern coast. There were convoys consisting of all kinds of military vehicles and trucks hauling war materiel for the invasion, including munitions, bombs, shells, armor, etc. I frequently drove through Savernake Forest at the edge of Marlborough, and on each drive-through, I noticed the increasing size of the stacks and piles of bombs, shells, and other ammunition under the beech trees.

A staggering tonnage of war materiel was piling up all over England. There were farm fields containing thousands of tanks parked side-by-side in endless rows. Other fields held scores of parked trucks, jeeps, half-tracks, bulldozers, self-propelled guns, and trailers. Some supply depots were piled high with barrels of motor oil, pontoons, shells, bombs, and small arms ammunition. Some farmlands were converted into temporary airfields with partially assembled fighter planes, bombers, and gliders. Coastal seaports held warships including cruisers, destroyers, transports, and landing craft. In the late spring of 1944, a ten-mile belt along the southern coast of England was closed to British civilians, and their villages were turned into assault training centers so the troops could practice street fighting.

Food is a very important commodity used in fighting a war, so there was a huge buildup of food staples including potatoes, vegetables, flour, butter, canned fruits, and many others. There were semi-trailer trucks called "ice boxes on wheels," which were used to transport perishable food and meat. The top of each cab of these food trucks also carried a mounted machine gun for protection. The war effort had changed the way some foods were prepared for shipping to the war zone as well as keeping the foods from spoiling while in storage. Potatoes, milk, eggs, and meat were prepared in powdered form, but its flavor was not like the good-tasting real stuff, and the powdered foods were always the butt of jokes about food.

The city of Swindon in County Wilts was fifteen miles north of our camp in Marlborough Downs, but it was a very important place because of its huge airbase where the US Army Air Force trained its paratroopers and glider troops. The job of the paratroopers was to drop behind enemy lines in the battle zone, while the glider infantrymen landed with gliders that operated like sail planes without motors. An airborne division typically consisted of about four thousand glider infantry and eight thousand paratroopers.

The 9th Troop Carrier Command at Swindon consisted of tow planes and gliders that conducted their training flights on a frequent basis each week. Each tow plane with a glider behind it always flew over our camp at low altitude as they circled the airfield, and then cut loose the glider which made a landing. I noticed that in late April, the training flights accelerated into a daily routine and the nearly constant roar of engines became commonplace. I wondered if this was another sign that the invasion was getting closer.

The air force's glider training program was a complicated affair. The tow plane was a twin-engine C-47 plane, also called the "Dakota," and it was the old reliable workhorse of the air force. The CG-4 glider consisted of a fuselage without a motor, a very fragile contraption that had a tubular steel frame covered with fabric and a floor made of plywood. Cords and pulleys were strung along the ceiling and a hook at the front of the fuselage held the tow rope. The wingspan was eighty-four feet long, which gave it more lift and sailing time in the air. It carried thirteen infantrymen plus a pilot and copilot. In lieu of a human payload, the glider could also transport a tank, a 75mm howitzer, a jeep, or a bulldozer. The flight training for the tow plane and glider pilots at the Swindon airdrome was honed into a very smooth operation in preparation for the big day. The flights and the droning of the motors became more frequent during the days of May as I watched the flights with fascination as they flew in wide circles over our camp.

At the Swindon airbase, tow planes and gliders lined up in two long rows facing one end of the runway. As each tow plane moved into the takeoff position, a glider was hauled out of line and tied up to the tow plane. The tow rope, made of plaited nylon, was attached to a hook in the tail of the tow plane and the nose of the glider. The tow rope was three hundred feet long. A jeep with radio equipment served as a mobile control tower and radioed the C-47 pilot when all the slack had been taken up in the tow rope. The take-off speed was 80 MPH. Once all the units were airborne, they flew in tight formation. Piloting the glider was very tricky because of air currents and the wash from the two motors of the tow plane, making it very difficult to keep the glider flying in a straight line behind the C-47. When the control tower gave clearance for the glider to land, the glider pilot cut loose the tow rope which dropped down behind the tow plane. The glider descended to earth at the rate of one foot for every 15 feet forward. The glider then circled the airfield making two 90 degree turns before landing on a grassy area next to the runway. The glider was hauled off to the side and pegged into the ground until the next day when it again made its practice flight.

Our daily work activities at XX Corps Headquarters had increased considerably, and everyone felt the tenseness and anticipation of the approaching invasion. At the pubs in town, the local citizens also felt it and made small talk about the big day. General Walker and his officers visited the channel coast to observe preparations and maneuvers. Important brass from Army Headquarters visited us more frequently as we became the center of a beehive of activity.

The G-2 and G-3 offices were housed in one of the larger Nissen huts. The "war room" was a top-secret map room that contained a very large map about twelve feet wide that lay on top of a table. It was a large-scale map of southern England, northern France, and the English Channel. On this map was plotted all the important military installations, camps, and depots scattered around England, as well as the Channel ports, docks, and marshalling areas. The Normandy coast of northern France showed the locations of the big coastal guns and other gun emplacement further inland, as well as underground bunkers and other defenses.

Since I was a clerk-typist in G-3, I had security clearance and permission to enter the war room. Security was very tight at XX Corps Headquarters, and we had a full company of Military Police protecting our facilities. An MP guard was stationed daily outside the door of the secret war room. One day when I was typing at my desk in the G-3 office, my boss, Colonel Griffith, stopped at my desk and asked me to follow him. We walked down the corridor leading to the war room, and at its locked door, the MP was sitting on a chair with his carbine lying across his lap and his hands lightly holding the gun. He was *asleep*!

While I watched, Colonel Griffith gingerly leaned toward the soldier, grabbed his carbine, and jerked it out of his hands. The startled guard opened his eyes in horror when he saw us standing in front of him with the colonel holding his weapon. The officer of the guard was called, and the soldier was taken away. Colonel Griffith told me in strong words to remember what I had just seen. My heart sank because of this incident as I felt so deeply sorry for the MP and what he was now up against. A soldier who is caught sleeping on duty has committed an extremely serious offense, especially during wartime, so I was very troubled with the thought of what might happen to this soldier.

About a month later, this soldier was tried at a court-martial at a separate army camp where a court made up of judge advocate officers were in charge of the trial. Colonel Griffith and I were subpoenaed to be at the trial, and I remember how nervous and tense I felt on the witness stand as I testified and reported truthfully that I did see this soldier sleeping while he was on guard duty at the door of the top-secret war room. I felt awful and sad, and wondered what would happen to this young man who was probably my age. I never heard what kind of a court martial he received, but I'm sure he was sentenced to the brig for a period of time. This event was never talked about openly at corps headquarters, but it was a sobering experience for me.

Each enlisted man was issued a pup tent which was his personal "home" when sleeping in the field. It was made of thin, light, canvas, and it had no floor, so we slept directly on the ground. My buddy Joe Messner and I worked on the same shift, and we discussed the subject of pup tents and how undesirable they were as a comfortable shelter. Since we would be working together during combat Joe decided to design a new pup tent that was double in size and would comfortably accommodate both of us, like a duplex.

We found a store on High Street in Marlborough that sold canvas and leather goods, and one of the employees was a tentmaker. We asked him to make a tent for us, and it was a beauty. It was eight feet long, which provided an extra two feet of space for our duffle bags, toilet articles, or whatever personal items we had. It was wide enough to give us extra space for our sleeping bags and high enough to sit upright for easy reading and writing. Its best feature was its sewn-in, heavy canvas floor to keep out the damp, wet, and cold ground. Our cozy duplex served us well during combat in France.

"Operation Overlord" was the code name for the planned invasion of northern France. After President Franklin D. Roosevelt attended the Teheran Conference in December 1943, he had stopped in Sicily to brief senior army officers about Overlord. The decision was to move Gen. Dwight D. Eisenhower to England to become Supreme Commander of the Allied Expeditionary Forces in Europe. "Ike" arrived in England in January 1944 and set up his Supreme Headquarters (SHAEF) in London at 20 Grosvenor Square near the American Embassy. Here, on January 25, the forty-nine year old General Eisenhower began planning the invasion of the continent of Europe.

General Eisenhower's plans included a command job for General George S. Patton, so in late January, Patton, who had served earlier in the Africa Campaign and Sicily, received orders to go to the UK. Ike told Patton that he should put together and command the Third Army. Patton flew to the UK in a C-54 and set up his Third Army Headquarters at Knutsford, near Manchester and Liverpool, about 150 miles from Marlborough. Patton took formal command of his new Third Army on March 26, 1944, but Ike told him that his army would not participate in the Normandy landings. During the following days of April and May, Patton was busy building his new army command, choosing administrative Corps as well as infantry and armored divisions and supporting units.

On a sunny and warm spring day in early May, a tall, gray-haired man wearing a short jacket and cavalry boots strode into our XX Corps Command Post. A pearl-handled revolver was quite visible in the holster of his hip belt, and his cap displayed three stars. This man was Lt. Gen. George Smith Patton, Jr., the new commander of the US Third Army! The purpose of the General's visit was to ask General Walton H. Walker and our XX Corps to be part of the Third Army. This was very exciting news to our corps personnel because we all knew about Patton's reputation as a brilliant military strategist and his successes in the battles against the German Afrika Korps led by General Rommel in North Africa.

General Patton was fifty-eight years old when he took command of the Third Army. He was a tall man at six feet, two inches, and weighed 205 pounds. Our own General Walker was very short and portly with a height of five feet, two inches, so when the two generals stood together, the size difference was funny. I heard many quips about this combination, like "Mutt and Jeff," a pair of popular movie actors in Hollywood during the early 1900s. General Patton had one flaw that must have bothered him immensely. He had a high-pitched voice, almost feminine-sounding, and he must have felt that this trait was unbecoming for a "macho-type" general and a leader of men into battle. He thirsted for glory and victory in battle, and he boasted that he could inspire his troops into doing great things. He got the nickname "Old Blood and Guts." However, he probably was better known for his gross, vulgar, obscene, and profane speech.

As an example, the following words are an excerpt from his farewell speech to his troops when he left the Desert Training Center in California in 1942, after he had received orders to go to North Africa to fight the German army there.

"Well, they've given us a job to do, a tough job, a mansize job. We can go down on our bended knees, every one of us, and thank God the chance has been given to us to serve our country. I can't tell you where we're going, but it will be where we can do the most good. And where we can do the most good is where we can fight those damn Germans or the yellow-bellied Eyetaleans. And when we do, by God, we're going right in and kill the dirty bastards. We won't just shoot the sonsabitches. We're going to cut out their living guts—and use them to grease our tanks. We're going to murder those lousy Hun bastards by the bushel."

General Patton liked to give fiery speeches to captive audiences and to his officers and men. He was a genius of military strategy and kept a close relationship with his troops, thereby establishing a firm bond of respect and affection with them.

The German High Command, including Hitler and his generals, also had a great respect for General Patton, and held him and his military accomplishments in high esteem. The Nazi General Erwin Rommel faced the enormous power of Patton's tank corps in the North African desert. The Germans were afraid of Patton, and they strongly believed that he was preparing a huge army to invade France across the Strait of Dover, which the French called the Pas de Calais. The distance between the white cliffs of Dover in England and Calais in France was a mere twenty miles, the narrowest part of the English Channel. British intelligence had broken the German secret code, and they had intercepted messages and maps which indicated that Field Marshal Gerd von Rundstedt, the German Commander in Chief-West, had assembled his Fifteenth Army containing fifteen divisions near the Pas de Calais area, in contrast to only ten divisions in Normandy and eight divisions in Brittany.

Armed with this information, the British general who was in charge of planning the allies' invasion, Lt. Gen. Frederick E. Morgan, conceived an ingenious scheme to deceive the Germans into believing that the assault would indeed occur at the Pas de Calais. A fictitious army was created, and General Patton was the perfect character to be the commander of this "paper" assault group. As it turned out, the Germans swallowed this ruse and concentrated more divisions in the Calais region than in Normandy.

The code name of this fictitious organization was "Fortitude South," and General Eisenhower gave it his approval. The paper army was named "First United States Army Group," or FUSAG, and it contained more than one million men, including Patton's Third Army. British movie studios were major contributors to the plan because their set designers built dummy trucks, tanks, cannons, and other military equipment, all made with *inflatable rubber!* A phony dock was built near the port of Dover, and scores of landing craft crowded the harbor. They were made of canvas and wood, and floated on oil drums. There were large numbers of oil storage tanks which supposedly contained the fuel supply for Patton's tanks. Even King George and General Eisenhower visited the facilities and attended a dinner in Dover which honored the construction crews.

General Patton, as the commander of this huge fictitious army, played his role well. He began to give speeches, and he showed his theatrical talents which were carefully rehearsed and orchestrated to various segments of his Third Army located around England. It was during one of these speeches that Patton spoke these eloquent words about the desire of Americans to win, whether in athletics or in war.

"The Americans love a winner and cannot tolerate a loser. Americans despise cowards. Americans play to win—all the time. I wouldn't give a hoot for a man who lost and laughed. That's why Americans have never lost and will never lose a war, for the very thought of losing is hateful to an American. The real man never lets the fear of death overpower his honor, his duty to this country, and his innate manhood. An Army lives, sleeps, eats, and fights as a team. This individual heroic stuff is a lot of crap. We have the finest food, the finest equipment, the finest spirited men in the world. Why, by God, I actually pity these sons of bitches we are going up against—by God, I do."

The roads in England were becoming more crowded with lots of military traffic. Truck convoys were heading for the channel coast carrying all kinds of combat equipment including tanks, trucks, and ammunition. British lorries rumbled through the narrow streets of town, carrying strange looking structures which were prefabricated hulls for barges to be used in the invasion. There were frequent inspections and checks of tactical training of all the units that were assigned to the XX Corps.

General Patton met with the four Corps commanders which he had chosen to be in his Third Army on May 29. They were Maj. Gen. Walton Walker of the XX Corps, Maj. Gen. Wade Haislip of the XV Corps, Maj. Gen. Gilbert Cook of the XII Corps, and Maj. Gen. Troy Middleton of the VIII Corps. These four Corps were the units that would lead the Third Army thrust across Northern France to the German border.

The United States Air Force in the UK was divided into two major categories with two different functions. The Strategic Air Command's function was the long-range bombing of mainly industrial targets located throughout Germany and Eastern Europe. This was done by long-range heavy bombers, such as the B-17 (the Flying Fortress), the B-29 (Super Fortress), and the B-24 (Liberator). The Tactical Air Command was the other type of air support, which consisted of fighter planes and fighter bombers whose jobs were to strike ground targets such as bridges, and to give close support to infantry, troops, and tank divisions.

Patton knew nothing about air support for ground troops until he arrived in England. This changed after the arrival of two US Air Force generals who were innovative tactical airmen. Their names were Maj. Gen. Elwood Quesada and Brigadier General Otto P. "Opie" Weyland. Their strategies consisted of employing fighter planes to work closely with the ground troops. Quesada was assigned to support the first army group, and Weyland was assigned to Patton's Third Army. General "Opie" Weyland commanded the 19th Tactical Air Command, and he and Patton had many meetings in which Weyland briefed him about the nuances and techniques that would be helpful for the infantry and armored troops. The attachment of the 19th TAC to the Third Army was a significant happening which would later change my job because it resulted in creating a new unit in G-3 when we entered combat in France.

June arrived, and our daily activities got busier than ever. The traffic into and out of the war room was incessant, and there were numerous visits of high army brass. The flights of aircraft towing gliders went on all day long. We all felt that the coming invasion was imminent. Monday, June 5 was another exhausting day, and I was dead-tired by evening. At eleven o'clock, it was "lights out" in the barracks, all talking stopped and I went to sleep.

All was quiet and peaceful.

CHAPTER 12

D-Day: June 6, 1944

MY SLEEP WAS INTERRUPTED BY the sound of aircraft, a continuous, loud, droning of motors. Everyone in our barracks woke up because the powerful sound vibrations rattled the windows in our Nissen hut. I looked at my watch—it was almost two o'clock. Everybody in the barracks shouted in unison "This is IT! This is D-Day!"

We leaped out of our bunks and ran outside. What we saw in the night sky was awesome. One by one the C-47s, each towing a glider, flew over us as they took off from the airdrome at Swindon, a few miles north of us. The noise of groaning engines shook the ground as hundreds of them with their silent gliders followed behind on a tow rope. The aircraft, with landing lights blinking in the darkness, circled in the sky over central England where they rendezvoused and formed their flying formations before they turned south to their drop sites in Normandy, where the gliders would be cut loose from the tow planes. In the darkness other C-47 transports from various airfields carried paratroopers of the 82nd and 101st Airborne Divisions, which were to be dropped behind German lines at the Utah and Omaha Beaches.

The abrupt wake-up call from the roaring aircraft stirred my emotions, and it was hard, if not impossible, to get back to sleep. When reveille arrived at six o'clock, we assembled outside of the headquarters building where Colonel Collier, Chief of Staff, told us that the long-awaited invasion had begun. During this assembly, I looked up at a returning C-47 which was flying very low over our camp on its approach to the Swindon airfield. I noticed that this plane had a huge hole in the tail fin. Another plane followed, and I saw shell holes in its fuselage and wing. They were hit by German anti-aircraft fire and were limping home. It was awesome.

The greatest military invasion in the history of the world began during the early morning hours of June 6. However, the first naval and troop movements actually began several days earlier. In England, General Eisenhower and his staff of Allied Commanders had moved their SHAEF Headquarters from London to a forward location near Portsmouth, a large naval base on the English Channel. Here they occupied an elegant Georgian mansion called Southwick House, which was surrounded by gardens and overlooked the city and harbor of Portsmouth. This was the place where the final decisions for the invasion took place. General Eisenhower's staff of allied commanders consisted of the following officers:

Southwick House, Portsmouth, England

Supreme Commander: Gen. Dwight D. Eisenhower
Deputy Supreme Commander: RAF Chief Marshall Arthur Tedder
First Army Commander: US General Omar Bradley
Naval Forces Commander: Admiral Sir Bertram Ramsay
Air Forces Commander: Air Marshall Sir Trafford Leigh-Mallory
Chief of Staff: Lt. Gen. Walter Bedell Smith
Ground Forces Commander: Gen. Sir Bernard Montgomery

In early May, General Eisenhower had set the date for D-Day to be Monday, June 5, with a possible delay to June 6 or 7. According to this timetable, some troop movements to ports and airfields got underway by Saturday, June 3, and some naval warships began to weigh anchors on Sunday, June 4. Advance movements of the invasion forces, both land and sea, had started.

The most critical subject this first weekend in June, however, was the *weather*. Operation Overlord's chief meteorologist was James Stagg of the Royal Air Force. His forecast on Saturday night was quite disturbing because a series of low pressure areas were moving across the North Atlantic which would bring high winds, rough seas, and low clouds for the next two days.

At 4:00 a.m. Sunday morning, June 4, the forecast included a strong possibility of formidable wave action in the channel, which would make shore landings extremely hazardous. The Allied Commanders had differing opinions about a "go or no go" but finally Ike decided to postpone D-Day for one day, to Tuesday, June 6, hoping for an improvement in the weather. However, by this time, hundreds of ships were already heading to France, and they got the order to head back. This order had the code name "Ripcord plus 24."

On Sunday night, meteorologist James Stagg announced an unexpected change in the weather. A high-pressure system was pushing north from Spain, and if it continued its projected path, it would present some marginal landing possibilities on June 5 until mid-day on June 6. Eisenhower had a difficult decision to make, as the weather forecast for June 6 was not ideal, but if the landings were postponed to June 7, it might be worse, because the right combination of tide and dawn sunup would not occur again until June 19. Such a postponement would cause new concerns for beach landings, security, and morale.

The Allied Commanders met again Sunday evening. It was very tense in the room as they waited for Eisenhower's final decision. Finally, Ike said, "I am quite positive we must give the order. I don't like it,

Briefing Room at Southwick House

but there it is. I don't see how we can do anything else." It was a short night, because at 4:00 a.m. on Monday morning, June 5, the allied commanders met again for a final time. Stagg reported that there was no change in the weather forecast since the previous evening, and besides, the huge fleet of all invasion forces was already on its way. The time had arrived for the final, irrevocable decision. There was a very tense silence in the briefing room at Southwick House as General Eisenhower looked directly at his commanders. Then he said: "OK Lets Go"!

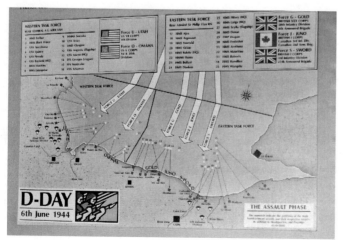

Map at Southwick House briefing room showing the Normandy beaches

The Naval Invasion Fleet
"Operation Neptune"

During the weekend of June 3–4, 1944, the American and British naval forces began to stir in various ports of southern England from Falmouth in the west to Felixstowe in the east. All of this activity was the beginning of "Operation Neptune," the gathering of the huge invasion fleet for the cross-channel assault on Fortress Europe. The following statistics show the enormous size of this gigantic seaborne attack:

- 7,000 ships (combat, cargo, and landing craft)
- 200,000 sailors and merchant seamen
- 50,000 troops in the first wave
- 100,000 troops in following waves
- 1,500 tanks
- 20,000 vehicles
- 11,000 fighter planes, bombers, transports and gliders

The naval fleet of seven thousand ships included seven battleships, twenty-three cruisers, one hundred destroyers, one thousand merchant and supply ships, four thousand landing ships and crafts, and six hundred frigates, corvettes, torpedo boats, and small coastal crafts. Over three hundred mine sweepers sailed ahead of the vast landing fleet in order to cut five main swaths through the German mine fields. They were followed by other small craft that marked the cleared lanes with blinker buoys. Layers of fighter planes filled the skies above the fleet, while patrol bombers, fighter planes from aircraft carriers, and destroyers guarded the flanks of this enormous invasion armada from German U-boat and torpedo attacks.

Operation Neptune resembled a huge funnel with its wide mouth being the two hundred miles of coastline of southern England, and its narrow neck extending from the middle of the Channel to the fifty-mile-wide coastline of Normandy. The ships of this armada made a rendezvous at a location designated "Zone Z" nicknamed "Piccadilly Circus" which was a circle about eight miles in diameter southeast of the Isle of Wight, near Southampton. Zone Z was chosen to keep the Germans guessing as long as possible as to where the assault would be, whether at Normandy or at Pas de Calais. In this zone, the ships formed assault groups for the final voyage to Normandy. These groups were divided according to which of the five landing beaches they were destined for, as follows:

- Twelve groups for Utah Beach (US)
- Nine groups for Omaha Beach (US)
- Sixteen groups for Gold Beach (British)
- Ten groups for Juno Beach (Canadian)
- Twelve groups for Sword Beach (British)

During this first week in June, the weather over the English Channel was the worst it had been for many years. Strong westerly winds whipped up the waves into a rough sea along with rain showers. The Germans believed that the weather was too awful to permit an invasion, so they altered their behavior. The Luftwaffe stayed on the ground, and naval patrols were cancelled. This lull in activity prompted General Rommel to leave his headquarters in Normandy on Sunday, June 4, and he drove to Germany to celebrate his wife's fiftieth birthday. He gave her a new pair of shoes from Paris, an elegant present during the wartime shortages prevalent in Germany. Rommel also had an appointment with Hitler on Tuesday, June 6, to try to persuade him to send two more panzer divisions to Normandy.

Adolf Hitler was in Berchtesgaden, and at about 2:00 a.m. on the morning of June 6, he took a sleeping pill because he had insomnia. At the White House in Washington, President Roosevelt got ready for bed late in the evening of June 5, but before retiring he told his wife Eleanor, that the invasion was happening at that moment. In London, Prime Minister Churchill stayed up late in his war room at Number 10 Downing Street, sipping brandy.

The Airborne Invasion

In late afternoon on Monday, June 5, General Eisenhower drove to one of the airdromes with his jeep driver. It was only a few hours after Ike had given his command to start the invasion with the words "OK Lets Go!" He made this unexpected visit to the 101st Airborne Division where the "Screaming Eagles" paratroopers and glider troops were preparing for their night flights to Normandy. The supreme commander chatted with many of the men gathered around him, making small talk and wishing them good luck. Ike later recalled that "I was sending these men into battle—some to their deaths. I felt I had to look them straight in the face."

There were two US airborne divisions in England, the 82nd Airborne and 101st Airborne, totaling some fifteen thousand troops. At the moment that General Eisenhower visited the 101st Division, they were battle-ready for their mission, which was only a few hours later that night. Each man had a small

American flag sewed on the right shoulder of his jacket. His division patch was on the left shoulder. Strips of green and brown burlap hung from the helmet netting as camouflage. Many of the men blackened their faces with burned cork. Each man carried weapons and equipment including his rifle, a 45-caliber pistol, a fighting knife, fragmentation grenades, hacksaw, compass, escape route map, K and D rations, and two cartons of cigarettes. The paratroopers also wore a chute for their drops. It was a heavy load!

These same men that General Eisenhower visited were aboard the C-47 "Dakota" transports and gliders that flew over our barracks in Marlborough and awakened us at 2:00 a.m.

We watched the blinking red and white lights on the wings and fuselages of these planes as they gradually formed flying formations with their gliders silently following behind, and with each glider loaded with up to twenty infantry doughboys who were feeling anxious and scared. I had goose bumps running up and down my spine as I watched this awesome sight. Airborne troops from other airfields in England joined this huge assault group totaling fifteen thousand men and more than eight hundred C-47 aircraft.

The rendezvous area for all the airborne planes was over central England, where they formed groups of forty aircraft that flew in V-formations. Over two thousand fighter planes escorted the armada across the Channel. The earth and sea must have trembled from the enormous noise and turbulence of the air caused by thousands of roaring engines. The American airborne troops flew to the west of the naval assembly area in the Channel as they were scheduled to cross the Cotentin Peninsula south of Cherbourg to the drop area behind Utah Beach. Meanwhile, the British airborne troops flew to the east of the naval assembly area to their jump zone at the east end of the Normandy Beaches, near Caen.

The first American planes approached their drop zone with the mission to drop twenty teams of "pathfinders," twelve men to a plane. Their job on the ground was to set up radar beacons and lights that would mark six main drop zones. These men were supposed to jump at five hundred feet to avoid anti-aircraft fire and enable the men to land close together. This plan was not completely successful because there were low clouds, and the air was very turbulent causing some paratroopers to miss their drop zone. They received heavy anti-aircraft fire as German searchlights lit up the dropping soldiers and their parachutes.

The paratroopers landed in the darkness among cattle, in hedgerows, orchards, plowed fields, gardens, and dung heaps. Many guys fell in lowlands and marshes which the German army had deliberately flooded, so some soldiers died in the water because of the heavy weight of their backpacks and weapons.

The glider troops also had their problems. Before landing, some gliders were hit with enemy flak which ripped through the flimsy floor. Many gliders careened into trees and the bocage (hedgerows) at eighty miles per hour and were smashed to pieces, with heavy casualties. Others were ripped apart by "Rommel's Asparagus," which consisted of poles set in the fields and connected with webs of wire.

The troops of the 101st Airborne Division used tiny toys called "crickets" which were sold in dime stores back home. They were about an inch long and looked like a beetle bug, and when you pressed its thin, wafer-sized piece of tin attached to one end, it clicked like the sound of a cricket. The troops used these tiny crickets in the darkness for identification of friendly soldiers; one click-clack was answered by a double click-clack. (Note: I played with these cricket toys when I was a kid, and every boy owned several of them. It was lots of fun to use them in school classes, but the constant click-clack noise drove the teachers and our elders crazy.)

The village of Sainte-Mère-Eglise was in the drop zone of the 82nd Airborne Division, only six miles west of Utah Beach. In the darkness, about forty soldiers landed right in the center of town amid German searchlights aimed at them and with some of them shot before they hit the ground. The parachute of one soldier, named Private John Steele, got snagged on the steeple of the old Norman church in the town square. He hung helpless on the steeple for two hours and pretended to be dead, but finally the Germans cut the wounded man from his hook on the church.

Private Steele died later at the hands of the German army. After some fierce fighting on the morning of D-Day, American paratroopers captured Sainte-Mère-Eglise by 9:30 a.m. They raised the American flag in the central square, thus liberating the first town in France, and setting the stage for the seaborne landing at Utah Beach.

The men of the 82nd and 101st Airborne Divisions suffered heavy casualties during these few hours in which they dropped into the combat zone and engaged the enemy in the flooded marshes and orchards and fields and village streets. The number of casualties suffered by these two divisions totaled 350 killed, 900 wounded, and 1,700 missing. In spite of the great cost, a tiny area of land near the Normandy beaches had been secured, and the airborne operation was deemed a success.

La Pointe du Hoc

Half-way between Utah and Omaha Beaches, La Pointe du Hoc dominates the sea because of the vertical cliffs that rise a sheer 120 feet above the narrow, rocky beach. These cliffs were protected with heavy gun batteries and concrete bunkers. The German troops manned 155mm guns that could reach up to ten miles offshore and also shoot at any assault troops and landing craft on the beaches. These guns could reach as far as Utah Beach to the west and Omaha Beach to the east, which made them a big threat that had to be eliminated. On previous days, bombers had hammered these gun batteries and bunkers but a US Army Ranger unit was needed to destroy it before the assault troops arrived at the beaches. Unknown to the Rangers, however, was the fact that the Germans had moved the big guns to a new site farther back from the cliffs.

Lt. Col. James Rudder commanded the elite 2nd Ranger Battalion, containing three companies totaling 225 men. This unit had practiced for months scaling cliffs and precipices along the English coast. Now their real mission was at hand, which was to arrive at Pointe du Hoc at 6:30 a.m., scale the cliffs, and destroy the guns. The job had to be completed by H-Hour when the first waves of troops would be hitting Utah and Omaha beaches.

At dawn, American bombers arrived to hit the cliff batteries. The battleship "Texas" pounded the top of the plateau making craters thirty feet across and ten feet deep with their fourteen inch projectiles. An unfortunate mistake was made by the British guide craft that was leading the landing boats with the Rangers aboard as they headed for the wrong cliff in the pre-dawn darkness. They were too far east of Pointe du Hoc so they turned west and followed the cliffs to the right spot, arriving forty minutes late at 7:10 a.m. Nine assault boats arrived safely but two were lost at sea.

The Rangers disembarked onto a narrow shale beach that was very rocky. Here they took their rope ladders and used mortar rockets to fire these rope ladders to the top of the 120 foot cliffs. The ladders had grapnel hooks which snagged rocks at the top of the cliffs to hold these ladders firmly. The men quickly climbed them hand-over-hand and step-by-step while carrying heavy backpacks and rifles. It was a very strenuous effort to reach the top, while German defenders above them shot straight down at the climbers with their automatic weapons as well as dropping grenades at the Americans. This point blank range caused heavy losses to the Rangers.

The Rangers climbed to the top of the plateau in about ten minutes, but no big guns were there, only several decoys of telephone poles set at a slant to resemble gun barrels. The Rangers fought their way inland from the cliffs and discovered vehicle tracks leading through the bocage to an apple orchard. The tracks led them to five newly-hid coastal guns covered with camouflaged netting. These were the big guns of La Pointe du Hoc that originally were placed at the edge of the cliffs. The guns were arranged in a wide arc with elevated barrels that were sighted directly at Utah Beach, with stacks of shells nearby. It was imperative that these guns be destroyed before they could shoot at the troop landings at Utah Beach at that very hour. The rangers melted the firing mechanisms of the big guns with thermite grenades and bashed their sites. By 8:30 a.m., the guns were silenced.

The cost of capturing La Pointe du Hoc was very high, with about half of the 225 troops of the 2nd Ranger Battalion being killed or wounded. However, these courageous Rangers had destroyed the huge guns on these cliffs and had blocked the German coastal highway and established a tiny beachhead on D-Day.

Utah Beach

Just past midnight on the morning of June 6, over fifteen hundred heavy bombers of the British Royal Air Force crossed the Channel and dropped five thousand tons of bombs along the entire invasion coast from Cherbourg to Le Havre, the area that contained the five landing beaches. There also were about one hundred Flying Fortresses and Lancasters which dropped bundles of "window" that were actually long shreds of aluminum foil, which on radar looked like hundreds of aircraft. Small boats moved through the invasion fleet that was stationed in the assembly area, with a barrage balloon tethered to the deck of each boat. Each balloon held a device that reflected electronic impulses, or blips, that made it appear to be a huge invasion fleet. Some aircraft also flew radar and radio-jamming missions.

On shore, German radio operators were bewildered as they monitored their instruments, and it wasn't until 3:00 a.m. that they finally realized that there was an *actual* invasion fleet headed toward the Normandy coast, but strangely the shore batteries held their fire until daybreak. The leading vessels of the invasion fleet consisted of the following types:

- LST—landing ship, tank
- LCI—landing craft, infantry
- LCT—landing craft, tank
- LCVP—landing craft, vehicle, and personnel

The transport ships that had rendezvoused at Zone Z, or Piccadilly Circus, were packed with GIs and "Tommies" (or "dogfaces," as these infantrymen were nicknamed). The armada stretched out in an array thirty miles from east to west. The villages along England's southern coast where some of them had trained were suddenly deserted, and now the troops were at anchor in the English Channel, waiting for their orders. These orders came at 3:00 a.m. for the first wave of assault troops to leave the transports that were in their holding positions about 12–15 miles from Utah Beach. H-Hour for hitting the beach was 6:30 a.m.

The Utah assault force was planned to arrive at the beach in four waves. It consisted of thirty thousand troops and thirty-five hundred vehicles of the 4th Infantry Division and the 90th Infantry Division.

- The first wave comprised twenty LCVPs each with a team of thirty men.
- The second wave numbered thirty-two LCVPs with the remainder of two assault battalions, some engineers and eight teams of Marine sappers.
- The third wave was timed to land at fifteen minutes after H-Hour and comprised eight LCTs loaded with bulldozer tanks.
- The fourth wave followed two minutes later and was composed of engineer battalions who had to clear the beaches.

After receiving the orders to go, the assault troops of the 4th and 90th Infantry Divisions assembled on the decks of the transport ships and climbed down cargo nets on the ship's sides into their specific landing crafts below. Each craft held thirty men with each one carrying fifty pounds of battle gear. Each infantryman carried an M-1 rifle, ammunition bandolier, entrenching tool, canteen, rations, and first aid kit. Each wore a steel helmet, olive drab pants, field jacket, and canvas leggings. While on the landing craft, they wore inflatable life vests.

Utah Beach forms a crescent several miles long located in the bend of land where the east-west line of the Normandy coast joins the north–south direction of the Cotentin Peninsula. This beach contains beautiful golden sand and a few feet beyond the water line at high tide there is a line of sand dunes about six to eight feet high that run parallel to the beach. Access to the land across this flat beach and low dunes is quite easy because there are no natural obstacles, only a few low-growing plants sticking out of the dunes. The terrain at Utah Beach is completely different from Omaha Beach, which is about twenty miles to the east, where there are cliffs along that beach. The sheer cliffs of La Pointe du Hoc are only ten miles east of Utah Beach.

At 5:30 a.m., which was one hour before H-Hour, the big guns of the US Navy, along with 276 attack aircraft of the 9th US Air Force, began a tremendous bombardment of Utah Beach. The German gun batteries, pillboxes, and machine gun positions were demolished. American destroyers moved close to shore where they fired five-inch shells at a rate of eight per minute. This pounding lasted fifty minutes, and at exactly H-Hour at 6:30 a.m., the assault infantrymen of the 4th Division hit the beach. They came with tanks, artillery, and engineers. The troops of the 90th Division followed with their mission to seize four causeways along the beach and move inland to link up with the men of the 82nd and 101st Airborne Divisions who had landed several miles behind the beach.

The guide craft that were leading the troops to the main landing area of the beach missed their target due to strong currents that pushed them a mile further away. This turned out to be a fortunate event because they would have been caught in a crossfire from two enemy casemates at the designated landing area. The LCTs that carried tanks had planned to release them into the water about three miles from shore, but instead they released them closer to shore. Each thirty-ton tank had propellers and a seven foot high canvas flotation collar. The German defenders were quite puzzled when they saw thirty of these tanks reach shore and called them "floating boxes."

The timetable of the landings of the various waves of invaders was quite accurate and went well, which confused and stunned the German High Command, who did not believe it was the real thing. Finally, at 10:00 a.m., General Rommel's chief of staff telephoned him at his home in Germany with the report that huge landings were occurring in Normandy. Rommel cancelled his planned meeting with Hitler and raced back to Normandy.

When the American troops reached the sand dunes along the beach, they encountered many small white signs with skeletons painted on them. This meant that mines were buried in the sand, so the engineers had to clear them out before the infantrymen and tanks arrived. As patrols moved further inland, they discovered that the Germans had flooded the marshlands with water three to ten feet deep. There was no way around this area so the troops waded through the marshes where the paratroopers had dropped a few hours earlier. In the afternoon of D-Day, the invasion patrols made contact with patrols of the 101st Airborne Division.

By nightfall on June 6, the 4th Infantry Division had landed 23,250 men, seventeen hundred vehicles, and seventeen hundred tons of supplies. The American casualties were quite low, totaling two hundred men and included twelve killed, sixty missing and presumed dead, and 128 wounded. The landing at Utah Beach was successful, and nearly all of its objectives were attained.

Utah Beach as it appears now (2010)

Omaha Beach

The terrain of Omaha Beach was considerably different from that of Utah Beach and Point du Hoc. At Utah, the assault troops landed on a flat and sandy shore with low dunes, whereas at Point du Hoc the rangers had to scale high cliffs, but here at Omaha Beach the incoming troops encountered a mixture of terrains including sand, dunes, bluffs, and cliffs. This Normandy beach was a broad six-mile crescent of sand some three hundred yards wide. Beyond this was a stretch of stone shingle, followed with sand dunes and rising into bluffs which were a hundred feet or more high. Four narrow valleys, or "draws," led up from the sea edge to high ground.

The Wehrmacht had prepared two types of defense systems: one type was in the sand under the high-water mark, and the other was on top of the bluffs and cliffs. Numerous underwater obstacles were planted in the sand, designed to rip apart landing craft and tanks, and they were invisible during high tide. The underwater obstacles included heavy iron frames, dubbed "Belgian gates," irons welded into criss-crossed shapes called "Czech hedgehogs," floating rafts armed with mines, concrete obstacles called "dragon's tooth blocks," huge coils of barbed wire along the shore, and hundreds of mines buried in the sand and dunes. The German defenses on top of the bluffs and hillsides consisted of concrete casemates containing 75mm and 88mm guns. There were eighty-five machine gun positions, forty mortar pits, and scores of anti-tank guns. Zigzag trenches in the ground connected the casemates and gun positions.

The American 1st Infantry Division was the vanguard unit assigned to make the first attack on Omaha Beach. Each rifle company was formed into five assault sections of thirty men each, composed of automatic rifle infantrymen, bazooka-bearers, and demolition specialists. They had this very precise timetable at H Hour:

- H minus ten minutes: amphibious attack
- H Hour: more tanks and armored bulldozers
- H plus one minute: infantry hits the beach
- During following minutes, demolition teams blast obstacles

Unfortunately, things went wrong from the beginning. The weather was bad; the winds were strong, and the seas were rough, which caused the landing craft carrying the first assault waves to take longer to reach the beach. Many soldiers were seasick. When the 450 bombers (Flying Fortresses, Liberators, and Lancasters) flew their missions at daybreak they found that thick clouds covered the targets along the shore, so they dropped their bombs further inland, which left the defenses on the bluffs untouched.

The heavy seas caused a huge loss of lives and equipment. Ten landing craft sank and all three hundred infantrymen aboard drowned. Forty out of seventy-two craft carrying 105mm howitzers and armored bulldozers also sank. Thirty-two amphibious tanks (the ones that the Germans called "floating boxes") disembarked from their LCTs, and one-third of them went down with their crews.

Combat engineers arrived at the beach obstacles ahead of the infantry troops in order to blast boat channels through the field of obstacles. They carried two-pound blocks of TNT in a canvas case strapped across their chests. They also defused the mines that were attached to the angle-iron objects that protruded when the tide was out. However, out of the sixteen lanes that were planned for clearing to the beach, only six lanes were opened.

At H-Hour, 6:30 a.m., the first waves of the 1st Infantry Division swept through the obstacle field of concrete dragon's teeth and fought through the draws to the top of the bluffs. Within a half hour, there were about one thousand infantrymen and combat engineers in the surf and on the beach, but they were subjected to an enormous amount of enemy fire. The beach became a killing field as the GIs desperately tried to dodge bullets and keep from drowning. By mid-morning about one thousand American soldiers lay dead or wounded on the sand or in the water. General Omar Bradley, commander of the 1st Army, ordered American battleships and destroyers to move closer to the shore, so they could knock out the German gun emplacements on the bluffs.

By noon, more waves of assault troops had arrived at the beach and about six hundred men had arrived on top of the bluffs where they encountered the German defenders and shot at them with rifles and machine guns. Some of the enemy soldiers ran out of ammunition and surrendered, but the German High Command was not able to attempt a counterattack at Omaha Beach because they had a very wide front to defend along the Normandy and Cotentin coastline.

By the end of D-Day, the men of the 1st Infantry Division had cleared a small bridgehead of high ground above Omaha Beach which was four miles long and only one and a half miles deep. More than 34,500 troops made it ashore, but unfortunately, only 100 tons out of 2,400 tons of equipment arrived safely on shore. Almost all of the artillery and most of the tanks and vehicles, along with their crews, were engulfed by the sea, which resulted in a very short supply of ammunition, artillery, and the means to continue fighting. By nightfall the American troops held a very tenuous position on this portion of the infamous Atlantic Wall in Normandy.

The cost in American lives was enormous during this day when the greatest military invasion in the history of the world occurred. Official figures indicated that twenty-four hundred men were killed, wounded, or missing, with most of the casualties happening during the first two hours of the beach landings. On balance, D-Day at Omaha Beach was considered a success.

Omaha Beach as it appears now (2010)

The British Sector
Airborne Landings

British and Canadian troops made landings on D-Day at three beaches about twenty miles east of Omaha Beach. Their codenames were Gold, Juno, and Sword. The large French city of Caen was located nine miles inland from the English Channel and was connected to the sea by a navigable waterway called the Caen Canal. The city was at a very strategic location, so its capture was critical in order to establish a bridgehead in this area of Normandy.

The Canal and the Orne River flow parallel to each other. There was only one bridge that crossed the Canal, called the Pegasus Bridge at Benouville, and another bridge, called the Horsa Bridge, crossed the Orne River a few miles south of Pegasus at the town of Ranville.

Fifteen minutes after midnight on June 6, three Horsa gliders of the British 6th Airborne Division crash-landed on the banks of the Caen Canal, a mere two hundred meters from the Pegasus Bridge. In the darkness, forty-five paratroopers scrambled out of the gliders and overpowered the German defenders of the bridge. Then the paratroopers dismantled the demolition wires attached to the dynamite that was set to blow up the bridge. The Pegasus Bridge was saved intact. Two other Horsa gliders landed on the west side of the Orne River near the town of Ranville, and they quickly seized that bridge without damage. Of the original six Horsa gliders, one got lost and missed these targets by nine miles.

Shortly after the glider landings and the capture of the two bridges, the British paratroopers of the 6th Airborne Division arrived over the drop area northeast of Caen as well as in the flooded lowlands further inland. The German's huge coastal gun battery at Merville, situated at the estuary where the Orne River enters the sea, was a major target for the paratroopers. It was neutralized after a fierce battle.

A total of six thousand British paratroopers and airborne infantry were dropped during the early hours of darkness on D-Day. Many of the gliders were wrecked during their crash landings, and about one hundred glider pilots were killed, wounded, or missing. The whole airborne operation resulted in heavy losses and casualties estimated at six hundred killed or wounded and six hundred missing. Many paratroopers drowned in the flooded lands, and a large proportion of equipment was lost.

Gold Beach (British)

General Sir Bernard Montgomery had set the H-Hour of the British landings for 7:30 a.m., which was one hour later than the American landings at Utah and Omaha Beaches. This gave the cruisers and battleships of the Royal Navy an extra 1 ½ hours of morning light to bombard German defenses, twice as much time as the American Navy had had. The British assault forces assembled only seven miles offshore, which gave them a shorter run to the beaches. At 4:45 a.m., two midget submarines rose to the surface a mile offshore, one at each end of the British landing sector. Their job was to guide the invasion fleet with radio beacons and signal lights. Frogmen arrived at the beach to clear various obstacles.

Gold Beach was at the center of the landing zones, halfway between the Cotentin Peninsula and the Orne River. This beach was flanked by steep cliffs. It was assaulted by the 50th Northumbrian Division at 7:30 a.m. between the towns of La Riviere and Le Hamel. LCTs brought "swimming tanks" right up to the shore. During the day, a total of twenty-five thousand men came ashore, where they destroyed German-built blockhouses, gun emplacements, and other defenses of the Atlantic Wall, including about twenty-five hundred mines and other obstacles encountered on the three-mile-long beach.

By evening, the 50th Division had fought for a bridgehead that measured 6 × 6 miles and reached to Bayeux, southwest of the beach. They also made contact with units of the Canadian troops which landed at Juno Beach on their left flank. British casualties at Gold Beach totaled 413 men killed, wounded or missing, with eighty-nine landing craft being lost.

Juno Beach (Canadian)

Juno Beach was just east of Gold Beach, situated between the towns of Courseulles-sur-Mer and Bernieres-sur-Mer. At 8:00 a.m. on June 6, the 3rd Infantry Division from Canada made its first landing at Juno. This division consisted entirely of volunteers numbering sixteen thousand men.

In spite of offshore shoals and heavy seas, the Canadians went ashore with infantry and tanks which destroyed some of the German strong points after fierce fighting. Nineteen Sherman tanks approached the beach, protected by an inflatable canvas skirt supported on a metal frame, and being moved through the water by their twin propellers at a speed of six knots per hour. Fifteen of these tanks reached shore and destroyed a 50mm anti-tank gun that had first knocked out four Canadian tanks. The Canadian infantry encountered some fortified houses and sniper fire in the villages as well as mines on the beach.

At the end of the day's fighting, the Canadians had obtained a bridgehead that was six to seven miles deep, and they made contact with units of the British 50th Division at Gold Beach, thereby joining the two bridgeheads. More than 21,000 troops landed with 3,200 vehicles and 1,100 tons of supplies. The human cost was 302 dead, 574 wounded, and forty-seven taken prisoner.

Sword Beach (British)

Sword Beach was the easternmost landing site of the British Sector that had a border of houses and villas in the village of Ouistreham, a fishing village at the mouth of the Orne River. Locks there allow entry to the Caen Canal, which flows to the city of Caen only eight miles to the south.

At 7:30 a.m., Maj. Gen. T. G. Rennie, commander of the 3rd British Infantry Division, made the first landings at Sword Beach, between Lion-sur-Mer and Ouistreham. Their mission was to capture Caen as soon as possible and establish liaison with the 6th Airborne Division. The beach was strewn with obstacles and mines down to the low-water mark. Higher up from the water, the defenders had built a network of trenches and minefields that linked with bunkers placed 100 meters apart and armed with 50mm canons.

There was strong enemy resistance, but some French townspeople even ran to the beach to welcome the Tommies. Sixteen Sherman tanks stormed ashore to open up the beach exits, and the enemy defenders were overcome with mortar shells and grenades. The British assault troops gradually moved inland where they shut down the underground bunkers by using flame throwers and dropping explosives down their ventilation shafts. By noon, the infantry had cleared the town of Ouistreham, and they linked up with the airborne troops at Benouville, putting them on the road to Caen, their next goal.

However, in late afternoon, the German High Command launched a counterattack by bringing up their elite 21st Panzer Division with its powerful 26-ton Mark IV tanks. These tanks smashed into a gap between Juno and Gold Beaches, and fierce fighting ensued. Soon British gliders brought in paratrooper reinforcements, and the Panzer attack was stopped, with many German tanks destroyed in the battle. The British goal of capturing Caen was not attained as they had hoped, and the city was not liberated until July 9. But on this D-Day, a solid bridgehead was won on Sword Beach. A total force of 28,845 British troops went ashore here, with losses of 630 dead or wounded on the beach alone.

D-Day Ended

As daylight faded into night on June 6th, the Allies had achieved a tiny toehold on the five landing beaches in Normandy. At Utah Beach, the American 4th Infantry Division troops had driven over five miles inland, and some had linked up with the paratroopers of the 82nd and 101st Airborne Divisions who had dropped far inland. At Omaha Beach, the American 1st Infantry Division encountered fierce fighting that was very costly in casualties, and by nightfall these troops held a toehold only one mile inland from the shore. The British and Canadian forces who went ashore at Gold, Juno, and Sword Beaches obtained spearheads up to six miles deep, but their main goal on this first day to capture the city of Caen was not accomplished.

On D-Day, Adolf Hitler was not convinced that the Normandy invasion was "real," and he still believed that the Allies would make their main landings at Pas-de-Calais. However, on this day, Hitler's mighty Atlantic Wall was breached, and the liberation of Europe was about to begin!

The enormous size of the invasion was mindboggling. The following statistics show the gigantic size of the naval, air, and land forces that participated on D-Day at this beginning of the Battle of Normandy.

Naval Forces

Ships:

138	warships
221	destroyers, frigates, corvettes
287	mine sweepers
495	smaller vessels
58	submarine chasers
4,000	landing craft of all types
441	auxiliary naval craft and small boats
864	Merchant Navy ships
300	+ other small craft
6,800	Total Vessels

Warship Distribution:

79.0%	British
16.5%	American
4.5%	Other Allies

Servicemen:

112,824	British sailors
52,889	American sailors
4,998	Other Allied sailors
170,711	Sub-total
25,000	Merchant sailors
195,711	Total Sailors

Air Forces

Aircraft:

5,510	British
6,080	American
11,590	Total Aircraft
3,500	Gliders

Air crew: 31,000 (Excluding airborne troops and their aircrews)

Land Forces

Vehicles:

20,000	(Including over 1,000 tanks)

Troops Landed on Beaches:
American Sector:

23,250	Utah Beach
34,250	Omaha Beach
57,500	Total American

British Sector:

24,970	Gold Beach
21,400	Juno Beach
28,845	Sword Beach
75,215	Total British

Parachute and Glider Troops:

15,500	American
7,990	British and Canadian
23,490	Total

Total land forces deployed on D-Day: 156,205

The enormous task of planning the greatest invasion in history and the vast amount of logistics needed to accomplish the feat showed the great ingenuity and military genius of the allied leaders and commanders. The total number of personnel involved in D-Day was the following:

Sailors	195,711
Airmen	31,000
Land troops	156,205
Total Personnel	382,916

Fighting continued into the night of D-Day in order to expand the toeholds that were obtained on the five landing beaches. Battle-weary GIs tried to get some rest as sporadic shooting continued and air raids went on overhead.

When it was midnight on this 6th day of June, it was early evening back home in America. In the White House, President Roosevelt sat in front of a microphone in the Oval Office where he gave his radio address to a nervous nation, citing the events of D-Day and the invasion of Hitler's occupied Europe by Allied forces. My mom and dad always listened to Roosevelt's "fireside chats," and on this night, I knew that they were listening to him intently. I can't imagine what their feelings of anxiety and uncertainty were like, wondering where I was and whether perhaps I, too, was involved in the initial landings. They had no idea where I was due to tight censorship of the letters I wrote. President Roosevelt ended his radio address with this very solemn prayer to Almighty God:

"Last night when I spoke with you about the fall of Rome, I knew at that moment that troops of the United States and our Allies were crossing the Channel in another and greater operation. It has come to pass with success thus far. And so, in this poignant hour, I ask you to join with me in prayer:

Almighty God: our sons, pride of our Nation, this day have set upon a mighty endeavor, a struggle to preserve our Republic, our religion, and our civilization, and to set free a suffering humanity. Lead them straight and true, give strength to their arms, stoutness to their hearts, steadfastness in their faith.

They will need Thy blessings. Their road will be long and hard, for the enemy is strong. He may hurl back our forces. Success may not come with rushing speed, but we shall return again and again; and we know that by Thy grace, and by the righteousness of our cause, our sons will triumph.

They will be sore tired, by night and by day without rest—until the victory is won. The darkness will be rent by noise and flame. Men's souls will be shaken with the violence of war. For these men are lately drawn from the ways of peace. They fight not for the lust of conquest. They fight to end conquest. They fight to liberate. They fight to let justice arise, and tolerance and good will among all Thy people. They yearn but for the end of battle, for their return to the haven of home.

Some will never return. Embrace these, Father, and receive them, Thy heroic servants, into Thy kingdom. And for us at home—fathers, mothers, children, wives, sisters and brothers of brave men overseas—whose thoughts and prayers are ever with them—help us, Almighty God, to rededicate ourselves in renewed faith in Thee in this hour of great sacrifice.

Many people have urged that I call the Nation into a single day of special prayer. But because the road is long and the desire is great, I ask that our people devote themselves in a countenance of prayer. As we rise to each new day, and again when each day is spent, let words of prayer be on our lips, invoking Thy help to our efforts.

Give us strength, too—strength in our daily tasks, to redouble the contributions we make in the physical and the material support of our armed forces. And let our hearts be stout, to wait out the long travail, to bear sorrows that may come, to impart our courage unto our sons wheresoever they may be.

And, oh Lord, give us faith, give us faith in Thee; faith in our sons; faith in each other; faith in our united crusade. Let not the keenness of our spirit ever be dulled. Let not the impacts of temporary events, of temporal matters deter us in our unconquerable purpose.

With Thy blessing, we shall prevail over the unholy forces of our enemy. Help us to conquer the apostles of greed and racial arrogancies. Lead us to the saving of our country, and with our sister nations into a world unity that will spell a sure peace—a peace invulnerable to the scheming of unworthy men. And a peace that will let all men live in freedom, reaping the just rewards of their honest toil.

Thy will be done, Almighty God. Amen."

CHAPTER 13

The Battle of Normandy

WHEN D-DAY WAS OVER, THERE were no more C-47s towing gliders over our camp at Marlborough because their missions of ferrying glider troops and paratroopers to Normandy were finished. As I watched the returning low-flying tow planes on their landing approach to the Swindon air base, I saw the damage that some of these planes sustained. Their wings, tails, and fuselages were riddled with holes caused by anti-aircraft shells. It was an awesome and sobering sight.

The time had arrived for the XX Corps Headquarters to vacate its quarters in the Nissen huts and prefabricated buildings on Marlborough Commons. We knew that the facilities we had occupied since our arrival in February were originally planned as a military hospital. Now that the war had started on the continent, these buildings were needed to treat the wounded from the war zone. Consequently, our Corps Headquarters moved to different quarters in a town called Ogbourne St. George, five miles north of Marlborough. We knew that our stay here would be short as we would be leaving for the continent before too long.

It was only a few days after D-Day that XX Corps Headquarters received a distinguished visitor. He was a tall, gray-haired man wearing a short jacket and cavalry boots—none other than Lt. Gen. George Smith Patton Jr. He brought the exciting news that he wanted General Walker and our XX Corps to spearhead his Third Army's drive across France after the bridgehead in Normandy was secured, and the breakout was ready to begin. All Corps personnel were delighted to learn that General Patton had chosen our XX

Corps for this important mission, and the success of our mission later on led to our nickname of the "Ghost Corps."

After Patton's surprise visit, our preparations became more intense. Various armored and infantry divisions were assigned and attached to the XX Corps, which meant that our officers made inspection visits to these units at their camps all around southern England. These inspections entailed tactical training and maneuvers, as well as unit administration matters concerning billeting, living conditions, morale, and the health of the troops. This knowledge gave the XX Corps officers valuable information concerning the combat efficiency of lower echelons in order to process them through the mazes of administration prior to their movement to the combat zone.

The planning also included the logistics of funneling all units attached to the XX Corps from their bases scattered around England and move them to the marshalling areas and ports where they would board transport ships. Corps officers made trips to London for staff conferences with representatives of the American and British army, navy, and air-force officials. General Walker flew to the Normandy beachhead on the continent to observe the fighting. Our XX Corps war room was a fascinating place during these days. The large-scale map of Normandy was covered with the plotted positions of the Allied units along with colored tacks that showed the locations of the enemy. It was exciting for me to work in this top-secret war room and to be privy to this information.

On D+1, the Allied armies were still engaged in fierce fighting to extend the beachhead in Normandy, but there was a serious lack of port facilities needed to land troops, equipment, and supplies. The three main ports in Normandy were located at Cherbourg, Le Havre, and Rouen (a few miles inland on the Seine River). During the months preceding D-Day, these ports were significantly destroyed by Allied bombers, and they were not yet liberated. So on the first day after the Normandy landings, combat engineers began to create prefabricated quays and harbor installations with artificial roads connecting them to the beaches.

Opposite the five landing beaches of Utah, Omaha, Gold, Juno, and Sword, a breakwater was built by scuttling the old merchant ships that sailed across the channel carrying troops and equipment for D-Day. The code names given to these offshore barriers were the "Gooseberries." The most unique prefabricated harbors, however, were the two *Mulberry Harbors* that were constructed offshore from Omaha beach at Saint-Laurent-sur-Mer and offshore from Gold beach at Arromanches. It was here that rows of huge concrete caissons were sunk into position to form artificial quays and floating pontoon roadways.

Caissons at Mulberry Harbor (Gold Beach)

Before D-Day, the British built huge reinforced concrete caissons, called "Phoenix," in various ports along the south coast of England. These caissons were designed to form a breakwater around a system of floating roadways and pier heads that could move up and down with the tides. Within this caisson wall, transport ships would be able to tie up alongside the floating quays to discharge their cargoes of troops, equipment, and supplies, which would then be transported to shore on pontoon roadways.

This was an ingenious plan which the German High Command did not comprehend. They did not believe that Normandy was the probable landing site of the invasion because of its lack of ports, but instead, they continued to think the invasion would occur at Pas-de-Calais. The German Wehrmacht knew about these large contraptions that were being assembled in British ports, but they thought their function ranged anywhere from floating grain elevators to substitute piers to use in a captured harbor. But to guess the real purpose that the Allies had in mind was preposterous and in contradiction to all military reasoning.

The first day after the invasion armada had delivered the assault troops to the Normandy beaches, another armada of 160 tugs and ferries began towing these huge caissons across the English Channel and positioned them near Omaha and Gold beaches. Then the air spaces inside the caissons were flooded with sea water, so they would sink into the sand and rest on the bottom of the sea in a permanent position. A total of 115 caissons were towed from England

and formed a breakwater five miles long that enclosed an unloading area of five hundred acres.

The Mulberry Harbor at Omaha beach was fully operational on June 18. Unfortunately, on the following day, a violent storm lashed this artificial harbor and completely destroyed it, so it was abandoned. However, the Mulberry Harbor at Arromanches had less damage and was quickly repaired. This one played a vital role until Cherbourg was captured, and its harbor and docks were restored to a useful condition. During this time, Mulberry Harbor at Arromanches handled 500,000 tons of war materiel, which made it a successful endeavor during the enlargement of the bridgehead and the liberation of Normandy.

Historians identified three phases of the Battle of Normandy—June 7 to July 31:

June 7–18:   Enlargement of the bridgehead.
June 18–July 8: Consolidation of the bridgehead.
July 8–31:   Increase in military strength and the breakout, including the "COBRA" offensive July 25–31.

The Enlargement of the Bridgehead

On D-Day + 1, American troops slowly advanced south of Omaha Beach, where they were subjected to considerable firepower from automatic weapons of many calibers, and some patrols established contact with British troops. They faced the German 352nd Division which was deeply scarred on D-Day and did not receive any reinforcements, so by the evening of June 8 the American bridgehead at Omaha was extended to a depth of six miles, and the final link up of American and British sectors was achieved west of Bayeux.

Then Eisenhower and Bradley decided to unite the two bridgeheads of Utah and Omaha before moving up the Cotentin Peninsula to Cherbourg. By June 12, the 29th Division from Omaha and the 101st Airborne Division linked up after capturing Carentan in the east and Sainte-Mère-Eglise in the west. The bridgehead was now fifty miles wide and ten to twenty miles deep, and it contained sixteen divisions (nine American and seven British and Canadian), with 326,547 men, 3,186 vehicles, and 104,428 tons of supplies.

The Allies had accomplished a tremendous success during this first week of the Battle of Normandy, and the German General Erwin Rommel made this gloomy statement about the situation his Army Group B faced:

"The enemy is being reinforced, under the umbrella of his air superiority...

the enemy is being reinforced much more rapidly than our reserves can reach us... our position is extremely difficult.

The enemy has complete air superiority over the combat zones and up to 100 km in the rear of them."

By June 18 (D-Day +12), the bridgehead was large enough to begin the offensive from Carentan at the base of the Cotentin Peninsula, and at Sainte-Mère-Eglise by Utah Beach, north to the port of Cherbourg.

The Consolidation of the Bridgehead

The port of Cherbourg at the tip of the Cotentin Peninsula was a very important goal because it was the only large harbor available to the Allies in the bridgehead area until the armies were able to cross the Seine River and liberate the port of Le Havre. Cherbourg was an important base for the French Navy before the war, and it was the terminal for the great transatlantic liners. There was an outer harbor wall that Emperor Napoleon III had finished in 1853, and the hills overlooking the town were fortified with defensive structures. When the Germans occupied Cherbourg, they added more defenses of artillery batteries that were able to fire out to sea. They used the harbor as their base for fast patrol boats called E-boats, which attacked allied shipping in the channel.

General Joseph Lawton Collins was the commander of the VII Corps of the American First Army, which pushed north from Sainte-Mère-Eglise. He got support from fighter-bombers and warship guns offshore, and was able to trap remnants of German divisions that were without armored support. There was some street fighting in Cherbourg, and finally on June 26, General von Schleiben of the German land forces, and Admiral Hennecke of the German navy, surrendered, along with ten thousand men. But before their surrender, the Germans had dynamited and burned the docks, cranes, warehouses, bridges, generators, and transformers.

This deepwater port was direly needed to unload heavy equipment like locomotives, but it took two months to repair the heavily damaged docks in the harbor of Cherbourg to permit Liberty ships to unload their cargo at the piers. On August 12, the first gasoline was pumped inland to Bayeux through a new pipeline called Pluto. In the meantime, the vicious Channel storm of June 19 destroyed the Mulberry Harbor at St. Laurent and severely damaged the artificial harbor at Arromanches. The St. Laurent harbor by Omaha beach was abandoned, but the other one was repaired and became an important artificial docking facility during the Battle of Normandy.

The Battle of Caen was fierce in the eastern zone of Normandy, where

British and Canadian armies were engaged with Rommel's 7th Panzer Division. The city was known as the "Venice of Normandy," the "city of a thousand steeples," and "the Athens of the North." It was a medieval city that the Allies had totally destroyed, ending the German stranglehold around the city. The enemy's losses were assessed at two hundred thousand dead, wounded, or taken prisoner, and the 7th Panzer Division lost over three hundred tanks. On July 9, British and Canadian troops entered the *ruins* of Caen.

The Push to Break Out of the Bridgehead

After the capture of Caen, the next objective was to move toward the city of St. Lo, about twenty miles south of Omaha Beach. This meant that American troops had to fight through some of the most difficult terrain in Normandy, called the "Bocage," or hedgerows. Bocage is a term that describes a terrain of mixed woodland and pasture, with winding side roads and lanes bounded on both sides by banks surmounted with high, thick hedgerows that limit visibility and are virtually impenetrable.

The American troops moved from the beaches into the bocage that divided the Cotentin Peninsula into innumerable enclosures. These hedgerows were three to six feet high and sometimes almost as thick, but they seemed to be even higher to the vehicles that had to cross them. It was impossible for tanks to traverse this region because as they would climb the hedgerow, their noses would go over the top, allowing the Germans on the other side to shoot through the bottom of the tank, where they had no armor. A different problem occurred for the troops who were fighting at the base of the Cotentin Peninsula, where the hedgerows gave way to lowlands and marshes which the Germans had flooded.

The Nazis used the following technique in the hedgerow fighting: they opened up with machine guns which stopped the American infantrymen. This was followed by five to ten minutes of mortar fire directed by an observer in a tree. At this point, the Americans called for artillery fire but while waiting for it they suffered more casualties. When the GIs were successful in thwarting an attack, the Germans moved to the next hedgerow at the cross hedge and repeated the procedure. An ingenious sergeant from the 2nd Armored Division, Curtis G. Culin, designed a device that enabled our tanks to penetrate the hedgerows. He fastened two iron prongs on the front of the tank, each one being about two feet long. When the tank ran against the wall of dirt and entwined tree roots it was able to plow through the hedgerow, the leading prongs pushing away roots, dirt, and trees, thereby blasting a road through the hedge.

When the tank personnel learned that this invention was effective they ordered all ordnance companies in the beachhead to fashion these devices for all armored divisions. The troops quickly found an adequate supply of iron to make the prongs because they gathered the angle irons from the beaches which the German defenders had used as underwater obstacles. Each angle iron was the proper three to four inches wide so the only job the guys had to perform was to cut them to size, sharpen the points, and bolt them to the front of each tank. By the time of the breakout in late July, more than half of American tanks were equipped with these iron prongs, and new attacks through the hedgerows surprised the enemy and overcame these obstacles.

Operation COBRA

COBRA was the code name for the offensive that General Omar Bradley had planned to exploit the breakthrough from the beachheads. This operation was to take place along a four-mile front between Periers and St. Lo that was defended by the weakened Panzer Lehr Division. Operation COBRA was scheduled to begin on July 20, but adverse weather postponed the offensive to July 25. The American Air Force carried out carpet bombing, but some of our planes mistakenly attacked American targets. An errant bomb landed in the slit trench of Gen. Leslie J. McNair, the sixty-one year-old chief of Army Ground Forces in Washington, who had arrived in France just two weeks before. This was a very tragic loss in the early days of the war. General McNair's grave is in the American Military Cemetery at Omaha beach.

Operation COBRA was a success when the American 4th Infantry Division finally broke through the breach and began the push south, with St. Lo and Coutances falling to the American troops. The bridge at Pontaubault was captured intact, thereby opening the road to Brittany and the Loire Valley, while General Woods's 4th Infantry Division made a lightening dash to Avranches at the base of the peninsula.

With the capture of Avranches on July 31, the breakout from the Normandy beachhead was achieved. Avranches now would be the initial starting point of the XX Corps' entry into combat.

CHAPTER 14

My Journey to Utah Beach

THE ORDER FINALLY CAME!

The XX Corps was alerted for movement to a marshalling area in Southampton. Our busy days became more hectic as combat equipment was packed into wooden boxes which were loaded into the vehicles. We removed our shoulder patches of the XX Corps insignia, so our unit could not be identified. Each vehicle displayed on its windshield a card that gave its weight and dimensions to aid the dock workers in loading the vehicle on the ship. Final checks of weapons and equipment were made, and the gas tanks of all vehicles were filled with fuel. Our duffle bags were fully packed with all our worldly possessions. We were ready to go.

Meanwhile, we got the news that General Patton had arrived in France on July 6, and since we were under his command, we concluded that our time to enter combat was near at hand. Patton's presence in Normandy was well-known as he traveled along the allied beachheads, conferred with various generals, spoke with reporters, and even served as a pallbearer at several funerals for servicemen. But it was amazing that German intelligence stubbornly believed that Patton was still in England, training his troops for their projected invasion from Dover to the Pas-de-Calais area of France, where the allies made large-scale raids on coastal fortifications. Even as late as July 23, Joachim von Ribbontrop, who was the Foreign Minister of Nazi Germany, and the German War Ministry thought that Patton's invasion of France was still several weeks down the road, mainly because they heard that Patton had sent three divisions to London to help stabilize the chaos created by the German V-1 rockets that had pounded the city, and therefore these forces were not available for the landing in France. The Nazis were completely fooled!

At 1100 hours on July 15, the XX Corps Headquarters crossed the initial point (IP) with a long column of jeeps, staff cars, trucks, and half-tracks. The five-month sojourn of our Corps in England now had ended. Our convoy slowly moved along the narrow roads leading to Southampton, and as we drove through the small towns and villages, the British men, women, and children paused to wave a final farewell. When our column of vehicles stopped in small towns, we were treated to tea and biscuits.

Upon our arrival in Southampton, we parked the corps' vehicles on a quiet street in a neighborhood of row houses. The mixture of jeeps, trucks, and trailers were tightly packed, bumper to bumper. We stayed on this street for an entire afternoon, and to pass the time, we walked around the neighborhood or stayed by our vehicles while waiting for orders to move to the marshalling area. My G-3 jeep was parked by a row house where two teenaged girls were living. They were about fifteen years old, friendly and talkative, so Joe Messner and I spent several hours kidding around with them and enjoying their charming English accents. They promised that they would write to us when we got to the Continent, and Joe and I did receive several letters and pictures from them later during our summer in France.

In late afternoon on the 15th, we drove to the marshalling area outside the city of Portsmouth where we spent the night at a very large open field that was jammed with vehicles, equipment, and thousands of troops. Portsmouth was the huge naval base and shipping port about fifteen miles southeast of Southampton. An army service unit provided chow kitchens, toilet facilities, and large pyramidal tents where we slept. The next day was one of waiting, but it also included a final check of weapons and equipment. We were issued K-rations (small boxes containing a can of soup, crackers, and cheese), seasick pills, sulfa pills, water-purifying tablets, and extra portions of cigarettes and candy bars. The payroll sergeant changed our money from pounds and shillings to French francs, which we called "invasion money." The francs were not real French currency which then had no value, so a new "fake," or artificial, currency was issued which we used during our entire time in France.

Two days later, on July 17, XX Corps Headquarters departed from the marshalling area and moved to the Southampton docks where the transport ships were docked and waiting to be loaded with troops and their equipment. It was an awesome sight to watch the troops embark on the ship, unit by unit, and see the big cranes pick up their vehicles in nets and slings and swoop them onto the ships' decks and into the holds. Our ship was not ready to load our unit, so we spent the night in the dock area, and we slept wherever we found a spot, whether in our vehicles or on piles of baggage or supplies. I tried to settle down on a bunch of duffle bags in the back of a 6x6, but sleep was difficult, not only because I had no bed, but I was very excited about the events that were about to happen. At midnight, an air raid alarm sounded in Southampton that kept me awake for a while.

The transport ships that were used in all English ports to carry the troops to the Normandy beaches were called "Liberty Ships." A huge supply of these cargo ships were needed to handle the sealift of war materiel after Pearl Harbor and America's entry into the war, so President Roosevelt decided that US shipbuilders should begin to build hundreds of standardized cargo carriers on an assembly-line basis. They were named after politicians, patriots, scientists, artists, explorers, and people from all walks of life.

Liberty ships were approximately four hundred feet long and fifty-seven feet wide, and had a speed of eleven knots with a range of seventeen thousand miles. They had five cargo holds with a carrying capacity of 10,800 tons, and a crew of thirty-eight to sixty-two civilian merchant marine sailors, plus twenty-one to forty naval personnel to operate the guns and communication equipment on board. The useful life of these ships was five years. A total of 2,751 Liberty ships were built between 1941 and 1945, with an average production time of forty-two days. During the war, two hundred of these ships were lost to enemy action, weather, and accidents, with a total loss of life of more than nine thousand merchant seamen out of the quarter million mariners of the Liberty fleet.

Daybreak on July 18 came too soon, but our XX Corps personnel were up early because it was our turn to board the ship. Our entire organization and all our vehicles traveled together on the same Liberty Ship, named *John A. Campbell*. (This ship was built in a Brunswick, Georgia shipyard and was named after US Supreme Court Justice John A. Campbell, who was born in Georgia.) After several hours, our unit was completely loaded, and the *John A. Campbell* slowly moved south into the wide mouth of the Southampton Water into the Solent that surrounds the Isle of Wight on its north side. Behind the shelter of this island, our vessel dropped its anchor among a large group of other Liberty ships, all fully loaded with troops and their equipment headed for the combat zone. We spent the night north of the island; our morale was high, and our spirits were filled with excitement and anticipation. Card games broke out on the various decks. The waiting was difficult to bear.

The next morning was Wednesday, July 19, with weather that was clear and hot, and the English Channel was as smooth as a mill pond, so the vomit bags that were issued to us were not needed. At 0800 hours, the *John A. Campbell* weighed anchor and slowly sailed around the western side of the Isle of Wight, where we joined a large convoy of Liberty ships, along with other craft of various sizes. A couple of sleek British destroyers moved around the perimeter of the fleet and provided protection for our voyage.

By late afternoon, after about six hours of sailing we had crossed the eighty mile wide English Channel, passing by the eastern side of the Cotentin Peninsula. At this location, our column of transport ships was guided through channels that had been cleared of mines by hard-working vessels called mine sweepers. It was an awesome sight because wherever we looked we saw hundreds of freighters and transports, all heavily loaded with men and equipment, anchored close to the coast. The *John A. Campbell* dropped its anchor here too. We were at *Utah Beach*!

We arrived here forty-three days after D-Day when the first wave of assault troops came ashore and established a tiny bridgehead on this beach. This day the scene was different. Standing on the top deck, I gazed toward the shore where I saw a long, thin, crescent of light brown sand that was sandwiched between a sea of water that lapped gently onto this nice beach, and a long stretch of sand dunes that formed a wall about six to ten feet high. Utah Beach provided an easy access to land, with no bluffs or cliffs to climb as was the case at Omaha beach and Pointe du Hoc. The Nazi defenders had built huge casemates containing coastal guns along the crests of the dunes which was part of the Atlantic Wall and now lay in ruins. Anti-aircraft gun batteries were silent, and the beach area was strewn with the remains of German beach defenses.

There was no harbor at Utah beach, so the US Navy built a breakwater to protect the unloading of freighters from the high waves of the English Channel. The big arc of this sea wall was made with sunken ships left over from the initial assault of landing craft on D-Day. Within this protected arc of the breakwater and the calmer waters, I watched the uninterrupted unloading of troops and vehicles of all sizes and types. The cranes on the Liberty ships hoisted each vehicle securely nestled in a huge net from the deck onto a lighter or landing craft, to be shuttled to a low-floating steel pier. The men climbed down nets that were suspended on the side of the ship. All kinds of small craft, including ferries and whatever was available, were busy shuttling the stream of men and materiel to the pier and the sandy beach beyond the rolling dunes to a marshalling area where their units reassembled to make sure that everyone was accounted for. The troops gradually moved out to temporary camps spread around the liberated beachhead of the Cotentin Peninsula.

Our turn to disembark from the *John A. Campbell* had not yet come, so we spent the night on board and waited. The next morning was Thursday, July 20, and the weather took a sudden turn for the worse, so our debarkation was delayed indefinitely. Storms in the channel along with high winds had churned up the sea, and it was too risky to unload the ships, cargo, and men into the smaller landing crafts for fear of sinking in the surf.

The hours were long and restless as we waited for forty-eight hours for the storm and sea to subside. We spent a lot of time on the top deck. Sometimes we had to "fall in" for roll call and instructions or we field stripped our carbines, cleaned them thoroughly, and reassembled them again. Some of the guys played poker or craps to occupy the time. The dice were always tossed on a taut blanket spread out on the planks of the deck. Our Corps' barber even gave haircuts during these long days.

Our Liberty ship was one of hundreds of other ships that were anchored and clustered closely together outside of Utah beach. As I looked at these ships, I was amazed to see that each ship, including ours, had a barrage balloon tethered to the deck. These were large canvas balloons inflated with gas that looked like miniature blimps hovering about one hundred feet above each deck. Its purpose was a precautionary defense against low-flying enemy aircraft to prevent them from strafing the ships with machine gun fire. I marveled at this awesome sight of a sea of balloons floating above all the ships anchored in the channel.

In the evening, after chow, I was on the top deck with some of my buddies taking in all of the sights and sounds around us. I heard the roar of motors of several aircraft that were flying inland beyond the beach, and soon I realized that I was watching a dog fight between a German and an American fighter plane. I watched their spectacular aerial maneuvers chasing each other, diving and firing their wing guns. This encounter went on for perhaps fifteen minutes when I saw the Nazi fighter plane plunge vertically into the earth. Then I saw smoke rising from the spot of impact. This was an impressive sight!

The storm and the boisterous waves continued on Friday, July 21, so we were confined to the ship for a second day. All the other ships anchored around us had the same dilemma. During the anxious waiting, there were more card and dice games, small talk, writing letters, thinking of our families back home, and another dreaded night of sleeping on the crowded ship.

Saturday morning dawned sunny and clear, and the high waves of the English Channel had calmed down to little more than ripples. It looked like the beginning of a beautiful day. Besides, today was July 22—my 21st Birthday!

The order came for the XX Corps personnel to disembark the *John A. Campbell*, our temporary quarters for the last four days and nights. A LCP (landing craft personnel) arrived at our ship and tied fast to the port side, where the stairway was lowered from the top deck to the floor of the LCP. I descended the steps into the boat as a soldier in full battle gear. After all personnel were on the LCP, crowded together, the craft headed for the beach, guided by an escort craft that gingerly led us through the channels that were cleared of mines and other underwater obstacles. The short trip across the shallower waters of the channel, between the anchored ship and the sandy shore, took only a few minutes, as the LCP eased up against one of the many steel piers that jutted out from the beach to deeper water.

My heart beat a little faster as I looked back to our ship and the many, many transport ships all anchored within the artificial breakwater of sunken ships. The sea was a beehive of activity, with hundreds of small craft ferrying troops and equipment to the shore. I noticed that some of the landing craft that headed back to the ships were not empty but were transporting wounded GIs, and in some cases, even German prisoners of war, back to the anchored ships to be returned to England. I thought that perhaps some of the wounded men might be taken to the hospital that we had vacated in Marlborough where we had our headquarters. The activity at Utah Beach was a massive movement of thousands of men and the equipment of war that was happening before my eyes. It was all so awesome that I couldn't take it all in. Wow!

Utah Beach and its sand dunes
as it appears now (2010)

When the LCP reached the floating pier, I stepped out of the craft and walked toward the sandy beach. It was a beautiful stretch of fine-grade yellow sand, and I thought to myself that this must have been a wonderful place to enjoy for recreation before the war, and before the Nazis turned it into a part of the infamous Atlantic Wall. I trudged across the soft sand with my load of heavy gear and onto the narrow path over the crest of the sand dune, which was about fifteen to twenty feet high. This trail was marked by the engineers with white tapes on both sides of the path to keep us from wandering into unknown ground, because I noticed the free-drawn signs sticking out of the sand that showed a skull and cross bones and the words "Achtung, Minen" (attention, Mines).

Wow! Today was a very memorable day, as I, on my 21st birthday, along with my XX Corps buddies, walked onto *Utah Beach* and the soil of France. My emotions were running high, and my adrenalin surged within me as I now began to realize that I truly had entered a combat zone. My daily life was about to change.

Today was D-Day +46, and as I walked across Utah beach my thoughts turned back to June 6, when this ground was a bloody battleground where thousands of my fellow soldiers had fought so valiantly to capture this ground at an enormous cost of lives. On the beach and the dunes, I saw the wrecked remains of battered and burned trucks, landing craft, tanks, and weapons of all kinds scattered everywhere. The destroyed anti-aircraft gun emplacements and enormous concrete casemates that showed direct hits from American bombs stood silently as a reminder of that awful day when this ground was covered with the wounded and dead of friend and foe.

My thoughts were interrupted when I arrived at a narrow two-lane road beyond the dunes where there was a long line of trucks waiting for us. I threw my duffle bag into the back end of one of the cargo trucks which already contained a huge pile of bags, and I climbed into a different 6x6 along with twenty other guys. Soon our convoy of trucks left the beach area and traveled inland to the west side of the Cotentin Peninsula, which was a cleared part of the beachhead now held by American troops. After a drive of perhaps an hour on winding rural roads, we arrived at the village of St. Jacques de Nehou, about twenty miles southwest of Cherbourg. At the edge of the town, we set up our first Command Post. My first impression of this land of Normandy reminded me of Wisconsin because this was farming country with a rolling countryside with small fields and many apple orchards. No cows and other farm animals were around because the farms had been devastated by the fierce fighting during the past couple of weeks.

Command Post No. 1

St. Jacques de Nehou, France
(In an apple orchard)
July 22–August 3, 1944

Our first Continental Command Post was in an apple orchard! We were in the bloody *bocage*, the hedgerow country of Normandy. The fields were surrounded with the green and thick summer foliage of tree roots, vines, and earth, all bound together in an impenetrable barrier several feet high. Visibility through this entanglement was impossible. The "Achtung, Minen" signs were still standing along the edges of the hedgerows, and a vast amount of discarded gear, both German and American, lay along the hedgerows that encircled the farm fields. This included dented helmets, broken weapons, parts of uniforms, the litter of K-ration boxes, and smashed artillery or burned-out tanks. Much of this American debris was left over from the airborne invasion by the paratroopers of the 82nd and 101st Divisions.

The nauseating smell of corpses hung like a pall over the fields, and sometimes a dead soldier, either German or American, was found wedged in the entangled vines and roots of the hedges, where perhaps the wounded soldier had crawled to hide and then died. Some of these men were found through the foul odor of their rotting flesh.

At our apple orchard CP, XX Corps personnel settled in doing various tasks such as digging slit trenches next to a hedgerow to be used as a toilet. Whenever it rained, water filled these trenches and the edges became slippery which brought out various derogatory jokes. All of our command tents and vehicles were covered with camouflage netting. The cooks set up their kitchen stoves under apple trees which now had little green apples, and we ate our meals from our aluminum mess kits while sitting on our steel helmets. Helmets became an important accessory, because in addition to its protection against bullets and shrapnel, we used it as a seat and a wash basin. The drinking water supply was stored in a huge canvas bag called a "lister bag," which was suspended from a tree branch. The water always had an odd taste because it had purifying chemicals added to it. The cooks now served us hot food, which was so much more appreciated than the awful K-rations. Now that we were camping in the field, Joe and I set up our new "duplex" pup tent under an apple tree, and this new arrangement of living was off to a good start.

Here in Normandy we discovered an interesting French commodity: the very potent and famous Normandy liquor called "calvados." Its alcohol content was very high, and it made you shudder when drinking a shot. When a GI poured it onto a board and lit it with a match, it burned brightly. Calvados is distilled from apples common in this countryside.

We were now constantly reminded that we were in a combat zone by the sounds of heavy artillery in the distance and German bombers, which we called "Bed-check Charlies," kept us alert and sometimes awakened us during the night. The most spectacular event occurred on the morning of July 25, when a huge armada of American aircraft roared overhead from bases in England. First there was squadron after squadron of four-engine Super Flying Fortresses and Liberators, followed by medium bombers, and finally by scores of P-47 and P-51 fighter planes. More than eighteen hundred aircraft dropped forty-seven hundred tons of bombs on the Normandy town of St. Lo and the surrounding area where there was stiff German resistance. This sight was awesome and unforgettable, and this enormous strike of carpet bombing blasted an opening in enemy lines. This mission was the opening salvo of Operation COBRA which allowed American troops to clear out much of the Cotentin Peninsula and began the drive south to Avranches. St. Lo was twenty-five miles southeast of our CP in the apple orchard, and a few days later we drove through St. Lo on our way south. As we passed through the rubble-strewn streets of the city, we witnessed the terrible destruction of the bombing. This was my first sight of the horrible and nearly complete destruction of an entire town, and it affected me greatly.

Destruction in a Normandy town (August 1944)

Destruction in a Normandy town (August 1944)

Destruction in a Normandy town (August 1944)

During the latter days of July, when Phase 3 of the Battle of Normandy was developing into a push to break out of the bridgehead and sweep into the rest of France, these liberated areas of Normandy were being filled with large numbers of troops as well as huge quantities of trucks, tanks, ammunition, and supplies. The time for the allied offensive was at hand.

During the last week of July, XX Corps staff officers were very busy as they met with the commanders of each of the infantry and armored divisions that were attached to our Corps. These units were camped in various locations in the Cotentin Peninsula. Patton, who had arrived in Normandy on July 6, was also making the rounds of visiting his Corps commanders. He appeared in our apple orchard too and strode into the war tent where he conferred with General Walker and all of the department heads including my boss, Colonel Griffith. I wasn't present because I was involved in other camp duties.

On July 31, Patton and his Corps Commanders were ready for action, and his Third Army was waiting for its official activation. The great day of August 1, 1944, had arrived, and Patton was quoted as saying, "I was very nervous all morning because it seemed impossible to get any definite news and the clock seemed to have stopped." Finally, at noon, Patton and his Chief of Staff, Col. Paul D. Harkins, who were alone at his headquarters, celebrated the

Patton's Third Army Insignia

activation of the Third United States Army by taking "a drink of horrible brandy."

General Omar Bradley was in command of the Twelfth Army Group, which now consisted of the First Army, commanded by Gen. Courtney Hodges, the Third Army, under Patton, and the Ninth Army commanded by Gen. William H. Simpson. The divisions that were under the command of the XX Corps were the 5th Infantry Division under Maj. Gen. Stafford L. "Red" Irwin, the 35th Infantry Division commanded by Maj. Gen. Paul W. Baade, and the 2nd French Armored Division led by Brigadier General Jacques-Philippe LeClerc. The French 2nd Armored Division, which had a complement of twelve thousand men, had just arrived in France from its training "in exile" in England.

Just after noon on August 1, the Third Army and its attached Corps became operational. At the same time, the 19th Tactical Air Command under Brigadier Gen. Otto P. "Opie" Weyland was added to the Third Army. This was the moment that we had trained for during the past year and a half. Now we were officially a fighting organization, and we were in *combat*. The XX Corps was eager to get going!

CHAPTER 15

The XX Corps Enters Combat

Command Post No. 2

Fleury, France
(On a farm south of Fleury and east of Champrepus)
August 3–5, 1944

ON AUGUST 3, XX CORPS Headquarters began the practice of always moving closer to the fighting front, so we moved to our second CP after living in the Normandy apple orchard for twelve days. We set up our bivouac in a farm pasture next to the village of Fleury on the west side of the Cotentin Peninsula. We were aware of our being close to the front because we saw the flashes of fire and heard the deafening boom of American artillery gun batteries that supported the infantry. In a wooded area of this CP, some of our guys discovered the abandoned rocket ramp that the Germans used to launch and guide the V2 German rockets to London during the Blitz. It was a grim discovery.

Now that we were in actual combat, XX Corps Headquarters organized its personnel to utilize a more efficient use of men and their duties. We were divided into two work units with equal numbers of men and their skills with each unit working a twelve-hour shift. The day shift worked from 0900 hours to 2100 hours, and the night shift worked from 2100 hours to 0900 hours the next morning. Joe Messner and I were on the night shift. I was the clerk typist responsible for typing the orders of battle that were delivered to division commanders by liaison officers. Joe was the chief clerk of our night shift and the head draftsman, who was in charge of keeping the war map current regarding the enemy's positions and the location of the various units under the command of the XX Corps. The second draftsman in our group was John Massa, who was from Ohio.

The actual nerve center of the XX Corps Headquarters was the huge "war tent," in which I spent many of my working hours. The tent was made of heavy canvas and about 16x20 feet in size and 8 feet high. Each side was held up with wooden poles, and several poles supported the middle of the tent. It took four guys to set it up and take it down. There was an opening with a flap on each of the narrow ends attached to a smaller tent that was an office. The tent on the left was the G-2 Intelligence Department, and the tent attached on the right was the G-3 Operations Department, where I worked. I had my own L. C. Smith typewriter, a work table, and chair.

Huge war maps were taped to a large piece of sturdy plywood that was leaned against the long side of the war tent. We carried a map case that contained a supply of large-scale and very detailed topographical maps of the entire war zone where our troops were located, as well as the geographical positions of the enemy fighting units. Some of these maps showed minute details of all roads and lanes, fence lines, creeks, isolated buildings, farm buildings, and villages. After the maps were tacked to the board, they were covered with a sheet of transparent acetate so the map was clear underneath. Joe's job was to plot the positions of each division and battalion that was under the command of the XX Corps. He used grease pencils of different colors that showed whether these units were armored, infantry, or artillery. Each unit had a unique symbol, such as an "X," oval, or circle within a rectangular box that was instantly recognizable. The movements of all military units were always fluid, so the draftsmen needed to constantly update the location of the symbols. This was done by using a rag dampened with alcohol as a solvent to wipe the acetate clean.

The draftsmen in the G-2 Section plotted the locations and types of the German army units that were facing our troops on the same war map. This intelligence information was gathered by G-2 personnel from many sources. At the front lines, American patrols reported their information to G-2 via field telephone, radio, or in code. We also used single-engine light planes, like Piper Cubs or Stinsons, that flew near the front to gather information. We had spies who infiltrated enemy territory, including several German-speaking soldiers, some of whom had fled from Germany during the rise of Hitler and later became US citizens. At night, these men dressed in civilian clothes and walked through enemy lines to go into the towns where they visited bars, bier stubes, and other places, where they mingled with the German townsfolk and listened for news about activities of the German army units and personnel. In the morning, these GIs returned to our Corps Headquarters and donned American uniforms again and related what they had seen and heard on their trips into town. With this information, the war map was updated to show the locations and strength of German army units.

When all of this information was plotted on the situation map, it was ready for analysis by the XX Corps staff officers. General Walker, his Chief of Staff Colonel Collier, my G-3 boss, Colonel Griffith, the G-2 director Colonel Zeller, and other general staff heads stood before the map and discussed strategy, timing, and the execution of battle plans. Colonel Griffith would then draft the orders of attack, which units would be involved, the time and direction of attack, including artillery and air support for the divisions, battalions, and companies of the involved units. Colonel Griffith handed me these orders of attack, and I typed them on my typewriter using mimeograph stencils. They were reproduced on mimeograph machines using black ink, which was always a messy job. Two or three liaison officers, usually second or first lieutenants, were standing by waiting for me to finish, and they placed the orders into their attaché cases, leaving our headquarters with their jeep drivers and headed for the front lines to deliver these orders to the division or battalion commanders.

General Staff of XX Corps Headquarters

Functions and Duties

Chief of Staff: Supervise and coordinate the execution of plans and orders of the XX Corps and its attached troops.

G-1 (Personnel): Find fresh reinforcements for the depleted ranks of the corps' divisions from combat operations, process casualty reports, and process prisoners of war.

G-2 (Intelligence): Compile information on enemy movements gained from reconnaissance reports and interrogation of prisoners in order to determine the enemy's weaknesses and strengths. Disseminate tactical maps of enemy locations to commanders of units for them to execute the orders for attack.

G-3 (Operations): Administer the tactical plans and develop the orders for battle in conjunction with the location and strength of the enemy as determined by G-2. Battle orders are written by G-3 and sent to the units that were assigned to execute them.

G-4 (Supply): The nerve center of supplies, gasoline, ammunition, and food, thus providing for the needs of men and machines. Administer transportation and delivery of all vital materiel throughout the far-flung Corps' zone.

G-5 (Military Government): Administer the needs of the helpless victims of the war, the refugees who were deprived of their homes and needed housing, food, and clothing. In conquered lands, G-5 supervised every civilian activity through interrogation and close supervision in order to preserve military security.

Table of Organization of XX Corps Headquarters

Commanding General

    Chief of Staff and Deputy Chief of Staff

        G-1 Personnel, replacements, administration, decorations
           AG (Adjutant General-assistant)
           JA (Judge Advocate)
           Special services
           IG (Inspector General)
           Chaplain

        G-2 Intelligence, counter-intelligence, situation map

        G-3 Plans, operations, air support, situation map
           Infantry
           Armor
           Artillery
           Cavalry
           Anti-aircraft
           G-3 Air
               Air reconnaissance
               Tactical air support (fighter-bombers)

G-4 Supply, evacuation, maintenance, truck movement, army depots
    Quartermaster
    Chemical Warfare
    Medics
    Ordnance
    Signal Corps
    Engineers

G-5 Civil affairs, military government, displaced persons

Military Map Symbols

I. Military Unit Identification Symbols

Infantry

Armored Unit

Artillery

Cavalry, mechanized

Quartermaster Corps

Chemical Warfare

Medical Corps

Ordnance

Signal Corps

Engineers

Transportation Corps

II. Size of Military Organization Symbols

These symbols are placed either in boundary lines or above the rectangles, triangles, or circles of the unit identification.

●	Squad
●●	Section
●●●	Platoon
I	Company (or Battery)
II	Battalion
III	Regiment (or Combat Team – Armored)
X	Brigade (or Combat Command – Armored)
XX	Division
XXX	Corps
XXXX	Army
XXXXX	Group of Armies

III. Examples of Unit Identification

The letter or number to the left of the symbol indicates the unit designation, that to the right identifies the parent unit to which it belongs, or the unit identification if there is nothing to the left. Letters or numbers above or below boundary lines designate the units separated by the lines.

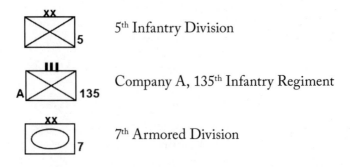

5th Infantry Division

Company A, 135th Infantry Regiment

7th Armored Division

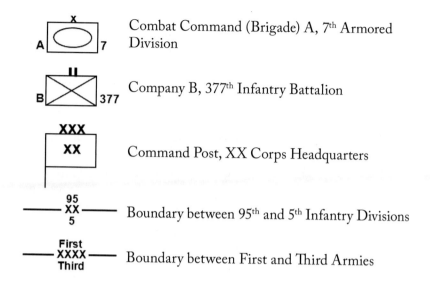

Combat Command (Brigade) A, 7th Armored Division

Company B, 377th Infantry Battalion

Command Post, XX Corps Headquarters

Boundary between 95th and 5th Infantry Divisions

Boundary between First and Third Armies

Command Post No. 3

St. Martin de Landelles, France
(West of St. Hilaire)
August 6–7, 1944

On the fifth day after we entered combat, our Corps Headquarters moved about thirty-six miles further south into some bocage fields near St. Martin de Landelles. The night we arrived, our Corps troops got its first real baptism of fire when the German Luftwaffe launched a fierce bombing attack in an attempt to stop our quick advance. It was exhilarating and fascinating, yet terrifying, to see the night sky turned bright from flares dropped by enemy bombers while bright-red streaks from tracer bullets going skyward tried to reach the planes. The tracers traveled along with the deadly shells fired from the 90mm anti-aircraft batteries from our own XX Corps Artillery, who were always stationed a few miles from our headquarters. The loud, monotonous droning of the motors of bomber squadrons filled the air, interspersed with the staccato bark of the ack-ack guns, and then the deafening crash of bombs hitting the earth in a violent explosion of brilliant light that turned the darkness into daylight for a few moments. As I watched this aerial attack, I even had moments of exhilaration, even bursting out with a cheer, when I saw a huge burst of bright red flames high in the sky, and then watched the long, slow, spiral of a German bomber falling to the earth with its crew inside. For the first time I thought to myself, "So this is what war is like." This was no longer a training exercise or war games. German air attacks continued in our area for three consecutive nights, without any injuries or casualties to Corps Headquarters' troops. During these three nights, 291 enemy planes flew over our area, of which thirty were destroyed and the balance driven away.

On August 6, our Corps received its first mission from Third Army Headquarters to drive south and cross the Selune River, but the previous night's air raid had destroyed the bridge, so XX Corps engineers immediately built a double Bailey bridge which opened up to traffic before nightfall the same day. It was the only route to bring men and equipment to the fast moving infantry and armored divisions. Anti-aircraft units set up a seven-mile zone around a critical dam to prevent its being bombed. If the dam broke, there would have been extensive flooding, but it was saved. However, several German panzer divisions began a counterattack against the narrow corridor held by American troops, so Patton ordered Walker to divert part of XX Corps troops to assist in stopping the counterattack.

In the meantime, other XX Corps divisions were advancing south so rapidly, that Chief of Staff Collier moved half of our Corps Headquarters to Vitre to establish an advance command post. I was not in this advance group because some of our corps divisions were still involved in disposing of some German SS Panzer regiments that put up strong resistance. These rapid advances of Corps Headquarters troops gave the XX Corps' 69th Signal Battalion some big challenges to maintain communication between the headquarters staff and its attached divisions with their regiments and battalions. They worked day and night, often under fire from enemy patrols and snipers to install miles and miles of telephone wires and cables on the ground, along the roads and hedgerows. They had to search for breaks in the wires because they often were crumpled by trucks and tanks, or they were cut by enemy patrols. These telephone men had dangerous missions and suffered many casualties.

Command Post No. 4

Vitre, France
(One mile southwest of Vitre)
August 7–9, 1944

The other half of XX Corps Headquarters, which included my group, moved forward to join Collier's advance CP, which was camped in a wheat field near

Vitre. We did not have any concealment in this open wheat field, because this part of France was the "bread basket" of the country, consisting of many miles of flat land that looked much like Nebraska or Kansas. Walker's next objective was to capture the city of Angers and save the bridges over the Loire River. Consequently, the 5th Infantry Division had to open up a corridor to this city of eighty thousand, located about sixty-five miles south of Vitre. At first, there was not much German resistance, and the infantry "doughboys" even rode on tanks, artillery trucks, and jeeps. French civilians lined the roads and streets in towns along the way, and they greeted our troops with shouts of joy and tears, and showered them with wine, eggs, and flowers, a sudden and tremendous outpouring of emotions after four long years of Nazi oppression. The roads were lined with the battered litter of the retreating Germans, and the burned-out and twisted remains of their tanks and transports even caused a traffic problem for the advancing 5th Division. Their streams of armored vehicles, artillery trucks, huge tank transports, jeeps, and six-by-sixes packed with troops raced through this break in the combat zone. These troops were feeling great because they finally were getting out of the hated hedgerows of Normandy. Now, the battle of northern France had begun!

There was fierce fighting in Angers, but the railroad bridge was rescued before it could be destroyed by a box car loaded with explosives in the middle of the bridge. The infantrymen of the 5th Division raced across the bridge and engaged the enemy across the river. In the meantime, a US tank under fire from German snipers hooked onto the box car and pulled it off the bridge. The bridge was saved intact.

Angers was the first large city and strategic center to fall to the XX Corps and the Third Army. It had been an important communication and transportation center and the main supply depot for the Seventh German Army. The city also housed a Nazi naval command station which controlled the German Atlantic Fleet of Admiral Karl Doenitz by means of a huge underground radio station. The city also housed a submarine training regiment and a large Gestapo headquarters as well as naval artillery battalions, flak battalions, and the Angers Air Command. More than eighteen hundred German prisoners were taken, and the 16th Infantry Division was annihilated. The seizure of Angers on August 9 was an important victory in the battle of northern France.

Command Post No. 5

Soulge-le-Bruant, France
(East of Laval)
August 10–13, 1944

On August 10, Corps Headquarters moved to a new farm field a few miles east of Laval, about thirty miles from Vitre. On the military front, there was not much activity as German units had moved east, and their left flank was lightly held. However, the main event for XX Corps Headquarters occurred on August 11. Our bivouac was in the cow pasture of a farm without any trees around. The day was hot and sunny, and there was a lull in the fighting. Our cooks had set up the field kitchen, and we were treated to a nice hot dinner. The cooks provided orange marmalade to spread on our bread, and suddenly we were attacked by swarms of yellow jackets (wasps). They zoomed into this field from nowhere and landed on the marmalade, so it was difficult to take a bite of bread without a yellow jacket being in the way. We tried to shoo them off between bites, but they were persistent. Many of the guys ended up with yellow jackets inside their mouths, and we heard outbursts of yelps and ow-ahs from the guys who got stung. In the middle of a war zone, we long remembered this event of humans versus insects. I survived without any injury.

Command Post No. 6

La Ferte Bernard, France
(In the rose garden of a chateau)
August 13–15, 1944

Our Corps Headquarters advanced to its next command post about seventy miles to the east. This was a much longer move due to the cracking-up of enemy lines and the retreat of German divisions to the vicinity of Chartres. We set up our office tents in a beautiful rose garden surrounding a very old chateau because the building itself was not open for our use. There was a surprise visitor one day, a French woman named Madame Clavel, whose husband was the commanding officer of a battalion of the FFI Forces (Forces Francaises de L'Interieur). She was a beautiful woman, with long blond hair, and she became known as the "Veronica Lake of the XX Corps." Veronica Lake was a Hollywood actress in the 1930s and 1940s who was a sexy, well-loved, long-haired blonde, and a favorite pin-up girl of the troops. When Madame

Clavel visited our camp, she was dressed as a peasant and her blonde tresses were covered with a head scarf tied in a knot under her chin. She provided our G-2 Intelligence Division with information about the enemy because the FFI people moved behind the German lines, where they harassed German forces and committed acts of sabotage.

The divisions attached to the XX Corps had entered the flat countryside west of Chartres, and the 7th Armored Division was racing across the wheat fields without much resistance from the German defenders. This area was known as the "breadbasket of France." The time had come for Corps Headquarters to move forward to the next CP.

Command Post No. 7

Courville sur Eure, France
(In a woods one mile west of Courville)
August 15–22, 1944

Chartres Cathedral, Chartres France. (Photo taken in August 1944)

We settled into our 7th Command Post in woods outside the town of Courville sur Eure, about thirteen miles from Chartres, a city with a population of forty thousand people known as the "Gateway to Paris." Late in the day of August 15, the American 7th Armored Division arrived at the outskirts of the city. They were supported by units of the XX Corps Artillery Battalion that had quickly moved to Chartres from the rear area and was joined by the XX Corps

Cavalry units to form an arc around the city to prevent an escape by the German garrison, which had mounted a savage counterattack. The fighting went on all night, and most pockets of German resistance were eliminated by daybreak.

I was on duty along with Joe and several of the officers of G-2 and G-3 when we heard the reports of heavy fighting from liaison officers who had returned to the CP from the front lines of the 7th Armored Division. On the morning of August 16, Joe plotted this information on the war map, so it was up-to-date with the current situation in Chartres. Griffith, Walker, and several

other staff officers entered the war tent for a briefing of the situation in Chartres. The news was disturbing because there were stubborn pockets of resistance from German machine gun and mortar emplacements located at strategic spots within the city. It was also learned that the Corps Artillery had an order to shell and destroy the old and famous medieval Chartres Cathedral which stood at the center of the city.

The construction of this beautiful Gothic edifice began in the late twelfth century, and it was consecrated in the year 1260. The west façade is unusual because it has two contrasting or mismatched spires. One of the towers is in the shape of a pyramid, a Romanesque tower that is 349 feet high. The other spire is Gothic and is 377 feet high.

Chartres Cathedral, Chartres, France

Throughout the centuries, this cathedral survived damage from fires, lightning strikes, wars, and the French Revolution. In 1939, just before the German army invaded France, all the stained glass windows were removed and placed in safe storage.

The order to destroy the cathedral was given because it was suspected that the Germans were using the twin towers as observation posts. When Colonel Griffith heard about this plan, he decided to challenge this strategy and he took it upon himself to investigate. After the staff meeting ended, Griffith told Joe and me that he was going into the city of Chartres on a personal mission without giving any details. My parting words to the Colonel were, "Good-bye, be careful, and God be with you."

The colonel and his jeep driver left our G-3 office and drove into the city of Chartres. They arrived at the cathedral without incident and entered the

Colonel Welborn B. Griffith (Photo--courtesy of Alice Griffith Irving)

160

building. During their reconnaissance of the nave and adjoining chapels and rooms, no enemy soldiers were found. Griffith decided to climb the towers and found that no German soldiers were using them as observation posts. When Griffith was satisfied that the cathedral was not occupied by enemy troops, he immediately reported this information to higher authorities and the order to shell, bomb, and destroy the Cathedral of Chartres was rescinded, and it was saved from destruction.

Griffith and his driver left the cathedral and drove to the village of Lèves, which was on the outskirts of Chartres. He met a tank brigade of the 7th Armored Division and asked a tank crew for a ride into the city in order to determine why our troops had so much difficulty in liberating it. As the G-3 Operations Officer, Griffith was impatient that this mission had bogged down. The colonel climbed into the tank and stood up in the turret to give him a better view than if he squinted through the narrow slits in the tank. They drove through neighborhoods, and as they crossed an intersection of streets, a crew of German soldiers in a hidden machine-gun nest, opened up with a sudden burst of fire. The tank was stopped in its tracks, and the Colonel's body was shattered with a stream of bullets. He died instantly.

(Note: This was the story that we heard at Corps Headquarters that day. Years later, I learned more details of the actual events surrounding the Colonel's death which are written in the Epilog.)

About three hours after the Colonel had left our G-3 tent with his jeep driver, we received a stunning telephone call that our beloved boss, Colonel Griffith, had been killed. It was a shock that was so unbelievable that our senses were numbed, and we couldn't comprehend this news. As the news of this tragedy spread through XX Corps Headquarters, a pall of deep grief covered our camp, because we were a tightly knit unit of men who worked together like a family. Joe and I were devastated. This day, August 16, was only the sixteenth day that the XX Corps had been in combat, and now we had suffered our first casualty, my own boss. This event struck me deeply, because for the first time I realized the closeness of death at any moment while in combat. This incident prompted me to pray more earnestly to God for my safety and for the safety of all our troops, for every day that we were in combat with the enemy.

Funeral services for Col. Welborn B. Griffith Jr., were held two days later, and it was conducted by the XX Corps' Chaplain and attended by several officers from Corps Headquarters. I did not attend. He was laid to rest in a temporary cemetery that had been opened in a farm field by the US Military Graves Department to hold the remains of fallen soldiers in these early days of conflict. This cemetery was located at Savigny-sur-Braye, about fifty miles southwest of Chartres.

Col. Welborn B. Griffith's funeral (Photo--courtesy of Alice Griffith Irving)

* * * * * * *

Brittany American Cemetery

St. James, France
(Twelve miles south of Mont St. Michel, near Avranches)

Fifty years after D-Day, in the Autumn of 1994, I returned to France and Germany to retrace my military steps and to visit the Command Posts of the XX Corps during World War II. My wife, Eleanore, accompanied me on this nostalgic trip. I had contacted the American Battle Monuments Commission in Washington, DC, and they gave me the name and location of the military cemetery where Colonel Griffith was buried. His grave was in The Brittany American Cemetery and Memorial, a lovely area of twenty-eight acres of rolling farm country at the edge of the village of St. James. It was twelve miles southeast of Mont St. Michel, and very near to the city of Avranches, where the XX Corps had entered combat on August 1, 1944. This cemetery contains the graves of 4,410 American soldiers, most of whom perished in the Battle of Normandy, Brittany, and northern France.

Eleanore and I drove into this beautiful cemetery and stopped at the office of the superintendent, who was an American citizen because all American military cemeteries in the world are actually American soil, owned by the US government. He looked up the name of Welborn B. Griffith in the directory of grave sites. The grave was in Section B, Row 4, and I was excited when he found it. The superintendent said he would escort us to the grave, but I protested saying that we could find the grave by ourselves. He insisted, and then picked up two small galvanized pails and a paint brush. One pail contained wet, yellow sand, and the other held water.

We slowly walked past the many white granite crosses that dazzled in the bright sun, and soon arrived at the colonel's grave. His name, home state, and date of death were incised into the horizontal bar of the cross marker. The letters were deeply notched into the granite to a depth of about a half inch, but they were difficult to read because there was no contrast between the surface and the incised letters. At the colonel's grave marker, we watched the superintendent take a handful of wet sand from the pail and spread it across the incised letters on the granite cross, thus filling up the deep cuts of the letters. He then took the paint brush and brushed off the excess sand, and instantly, all the letters stood out clearly in yellow, as though they had been painted onto the stone. This was the inscription on the cross bar of the white marker:

WELBORN B. GRIFFITH
COL HQ XX CORPS
TEXAS AUG 16, 1944

The superintendent took our photos at the grave site with a Polaroid camera he carried in his pocket, and he waited while I took several pictures on my camera. After ten minutes or so, the superintendent dipped the paint brush into the pail of water and washed the sand out of the incised letters of the granite cross. When the last grain of sand was removed, the superintendent invited us to stay as long as we wished and wander though the cemetery, but he said that we should be sure to stop at his office before we left the cemetery.

We lingered at Colonel Griffith's grave, and then suddenly, the solemnity of this moment hit me. My emotions poured out into a flood of tears, and I cried and sobbed. This was my final moment to grieve for my beloved boss, even though it was now fifty years after his death. My memory of the Colonel went back to the very beginning of my army service, when I arrived at Camp Young, California, as a raw recruit. It was barely three weeks after my induction that I first met Colonel Griffith at the IV Armored Corps Headquarters, and from that day until the day he died, I was at his side working for him. He was very kind to me and was even like a father figure. He was a tall man, and his personality exhibited a gentle manner. I thoroughly enjoyed working for him, and his Texas drawl intrigued me. He had difficulty pronouncing my name "Schulz," and the best he could do was to say "Sergeant *Schoos.*" He was a great man in my eyes and helped to shape my character, instilling in me such traits as respect, discipline, and deep human concern for my fellow buddies.

Eleanore and I walked among the many graves in this hallowed field of the dead, and we read the names on the crosses. Occasionally there was a grave containing a soldier who could not be identified, and these grave stones held this poignant inscription:

HERE RESTS IN HONORED GLORY
A COMRADE IN ARMS
KNOWN BUT TO GOD

Before leaving the Brittany Cemetery, we stopped at the superintendent's office to thank him for his help. He handed me a small folder with Colonel Griffith's name on the cover, and the number of his grave site. Inside the card was the photograph that he took of us by the Colonel's granite marker. This was a wonderful conclusion to an emotion-filled afternoon, and we drove away from the cemetery with uplifted hearts and a feeling of closure to this traumatic event in my military service.

The Author and his wife at the grave of Col. W. B. Griffith,
Brittany American Cemetery, St. James, France (1994)

* * * * * * *

After Colonel Griffith's funeral in the field near Savigny-sur-Braye, General Walker introduced our new G-3 leader, Lieutenant Colonel Melville I. Stark. He was short and of slight stature with a distinguishing bushy, black mustache. Very few officers had mustaches, so Colonel Stark was easily recognizable. He was a respected and capable strategist and also a fine boss to work for.

Chartres was liberated and cleared of all Nazi troops, and the city residents poured out into the streets to welcome our troops. The "Gateway to Paris" had been opened! Excitement grew among the personnel at XX Corps Headquarters as we realized we were on the verge of capturing the greatest prize of all, namely Paris, the great "white city" and capital of France, which was a mere fifty miles east of Chartres. We thought that the liberation of Paris would be an enormous prize for our unit and would enhance our prestige among our peers. Unfortunately, that was not to be. On August 22, Corps Headquarters moved to its eighth command post.

Command Post No. 8

Oysonville, France
(In the woods surrounding a chateau)
August 22–23, 1944

This move took us through Chartres to our next CP in the woods that surrounded a chateau near the small town of Oysonville, about twenty-five miles south of Versailles, a suburb of Paris. The next objective of XX Corps troops was to cross the Seine River, which flows through Paris. German panzer divisions and infantry had retreated from Chartres to the next natural defense barrier, the Seine River, which they prepared to defend. The eastern bank of the Seine was held by some twenty thousand German troops of the 8th Division and supporting units of anti-tank battalions and 105mm howitzer battalions. The Seine River was about 250–300 feet wide in this area, with high hills that the river twisted and turned around on its way to Paris. The Germans had a large number of artillery batteries on the hills east of the river, which gave them an advantage of firepower aimed at our infantry and tanks which were approaching the river from the west in order to establish a bridgehead.

Tragedy hit our XX Corps again when we received the news that one of our liaison officers and his driver were killed near the Seine River. Major Alfred J. Scott III left our G-3 office to deliver some orders, which I had just typed, to division commanders at the front lines. He also had planned to personally observe the battle situation to bring back the latest tactical information for General Walker. Major Scott and his driver and jeep were hit by mortar fire from the German emplacements across the river. This was devastating news, coming less than a week after the death of Colonel Griffith, as both the Colonel and the Major were members of our G-3 office. This was another reminder of the danger that surrounded us, and my prayers to God for protection became more urgent.

Major Scott was an affable officer, a college graduate who had earned his rank at a young age. When he was present, life seemed to be a happy event because he livened-up the conversations with his outgoing personality and a happy-go-lucky attitude. He was the college guy who could have been the quarterback on the football team, or maybe the prom-king—just a popular kind of guy. Now he was gone! Sadness again fell over our office staff and the entire Corps.

Command Post No. 9

Milly, France
(In the gardens of the Chateau de Courances)
August 23–25, 1944

We moved to our ninth CP on August 23 to be closer to the front, where the 5th Infantry Division and the 7th Armored Division were poised to cross the Seine river. We set up our camp in the beautiful gardens of the Chateau de Courances. We were not permitted to occupy the chateau, but we set up our office tents in these gardens in which the shrubs were manicured and the flowers were in full bloom. A moat surrounded the chateau.

When Major Scott was killed, he left behind at Corps Headquarters a small two-wheeled trailer that he hauled from CP to CP. He carried a large supply of assorted liquor and wine in the trailer, a practice that was common among the top brass of Corps Headquarters. The officers helped themselves to a bottle or two of the top-shelf brands of booze in the major's trailer, such as Jack Daniels, Beefeaters, and Jamison Irish Whiskey. After the officers had picked their choices, they told us enlisted men to help ourselves. Joe and I looked over the remaining supply, and I chose a bottle of something called Cointreau while Joe chose Cognac. Neither of us knew anything about these French spirits.

Joe and I finished our night shift at nine o'clock in the morning. Our usual routine was to have breakfast and then spend a couple of hours relaxing before going to sleep, including letter writing, reading, or maybe washing some underwear or socks. However, this morning it was different. Joe and I had set up our "duplex" tent on a grassy spot in the gardens of the chateau. Our surroundings were lovely, and the weather was warm on this beautiful summer day. So I opened up my new friend—the bottle of Cointreau—and took a sip right out of the bottle. It had a surprisingly sweet and orange-flavored taste, and the liquid slid down my throat easily. I had never tasted anything so good before. Joe opened his bottle of Cognac, and he liked the effect of the very smooth brandy too. We also tasted each other's booze as we began our new "art" of drinking.

I loved the taste of Cointreau, but I was unaware of its power and effect on my stomach. Joe and I continued to enjoy our newfound activity, and finally we fell asleep in our tent. Not long after that, we both woke up, feeling very sick, and we vomited. I realized that I was drunk for the first time in my life. Sleep finally came, and later, when I started to work on my next shift my hangover was hard to handle. I learned later that Cointreau is a liqueur, or an after-dinner drink, which is highly flavored, sweet, and strong. I have not tasted Cointreau since that notable August morning in France when I "lived high" with Joe in the gardens of a lovely chateau.

The battle to cross the Seine river was fierce as the German defenses on the east side of the river were very strong, and they put on a tremendous fight. The troops of the three Corps of General Patton's Third Army had made lightning-fast progress during the first three weeks of August, covering over 160 miles deep into France and being at the doorstep of Paris. During this period, German losses were high, with an estimated capture of twenty-five thousand men by the Americans, and another twenty-five thousand captured by the British and Canadians. About ten thousand German troops lay dead on the field.

General "Opie" Weyland, commander of the XIX Tactical Air Command, had provided some very innovative close air support to the Third Army's troops. His fighter bombers operated from captured German airfields in France, which were usually located close to the fighting zones, so these planes did not have to travel long distances. The new techniques developed by the Tactical Air Corps were battle-proven and would soon result in a new reorganization of our G-3 Section that would change my job and duties. General Weyland described the new innovative tactics of air warfare in these words:

"We were making up new rules of engagement as we went along. I had armored-column cover, for example. All during the daylight hours when ground forces were fighting or advancing, General Patton advanced in parallel columns normally, and always spearheaded by armor. I had liaison officers up in the lead tanks in everyone of these columns—an Air Force officer guiding the lead tanks with a radio, so that he could talk to the aircraft. Then I had fighter bombers, which preceded the columns, knowing where they were supposed to go. They would locate enemy opposition tanks, troops, guns, or obstacles, or tank barriers, or what have you, let them know, and in most cases knock out the opposition before the American tanks got there."

On August 23, the Corps Artillery launched a massive attack against German infantry poised along the Seine river. Our engineers built four pontoon treadway bridges which enabled tanks, tank destroyers, and artillery to pour across the river. By the next day, the XX Corps had won a broad bridgehead on the east side of the Seine, and the German Armies of the West were in retreat. With the breaching of the Seine by XX Corps troops, the great city of Paris was now flanked on the south, and this situation stirred a renewed excitement among us that our next objective would be to capture Paris. What a glorious victory it would be for us to march into this romantic city and liberate the French citizens. The possibility brought many newspaper correspondents and reporters to XX Corps Headquarters with the hope of being among the first to enter Paris.

Events now moved more rapidly than ever, but Corpsmen were dead tired, worn out, and covered with dust, and when there were pauses in fighting, it was a welcome feeling for the men to rest on the hard, bare ground, or in a foxhole. Troop movements were so rapid that field kitchens could not be set up in the time available, so the tasteless cold rations were the only food available. Truck drivers worked around the clock shuttling troops, food, and ammunition to the fast-moving troops. On night trips, the trucks drove without bright headlights because they were covered with a black shield that had a narrow slit about 1 ½ inches long and ½ inch wide which allowed a dim beam of light to show the road ahead. This light was not visible from above and could not be seen by enemy aircraft. When the German troops retreated, they left behind huge stocks of war materiel, including fleets of vehicles that included the "Volkswagens," which we called the imitation jeep, and also huge troop carriers. Corps units used some of this captured booty to speed our own troops forward in pursuit of the enemy.

General Patton made a hurried visit to our Headquarters to personally congratulate General Walker and present the XX Corps with a commendation for the Seine river crossings, which stated: "For the aggressive and efficient manner in which this mission was carried out, you and the personnel of your command are hereby highly commended for your splendid accomplishment of this mission." Then Patton informed us that we would not get the mission to liberate Paris. This came as a major disappointment to all of us, but it also was a blow to Patton when Eisenhower and Bradley told him that the capture of Paris had evolved into a "politically correct" situation. The Third Army and its XX Corps units would be denied the honor and glory of entering Paris because of politics. Now the mission was given to the French Army to liberate their capital city, and since the French 2nd Armored Division was attached to the US Twelfth Army Group, they were given the job. General Jacques-Philippe LeClerc led his 2nd Army troops into the city and liberated it on August 25. It was a joyous and jubilant day and a great relief from the tyranny of the Nazi occupiers of Paris for the many years since the German Wehrmacht had captured it in 1940.

After General Patton gave us the disappointing news that Paris was not in our future, he presented the XX Corps with a new mission. We were ordered to continue the pursuit of the German Army eastward from the Seine river in the direction of Reims, so Corps Headquarters immediately moved to its next command post.

Command Post No. 10

Fontainebleau Forest, France
(In the Forest of Fontainebleau)
August 25–27, 1944

The convoy of vehicles carrying our headquarters personnel and equipment crossed the Seine river on several Bailey and pontoon bridges built by Corps engineers. We entered into a beautiful forest and set up our 10th Command Post at a place which was three miles west of the city of Fontainebleau. This large Foret de Fontainebleau covered an area of sixty-six square miles, or 42,500 acres, and it was the famous location used by French kings and their royal courts as their summer home to escape the heat in Paris. The royal palace itself was in the City of Fontainebleau which was about thirty-four miles south of the center of Paris. The Palace of Fontainebleau was first built as a chateau in the twelfth century and was occupied by all the French kings through the centuries. However, it was Emperor Napoleon Bonaparte who transformed this palace into its grandeur as an alternative to the Palace of Versailles. In 1814, Napoleon bade farewell to his Old Guard at Fontainebleau before he went into exile to the Island of Elba.

Within the vast area of Fontainebleau Forest were the royal hunting grounds that contained many species of animals and game birds. The forest itself consisted of many varieties of trees, including stately pines and elms and other deciduous trees. We set up our tents under these trees near the narrow roads that traversed the park, and we enjoyed this lovely setting, which was more enjoyable than some of the camping areas we had stayed in previously.

It was at midday on the second day at this campsite when we suddenly heard a lone fighter plane flying above the trees. I heard many voices throughout our CP yelling loudly, "Take cover now!" I was standing next to our G-3 tent, and I immediately dived under the G-3 half-track that was parked there. The German fighter plane made a pass over our CP and strafed the area with machine gun bullets. The plane returned again with another pass and strafing, and then there was silence. The enemy fighter pilot evidently had some knowledge that our Corps Headquarters was located in this forest, and he had somehow slipped past our anti-aircraft artillery defenses to attack us. We all escaped this attack without any injuries and none of our tents and vehicles were hit, but this event was very scary, and the alert status stayed in place the rest of the day. We never heard what happened to this lone enemy fighter plane, but it probably took off from a German air field which was very close to our CP, and we frequently camped very close to the front lines.

Command Post No. 11

Donnemarie-en-Montoise, France
(On the estate of the Chateau de Sigy)
August 27–28, 1944

New orders were received from Third Army Headquarters to swing to the north and head for Reims. General Walker decided that it was time to resort to more daring and aggressive tactics, so XX Corps Headquarters moved again, this time to the grounds of the Chateau de Sigy, one mile east of the village of Donnemarie-en-Montoise. The move from Fontainebleau Forest covered a distance of about fifteen miles. The divisions under the command of XX Corps continued to pursue the German army, and on August 27, the city of Chateau-Thierry fell to the XX Corps troops. This city was a historic battleground in World War I, and a huge granite Memorial to the American Dead was built in the center of this city.

On August 28, the Americans captured the city of Epernay, and the decimated and demoralized remnants of the German 49th SS Panzer Grenadier Brigade, the 48th Infantry Division, the 9th Panzer Division, and the 26th SS Brigade quickly fled north and east. The enemy's retreat was so swift that it compelled the XX Corps Headquarters to move again.

Command Post No. 12

Montmirail, France
(In the garden of the Chateau of Vicounte de la Rochefoucauld)
August 28–29, 1944

The countryside of France changed into a beautiful rolling landscape as we entered the famous French vineyards that covered thousands of acres. This was champagne country with Epernay as its capital. The city lay in a valley surrounded by hills which were covered with grapevines that stretched far to the horizon. It was an awesome sight.

On our trip to this CP, we traveled through the city of Epernay, and I rode in the open-roofed G-3 half-track which carried our big war tent and our personal equipment and a few of our crew. The city streets were crowded with thousands of French men, women, and children who had just been liberated hours before our arrival. The people ran into the streets and stopped our convoy of vehicles, and they cheered and cried while reaching out their hands to shake ours. Women hugged us and waved their French flags because they now were free again, and the people showered us with bottles of champagne. This demonstration of thanks from these liberated people warmed our hearts as they welcomed us as heroes. They were free again after living under the iron hand of Nazi tyranny for many years. It was on this day that I tasted champagne for the first time in my life, and to do this in the very heart of the French champagne capital of Epernay was a thrill.

Our stay at CP No. 12 lasted only a day and a half because all XX Corps units moved swiftly eastward toward Reims and Verdun, as the Germans continued their retreat.

Command Post No. 13

Louvois, France
(On the grounds of a chateau)
August 29–September 1, 1944

Our new CP was in a woods surrounding a chateau near the city of Louvois, only twelve miles southwest of the large cathedral city of Reims. On August 29th, the 5th Infantry Division swept into Reims and liberated it. The capture of the city was a special prize because it contained an airplane factory, an ordnance depot, and huge German supply dumps. Two excellent Luftwaffe airfields were captured intact and were immediately used by General Weyland's fighter bombers, which destroyed 833 enemy vehicles in one day. Also, 1,847 prisoners were taken and 446 enemy troops were killed in the battle. The American 5th Division suffered only thirteen killed and eighty-six wounded. The German forces were stunned and bewildered by the tactics of the XX Corps (a.k.a. the "Ghost Corps," by which we were now known), because our troops bypassed towns and strong points and then turned around abruptly to attack the town from the east, the opposite direction.

In Reims, in a display of justice, French gendarmes brought to our forces a young woman who had collaborated with the enemy. Her head had been shaved to mark her as a traitor, and thus she was put to shame by her countrymen. Crowds of Reims citizens swarmed into the streets to greet their liberators. The mayor and the city fathers held an impromptu "liberation day" ceremony in front of the Hotel de Ville. There were speeches while 5th Division troops stood at parade rest as the hundreds of city residents surrounding them cheered and cried for joy. The elegant Reims Cathedral, a twin-towered gothic building, stood silently at one side of the Centrum. It fortunately escaped the bombing and shelling without serious damage, and on this day the townspeople were inside the church attending masses and sending their prayers of thanks to God for their safety and liberation.

Command Post No. 14

St. Menehould, France
(On the grounds of a chateau)
September 1–2, 1944

After the capture of Reims, we moved our CP again, this time to the town of St. Menehould, about twenty-five miles west of the city of Verdun. The advance party found this chateau, and we set up our camp in the gardens surrounding the old mansion, which itself was off limits. The large Argonne Forest lay between our camp and Verdun, and the Corps' 7th Armored Division swept through the forest where they cleared out German installations. They seized the main bridge across the Meuse river and captured the city on August 31. This steel and concrete bridge had been mined by the Germans, but they kept it intact for the retreat of their rear guard, because all the other bridges in town had been blown up. Several combat troops of the FFI were able to sneak under the bridge where they found and cut the wires that were connected to the demotion charges. The 5th Infantry Division followed our tanks across the saved bridge into the city of Verdun and liberated it. In World War I, this city had been the site of one of the bloodiest battles of that war, and the French people had erected a large memorial monument in the city square. On the day of liberation in this war, the city leaders honored our Corps officers at a ceremony at the Hotel de Ville. Verdun city officials awarded the XX Corps the Medal of Verdun along with a certificate of commendation. Each of us at corps headquarters received this badge, which was attached to a ribbon, and the certificate was written in French and signed by the mayor of Verdun.

The capture of Verdun marked the end of the first major operation of the XX Corps and its supporting troops. During this first phase, the XX Corps had driven almost completely across France, had crossed six major rivers, and by the speed and aggressiveness of its attacks, had prevented the enemy from recovering sufficiently to form a cohesive line of defense. The route of the XX Corps in the campaigns of Normandy and northern France passed through some famous historical shrines: Angers and Nantes on the beautiful Loire River, Chartres, the cathedral city, Fontainebleau, the imperial city, Reims the crown of kings, and Verdun, the bloody battlefield of the First World War. There was plenty of fighting, and heavy losses too, that were strewn across the Corps' path to military glory. Because of the fluid nature of the campaigns on many fronts of the Third Army and the Twelfth Army Group, many divisions and units came and went through the command of the XX Corps.

The most spectacular achievements of the campaign of Northern France occurred during the last week in August. In only a few days, the XX Corps had driven through the fortified, historic places of World War I: namely, the Marne, the Meuse, Argonne Forest, Chateau-Thierry, and Verdun. Our fighting groups included combat teams and commands, task forces, artillery groups, signal and engineer battalions, quartermaster, and medical corps units. The 19th Tactical Air Command provided significant close air support to the advancing ground troops at the front. The success of the XX Corps was noticed in America and in the UK, as shown by the following paragraph written by a reporter named Joseph Driscoll and published in the *New York Herald Tribune*. It was dated September 30, 1944.

"The secrecy which for weeks has surrounded the mysterious 'Ghost Corps' was lifted today, revealing Major General Walton H. Walker's XX Corps as the spearhead of Lt. General George S. Patton's Third Army's great eastward drive across France, distinguished by bold tactics of encirclement which won Prime Minister Churchill's praise in Parliament the other day."

History was made as the XX Corps, the spearhead of the Third Army, had covered six hundred miles across France in thirty days, from August 3rd to

September 3rd. Our new nickname of the "Ghost Corps" became a footnote to World War II history!

Command Post No. 15

Brule Mill, France
(In a woods at the juncture of Route 3 and Voie Sacree)
September 2–8, 1944

On September 2nd, the Corps CP moved to a woods two miles west of Verdun, where we stayed for a week because the machines of war had abruptly ground to a halt. The supplies needed to keep our army moving became acutely scarce. The long, rapid drive across northern France brought the Corps and its supporting divisions too far from the original supply depots that were still back at the beaches of Normandy and the port of Cherbourg. Supplies were difficult to transport because the roads were torn up by battles, and many bridges were destroyed, so that the temporary Bailey steel bridges as well as pontoon bridges were the only way to cross the many rivers along the way.

The most serious problem, however, was the sudden shortage of gasoline. Combat vehicles were immobilized, and the infantry divisions at the front had barely enough gas for their cooking needs. At Corps Headquarters, we also felt the shortage, and General Patton sent out orders to use our vehicles as little as possible to conserve gas. Patton was extremely upset that his tanks were sitting idle in motor pools, and he desperately looked for gasoline supplies. The Third Army vehicles consumed an enormous quantity of 400,000 gallons of gas per day. Some of the gas was received by airlift, but it was minimal. By mid-August a cross-Channel gasoline pipeline became operational, and the much-needed supply began to flow. The next challenge was to move this gasoline completely across northern France to the front lines.

The challenge was met when the US Army Transportation Corps established a new service called the "Red Ball Express," a trucking system created to haul gasoline and petroleum products to combat units at the front. Back on August 1, when the Third Army entered combat, gasoline was moved in tens of thousands of five-gallon cans on trucks that hauled them from Omaha and Utah beaches to the fighting units. As the distances to the front got longer, the Motor Transport Brigade, the tactical organization of the Transportation Corps, shifted to using tanker trucks. There were seven hundred trucks belonging to fourteen companies that carried the POL (petrol, oil, and lubricants) to the combat zones.

As the distances to the front increased, the daily commitment for hauling POL was raised from 300,000 gallons to a million gallons, and the trucks that hauled this petrol consumed an astonishing 450,000 gallons themselves. An interesting fact is that on August 10, fifteen days before Paris' liberation, an emergency haul of 100,000 gallons of diesel fuel was delivered to the French 2nd Armored Division, because they were making preparations to move into the city.

The long-haul tanker trucks carried bulk gas rather than cans of gas. The trucks carried two drivers who alternated the time behind the wheel, as they often drove up to twenty-two hours per day. There were bivouac and rest areas placed at intervals between the fuel docks and the storage depots where the drivers could eat, rest, and sleep. The Red Ball Express trucks had a large, round, red ball painted on the doors, and as they traveled along the roads, some in bad shape with pot holes from mines and bombs, they often were the only traffic permitted on the roads, which sometimes were only one-way. The tanker trucks were also subjected to enemy fire or strafing from the air by the Luftwaffe. The Red Ball Express was a successful venture, and the severe gas shortage was alleviated by the time Patton's Third Army arrived near the great bastion of Metz. But soon rain and floods emerged, which caused a new disaster to our troops and the plans of operations.

During the week that XX Corps Headquarters camped in the woods at Brule Mill, several visitors arrived. His Royal Highness, Prince Felix of Luxembourg, joined Corps Headquarters. He was attached to our unit for a brief stint in order to observe our operations. The Prince's son, Prince John, came along with his father, and both were officers in the British Army. Our CP at Brule Mill was about sixty miles from Luxembourg City.

A famous Hollywood entertainer, Dinah Shore, was welcomed to Corps Headquarters for a USO show. She was perhaps the most popular pop singer during the war years, and she was one of my favorite vocalists. Dinah was a vivacious entertainer who was widely loved for her homey, heartfelt singing and her breezy Southern charm. Her voice was very sweet and mellow, and her beauty and easy-going personality made her a very popular entertainer. She spent a great deal of time in France and appeared at our CP on September 6, where she presented a two-hour show with her small ensemble of musicians. It was a mesmerizing evening for me, and I even got her autograph on a French franc, which we called "invasion currency."

Command Post No. 16

Mars-La-Tour, France
(In a woods two miles east of town)
September 8–24, 1944

XX Corps Headquarters moved again, this time to a woods about fifteen miles farther east, which brought us to within fifteen miles of Metz, the impenetrable fortress that the German Army had decided to defend at all costs. We set up our bivouac near a large chemical plant loaded with dangerous materials that the Germans had surrounded with explosives with a plan to blow it up, but they didn't get the chance to destroy it. These were nervous days for Corps troops because we realized the danger of living so close to such a hazard, but fortunately, nothing bad happened.

The fighting in the war zone shut down because of the severe gas shortage, and the German infantry and armored troops had retreated to the line of the Moselle River, the major line of defense along with the fortress of Metz. The Moselle started its northern route through a region of France called Alsace-Lorraine, flowing through the major cities of Nancy, Metz, and Thionville; then crossing the German border to join the Saar River at Trier and continuing northeast to enter the Rhine River at Koblenz.

During these days, the weather turned bad as big rains came, and the ground turned into mud. Tanks got stuck, and vehicles slid off the roads. The small streams and rivers rose and the Moselle became swollen. Fighting was limited to reconnaissance patrols and light exchanges of gunfire. An unexpected supply of 110,000 gallons of gasoline was flown into the Reims airport in C-47 aircraft, and this enabled the 7th Armored Division and the 5th and 90th Infantry Divisions to build a bridgehead across the raging Moselle in preparation for an assault on the outer defenses of Metz. Various task forces probed the enemy defenses at locations along the river.

At Mars-La-Tour, the Corps Command Post received a distinguished visitor: Cardinal Francis J. Spellman from New York, who was named the Military Vicar to the Armed Forces. Our own Corps Chaplain, Colonel Thomas L. Wolfe, assisted the Cardinal during a large Mass held in the woods of our CP camp. The Mass was held despite the heavy rain and mud, and my Catholic buddies were thrilled to be a part of it, especially since it was celebrated by this well-known cleric, who wore his elegant robe during the service, even in the mud.

The awful weather conditions and nearly continuous rain, along with low visibility and mud, made the fighting very difficult. The main objective during these early days of September was to cross the Moselle at several towns north of Metz and attempt to establish a bridgehead east of the river in order to attack the fortifications of Metz from the east. While XX Corps Artillery pounded the German fortified positions east of the river, infantry engineer units built a couple of pontoon bridges for vehicles, while infantry doughboys rowed across the river in assault boats that carried a company of a dozen riflemen. A pontoon bridge consisted of a row of rubber pontoon boats that were lashed together in a parallel row that stretched across the river. Two steel treadways were then fastened across the tops of the pontoons to form a roadway which was the width of the wheels of all vehicles and tanks. This was the most common and efficient way for our troops to cross rivers where no intact bridges existed. The XX Corps Signal Battalion was responsible for laying wires while following the infantry units as they moved forward. At the Moselle, the telephone personnel had to swim across the river near the pontoon bridge while carrying the wires across. They had to do this three times because the wires were cut by shelling from enemy defenders.

On the night of September 9, one infantry battalion was attempting to cross the Moselle in the town of Arnaville. One of our G-3 Liaison Officers, Major Terry Overton, left our office tent to go on a mission to check on the difficult attempt to cross the river at Arnaville. While he was with the infantry troops, the German artillery across the river laid down a barrage of heavy shelling, and a 120mm mortar shell landed close by, killing Major Overton. Tragedy had again struck our G-3 Section, and Overton became the third officer from our section that we lost during the first five weeks of combat. Sadness and grief again gripped our close-knit unit.

On September 23, Corps Headquarters personnel welcomed one of Hollywood's great entertainers and my favorite male singer during the war years. This USO show featured Bing Crosby, a lovable guy and the best crooner of popular songs in show business. He was even known to the Germans as "Der Bingle." He raised the morale of all GIs with his songs and lighthearted patter. Crosby, who was forty-one years old, arrived at XX Corps Headquarters with his troupe of two women and a small band. His improvised stage was a platform built on the back of a 6x6 truck, and the hundreds of troops sat on their helmets on the muddy ground. It was a great show, and I enjoyed listening to all the popular songs of the war years as well as hearing Bing's humorous quips. Bing left the stage at one point to walk among the troops, and in doing so he tripped on a small stone and fell flat on his face in the mud. This was very funny, and in spite of all the laughter, Bing took it in good stride and passed it off like a good trooper.

Bing Crosby spent a great deal of time entertaining troops wherever they were stationed in France. When he visited Third Army Headquarters, he was on stage wearing a soft cap. This infuriated General Patton, and he almost court marshaled Bing for not wearing a helmet in a war zone. Patton expected his troops and visitors to be properly dressed.

CHAPTER 16

The Conquest of Fortress Metz

Command Post No. 17

Jarny, France
(In a school L'Ecole Elementaire)
September 24–November 21, 1944

BY EARLY SEPTEMBER, THE HIGH-SPEED Allied advance had liberated most of northern France. The XX Corps was the spearhead of General Patton's Third Army, and the Corps made a remarkable story with its 600-mile dash across France in thirty days. This sensational military campaign earned the XX Corps its new nickname of "The Ghost Corps," and we became known as the "Ghost" in General Patton's Third Army. However, the speed of this drive had outdistanced army supply dumps, and the acute shortage of gasoline, oil, and ammunition had immobilized the infantry and armored divisions. Thus, any further advance into enemy territory became logistically impossible for the time being.

At the end of September, the three corps under the command of the Third Army were poised along a forty-mile front at the Moselle River, from Thionville in the north to Nancy in the South, with Metz between them. The German Army had retreated to the east side of the Moselle where they dug in for a planned fanatical defense, with Fortress Metz as their principal fortification. The enemy had a second defense line a few miles east of Metz, known as the formidable French Maginot Line. General Patton gave our XX

Corps the difficult mission to capture Metz! This task verged on the impossible, but our Corps Commander, General Walker, was up to it, and he had already earned the nickname of "Bulldog Walker" among his peers.

General Walker's new assignment prompted him to move our Corps Headquarters closer to the Moselle River to insure tighter control of the bridgehead battles that were currently carried out across the river and also to shorten the lines of communication to the Corps units involved in the fighting. So on September 24, we moved from Mars-La-Tour to Jarny, a city with about six thousand inhabitants, where we set up our offices in an elementary school and slept on cots in classrooms. We really appreciated working and sleeping indoors, because autumn had arrived and the weather was getting cooler. Until this date we had camped outdoors in sixteen CP's in fields and woods, from the apple orchard in Normandy in July to the woods at Mars-La-Tour in late September. The L'Ecole Elementaire enjoyed a prime location in Jarny because it was built on one side of the centrum, a large downtown central square where all the town's civic activities occurred. We held our assemblies in the square and mingled with the townspeople. Our Corps personnel enjoyed the wonderful feeling of living and working indoors in an urban setting, rather than the disagreeable field conditions of rain, mud, and yellow jackets trying to eat our orange marmalade sandwiches.

Ancient History and Development of Fortress Metz

In order to understand the impending Battle of Metz, it is necessary to look back at the ancient history of this city and the construction of its great rings of fortifications. The topography and terrain of this area was an important reason why a fortified city was built at this site. The Moselle River forms one of the greatest natural barriers anywhere, and the swift current of the river had cut the Lorraine Plateau to create a natural breastwork on the abrupt slopes of its western banks. (A breastwork is a temporary, quickly constructed fortification, usually breast high.) To the east of the Moselle, tributary streams, chiefly the Seille and the Nied Rivers, had cut hills and ridges that were steep and heavily wooded.

The city of Metz was first heard of around the years of 1,200 BC. It was then known as Divodurum, meaning "the town at the holy mountain," when it was the capital of a Celtic tribe known as the Mediomatrici, who controlled the region between the Meuse, the Moselle, and the Saar rivers. The abbreviated name of this tribe was Mettis, which eventually became Metz. Metz became the major city of Roman Gaul which is now known as France. The city also became a well-fortified town at the junction of several military roads, and it became rich from its exports of Moselle wine to Rome. The Romans also built a large amphitheater there.

In the fifth century, Germanic tribes arrived in Gaul, and in 451 AD, Attila the Hun captured and plundered this Roman stronghold. Christianity arrived in Metz at the end of this century when it became part of the Holy Roman Empire. From AD 742–814, Metz was part of the Empire of Charlemagne. In the twelfth century, the defenses of Metz were extended along the Moselle with the building of high ramparts that were protected by sixty-eight towers. In 1552, Emperor Charles V of Germany tried to capture Metz, but he failed after bombarding it for two and a half months. More defenses were added and by the early 1800s a complete circle of fifteen forts and eleven bastions were built for the outer defenses of Metz. (A bastion is the projecting part of a rampart.) In 1870, Prussian armies occupied Metz, added nineteen more bastions and eleven new forts, and dug moats around the fortifications, which extended the fortified zone to twenty-one miles around the city.

During World War I, the Germans occupied it, but they lost the war and also Metz. The city returned to France under the Treaty of Versailles in 1919. The French added still more defensive fortifications until the beginning of World War II when German armies captured it on June 17, 1940. With the new occupation by the Nazis, another round of construction of defenses was begun around the city. The new sites took advantage of the terrain when they added forty-three new forts in an inner ring and an outer ring. There were 128 artillery pieces of large caliber surrounding the city. The forts on various hills were linked by a huge series of underground tunnels and protected by pillboxes, armored outposts, heavily reinforced casemates, and mine fields. The Metz forts had large 210mm guns that fired from revolving steel turrets that protruded slightly above ground, and there were self-propelled 105mm guns placed in concrete reinforced caves as well.

Each fort in the outer ring was composed of a main or center fort with two or three smaller forts, batteries, or casemates. Each fort accommodated two thousand to three thousand men, and each battery required a crew of 150 to 200 men. There was communication with each fort, either directly or through a central exchange in Metz. The outer ring contained a string of seven minor forts, which the XX Corps assault units dubbed "The Seven Dwarfs," a reference to the Disney movie "Snow White and the Seven Dwarfs." In these minor forts, the Germans had placed the smaller 105mm howitzers and the 88mm anti-tank batteries.

Our new CP in Jarny was only seven miles from the outer ring of the Metz fortifications, and we were within easy striking range of the Nazis' huge

280mm guns across the Moselle. These guns shelled us repeatedly, and the Germans sent spies in civilian clothes to check American positions. In the areas where our troops had won some bridgeheads, the enemy had placed tightly strung steel wires across roads and lanes which were difficult to see, and thus riders in open jeeps were sometimes decapitated. They planted many booby traps, even on their own dead soldiers, preventing their removal for long periods of time because it was too dangerous to touch the corpses. Our G-2 Section gathered information that the enemy fully intended to hold Metz and its line of fortifications along the Moselle River at all costs.

In this part of Europe, Metz was at the crossroads of three classic invasion routes into Germany: (1) The valley of the Moselle River leading northeast through Trier; (2) The Kaiserslautern Pass, leading east into Mainz through Saarbrucken; and (3) The Savern Gap, pointing east to Strasbourg and the Rhine River.

The alternatives looming for the XX Corps if they were to bypass Metz and its vast areas of fortifications were *unthinkable*. To bypass the ring of forts would lengthen its supply lines by a hundred miles. It would leave a grave threat to rear installations and supply lines. To lay siege and contain the ring of forts with their strong garrisons would require several Third Army divisions, and thus prevent them from taking part in an all-out drive into the heartland of Germany. The Citadel of Metz and its surrounding ring of steel was a very formidable obstacle, and the mission to conquer it was assigned to the XX Corps by General Patton.

The enormous battle to conquer Fortress Metz was ready to begin!

Attack on Fort Driant

The most important and strongest fort defending Metz was named Fort Driant by the French, but its original name was Fort Kronprinz when the Germans held it. It was located five miles southwest of Metz on the western bank of the Moselle, which gave it a commanding position to cover the Moselle valley. The casemates on the ramparts had walls seven feet thick and contained huge batteries of guns with enormous firepower.

On September 27, the 5th Infantry Division of the XX Corps sent several assault battalions to Fort Driant to probe the defenses, but they were forced to retreat because of heavy artillery and mortar fire. Unfavorable weather postponed the next attack until October 3 when the fort was bombed with napalm bombs. These bombs were filled with jellied gasoline which ignited upon impact and generated tremendous heat. The bombing was followed by a combined force of tanks, infantry, and engineers that attacked the fort from north and south; however, the German firepower was too intense, and the attack forces were stopped.

During the attack, 5th Division troops discovered a few air ventilators on top of some barracks in the fort, so they dropped explosive charges into them, which eventually forced the German defenders out of the fort. A strange, confusing fight occurred in the eerie subterranean tunnels, like those found in old medieval castles. Deep in the fort, our troops saw the control centers of the garrison as they threw hand grenades at the steel doors and concrete walls. These tactics failed, and the fumes from the explosives made our guys sick. Walker conferred with Patton about the problems encountered here, and the decision was made to withdraw all our troops from Fort Driant on October 14.

The Town of Maizières-lès-Metz

The town of Maizières-lès-Metz was located on the west bank of the Moselle, six miles northwest of Metz. It was a steel mining town with three thousand inhabitants, and it was imperative to capture this town before launching the main thrust against the fortifications of Metz. On October 3, the 83rd Infantry Division was added to the XX Corps to help the 90th Division whose lines were spread quite thin. A squadron of P-47 fighter planes from the XIX Tactical Air Command bombed the town. Some progress was made at first, but the stubborn German troops fought back, and eventually the battle resulted in bitter house-to-house fighting.

Our troops were experiencing a dwindling supply of ammunition, but by October 24, the Third Army received a new supply of heavy-caliber ammunition which was sent to the XX Corps infantry engaged in the battle for this town. With renewed vigor, our troops shelled the City Hall in the town's centrum with heavy artillery, which disorganized the German defenders and caused them to surrender in small groups. Our task forces closed enemy escape routes south and east of the town. On October 30, remaining German positions were mopped up and the capture of Maizières-lès-Metz was complete. The XX Corps ruled the town!

A Lull in the Fighting

At the end of October, all the troops and officers welcomed a quiet interlude in the fighting, so many of the guys went through rotation or enjoyed time off in rest areas. It was also during this time that the generals and top officers urgently made plans for the upcoming final effort for the capture of Fortress Metz. Two new divisions were attached to the XX Corps: the 95th Infantry Division commanded by Maj. Gen. Harry L. Twaddle, and the 10th Armored Division commanded by Maj. Gen. William H. Morris.

Destroyed German fighter planes at a French airfield (1944)

Author by a destroyed German fighter plane (1944)

Meanwhile, back in the States, the national presidential election and Wisconsin's gubernatorial election was coming up on November 7, 1944. Corps Headquarters officers set up a "real election booth" by hanging a large canvas tarpaulin around a table to create a "secret" voting booth. The sign that hung on the tarp had the words "VOTE TODAY." Since I had turned twenty-one three months earlier, I was now eligible to cast my very first vote in an election. On October 6, I stood in line waiting to vote, along with my buddies. The OD (Officer of the Day) handed me an absentee ballot, and after I voted secretly behind the tarp, I put my ballot into a cardboard box nearby. This was a big thrill for me.

The candidates for the Democratic Party in the 1944 presidential election consisted of Franklin D. Roosevelt (who was running for an unprecedented fourth term), with Senator Harry S. Truman as his running mate. The Republican candidates were Thomas E. Dewey, Governor of New York, and his running mate, John W. Bricker, the Governor of Ohio. I voted for the Republican slate, and I knew that my family back home would also vote Republican. The final election result was the re-election of Roosevelt and Truman, who defeated the Republican team by a percentage of 53–46%. The gubernatorial campaign in Wisconsin resulted in the election of Walter S. Goodland as the new governor.

Many things were happening during our stay in Jarny. The reputation of the XX Corps brought about by its exploits and victories since the first day of combat on August 1 was noticed by the top brass at Eisenhower's SHAEF Headquarters. General George C. Marshall, US Army Chief of Staff from Washington, DC, visited us and conferred with General Walker and his staff. General Patton also showed up frequently. On one occasion our entire headquarters company assembled in the Jarny school auditorium, where we stood as a group wearing our steel helmets which was an order from Patton. The general stood on a platform with General Walker by his side. This was a really cool event for me to be in the presence of General Patton, listening to his "pep talk" about the impending assault on Metz. I felt like I was part of a big family listening to my father figure giving me encouragement, motivation, and inspiration, all laced with a colorful vocabulary that only George Patton could deliver.

One day some of our troops were snooping around in a warehouse that the German Wehrmacht used for storage of war materiels. Here they discovered a huge stock of top-shelf cognac and brandy still in their cases. The supply was so large that each of us at Corps Headquarters received a couple of bottles of these fine spirits, and there was enough remaining to supply all of the units attached to the XX Corps. Joe and I enjoyed sipping from a bottle of cognac when we were off duty and reading a book or writing a letter.

The American Red Cross Clubmobile visited our CP from time to time. The American girls who operated the canteen were a real joy and morale booster, and the coffee and doughnuts served by them were wonderful. The coffee vehicle was a trailer whose side panels opened up into a counter like in a restaurant. We drank the coffee from our own canteens. It was a highlight of our day to exchange small talk with these real American girls whose visit brightened the dismal days in Jarny.

Author (right) enjoying coffee and donuts at an American
Red Cross clubmobile, Jarny, France (1944)

Author with French family delivering milk to a creamery (1944)

A famous Hollywood singer and actress arrived in France to perform for the troops throughout the Third Army zone. Her name was Marlene Dietrich, actually a German woman who was born in Berlin in 1901. She began working on stage and in film in Berlin and Vienna, but in the 1930s, she moved to Hollywood where she starred in many movies in which her German accent became a classic. The German Nazi Party urged Dietrich to return to Germany, but she refused, and instead became an American citizen in 1939. Like many Weimar-era German entertainers, she was very anti-Nazi. Dietrich also recorded a number of anti-Nazi records in German for the OSS, and during the fall of 1944, she came to France to entertain troops, and we heard the exiting news that she would be in Jarny for one of her shows. Dietrich was a popular pin-up girl whose pictures were found in all the barracks where soldiers lived. We often listened to her songs on records which were played in every jukebox.

I was elated when I heard that Marlene Dietrich was to perform at the Olympia Theater on Friday night, November 10. Three of my buddies, Messner, Jacola, and Mengel, walked with me to the theater, and we carried our carbines on our shoulders into the theater, because in the war zone it was mandatory to carry our weapon everywhere. It was a thrill to see Marlene Dietrich and her supporting ensemble of musicians, and her songs were electrifying because she had a low, sultry and sexy voice with a lovely German accent. Of course, her concert included her signature song, which was anti-Nazi, called "Lili Marleen," and this song went to the top of the music charts during the war years. After the show when I was back at my quarters

Author at Olympia Theater, Jarny, France (1944)

and lying in my bed, the lyrics and haunting melody of "Lili Marleen" raced through my mind for a long time before I fell asleep.

The German Army was well aware of the presence of the XX Corps in Jarny. We were not far from the big guns in the outer ring of Metz fortresses, and their huge 280mm canons across the Moselle inflicted some heavy shelling on our location in the center of town. There were several casualties, including a Corps MP who stood guard outside our school building, who was killed by shrapnel. It was a sad morning for all of us. Hot fragments of steel ripped through several billets and installations. A huge piece of shrapnel from one of the shells cut completely through General Walker's car while it was parked outside our building. Fortunately, the General was safely inside the school.

During our stay in Jarny, approximately sixty shells hit our area which kept us on constant alert. One 660 pound shell, which fortunately was a dud, penetrated the ground close to our school building to a depth of twenty-seven feet. It was quickly removed by XX Corps Ordnance. It was an awesome sight when I looked into this deep hole at that huge inactive explosive, and I thanked God that we were spared from the danger that could have destroyed us.

The Battle of Metz

The new comprehensive plan that General Walker and his staff had developed consisted of two distinct operations to be performed concurrently: first, an attack to encircle and destroy the fortress of Metz and second, the seizure of a bridgehead over the Saar river near Saarburg, as a base to resume the attack northeast into Germany itself. The Corps Commander's reasoning was that during the assault against Metz, the enemy's troops would be siphoned into the Metz area, which would allow an infantry division to cross the Moselle north of Thionville and proceed into the Saar-Moselle Triangle. Interrogation of German prisoners indicated that Saarburg was the weakest part of the Siegfried Line, so the execution of this second operation was timed to coincide with the encirclement of Metz.

The plan for the attack on Metz was for the 5th Infantry Division to attack from the south in order to meet the 90th Infantry Division, which was designated to cross the Moselle River on the north, thus making a flanking attack along the ridges of the Maginot Line to link up with the 5th Division behind Metz on the east. The 10th Armored Division's plan was to move on the outside of the 90th Division and eventually meet up with the 5th Division to complete the encirclement of Metz. Finally, the 95th Infantry Division would get the order to capture the city of Metz.

The assault was set for the first week in November. During the preceding two-week period of relative quiet, Third Army forces regrouped and held training exercises. Meanwhile, the German commanders activated their forces for the anticipated attack as they had four divisions totaling thirty thousand troops holding Metz and the Moselle River line. They consisted of two infantry divisions: the 17th SS Panzer Grenadier Division, and the fanatical group of personnel from the VI Officer Candidate School Regiment.

Brigadier General Julius A. Slack, the commander of XX Corps Artillery, brought an additional eighteen field artillery battalions to supplement his normal artillery, which even included some large captured German guns. The Corps Artillery directed a tremendous volume of large shells at the casemates on the ridges where the 90th Division was headed. The artillery was located behind our Headquarters, and the shells made a screaming noise as they flew over the top of the school building where we lived to hit their targets. This was awesome, and the high volume of shelling went on for several hours. On November 3, the 5th Infantry Division began its mission to cross the Seille River south of Metz. These troops also received some support from the XIX Tactical Air Command which laid down a continuous bombardment on the strong points in this bridgehead.

On November 8, a new enemy appeared—floods! After three days of heavy rainfall, the Seille River, a tributary of the Moselle, rose rapidly and overflowed its banks to a width of three hundred to six hundred feet at the proposed crossing site. Because of this, the assault groups had to use boats instead of foot bridges, and they slowly crossed the river under heavy fire and through heavy fog and a smoke screen. Eventually, they captured a wooded hill at Fort L'Aisne. The next day, troops were slogging through mud, and because of low-hanging clouds and mist, the soldiers had no air support from the fighter-bombers of the XIX Air Command. However, the combat engineers were successful in constructing two treadway bridges across the swollen Seille River.

The German Army's elite defender of the Metz fortifications was the 17th SS Panzer Division. Their commander sent out a special patrol to penetrate behind XX Corps lines to determine the strength and composition of our troops facing Metz. This patrol had penetrated nine miles of Corps territory when they were captured and interrogated for two days in our prisoner of war enclosure. Eventually, they gave vital information about the location of their headquarters in the village of Peltre, as well as the strength and location of German troops in the area. Three days later, while the Germans were holding their morning staff briefing, our Corps Artillery made five direct hits on their G-2 and G-3 buildings, thereby killing sixty-seven high-ranking German officers and enlisted men.

Meanwhile, the XX Corps engineers were badly hampered in their work along the banks of the Moselle due to its swelling and the continuous artillery barrage from the German forts. The river grew wider and wider as the rains continued to fall. The engineers tried to lay pontoons while standing chest-deep in the icy, racing waters, but the angry river tore them loose. Finally, a treadway bridge was put across the river which could only tolerate dismounted troops and light vehicles. The engineers worked tirelessly on the construction of a 160 foot Bailey bridge under extremely grave conditions, and they completed the job in the early afternoon on November 10. Within a few hours, our tanks and tank destroyers moved across the raging Moselle River to support the infantry in its attack to the east.

American armor and infantry engaged the enemy in heavily defended towns as they continued to capture them one by one in their eastward drive. They were making progress in their plans to encircle the city of Metz and choke it off from reinforcement from the east. The next mission was to establish a bridgehead across the Nied river in order to cut the main escape route of the hard-pressed German garrison in Metz. Armor and infantry were subjected to counter-attacks but the German defenders were forced to pull back.

The 90th Infantry Division was fighting north of Metz in its mission to establish a foothold across the flooded section of the Moselle and capture Fort Koenigsmacher in the Maginot Line, from where they could envelop Metz from the north. Corps engineers brought assault boats to the crossing sites and began constructing support bridges, treadway bridges, and floating Bailey bridges. Shortly after midnight on November 9, the assault battalions of the 90th Division assembled at the pre-established boat stations. The crossing of the raging Moselle on this day became a more formidable foe than the enemy! The pouring rain continued, and by noon, the river had swelled to a width of eight hundred yards. The assault boats were tossed about and some capsized and sank with their crews and cargoes. Footbridge cables could not be anchored. Some assault craft were carried as far as one thousand yards downstream. The river was so high that enemy mine fields were covered with water, and our troops landed in deep mud on the far bank.

In spite of these extreme difficulties, our assault waves charged up the high ground at Fort Koenigsmacher and were able to cut through the barbed wire to reach the open trenches around the fort. The Germans were taken by complete surprise, thinking that they were secure because the Americans would never try to cross the Moselle at its flood stage. This was another instant in which the "Ghost Corps" displayed its bold tactics of striking where it was least expected. At the end of the first day, the 90th Division had moved eight battalions of infantry across the flooded river and penetrated to a depth of two miles without armored support. They overran seven towns before they entered Fort Koenigsmacher and captured two hundred prisoners. The American troops gradually moved from fort to fort through the Maginot Line.

During the evening of November 11, the Moselle River reached its crest, the highest in twenty-nine years. By November 13, the river began to recede rapidly, and as the water level dropped it uncovered extensive German mine fields along its banks. It took valuable time to clear these submerged mines before the engineers finally completed a Bailey bridge that then enabled our armored vehicles to race across into the bridgehead. This was the turning point in the entire Metz operation, as Metz defenses were pierced in the north and in the south; however, the most formidable obstacle had been overcome, namely, the *Moselle River!*

During these days when our Corps troops were battling the challenges of the flooded rivers as well as the German army, another enemy appeared to plague the infantry boys. This new problem was called "trench foot," which consisted of frostbite of the feet resulting from standing in cold water over long periods of time. The doughboys were exposed to continuous rain that flooded foxholes and turned the ground into mud and swamps. It was estimated that up to 40% of the assault troops were casualties of trench foot, so it was imperative for the guys to keep their feet dry as much as possible.

At Thionville, the 1306th Engineer Regiment constructed the largest Bailey bridge built in the entire ETO (European Theater of Operations). It was 190 feet long, built at the site of the original bridge which was destroyed. A large sign stood by the destroyed bridge on which its name was written in German: "Erich von Bloh Brucke." Our engineers showed their humor by painting over these words in bold letters: "Under new Management, 1306th Engr. Reg." The engineers built another pontoon bridge a few miles south of Thionville which was 765 feet long. This one enabled the 10th Armored Division to cross the river and take up positions on the east side of the Maginot Line. They moved from town to town with the infantry in spite of strong resistance. By November 17, the bulk of German forces began a retreat in long columns along the ridges of the Maginot Line, coming down from the heights and fleeing toward the Saar River, and surrendering along the way.

General Walker ordered the 90th Division to drive south to meet the 5th Division which was fighting its way to the north. Through this maneuver several escape routes were plugged east of Metz, and more towns were captured and prisoners taken. Meanwhile, a separate task force was given the mission to race south on the road built along the east bank of the Moselle. With speed and tremendous firepower, this task force stormed Fort St. Julien and Fort Bellacroix. On the evening of November 18, they were in the railroad yards of Metz, ready to sweep into the city itself at daybreak.

The 95th Infantry Division began attacking the forts from the west. The Germans began to blow up the Moselle bridges in Metz, thereby abandoning their own troops, who were still holding the garrisons in the forts on the west side of the river. On November 19, the 95th Division crossed the river in their own assault boats and began clearing out the city, block by block, under heavy artillery and machine gun fire. On this same day, the 5th Division moved into the southern suburbs of Metz along the railroad tracks, and made contact with the 95th Division whose job was to clean out the heart of the city. On the east side of Metz, the 90th Division blocked all escape routes through which the German remnants might pass. All XX Corps troops drove into the center of Metz from all directions, mopping up the "die-hard" German pockets. The next morning, a strong barrage of mortar shells and hand grenades caused the last defenders of the garrison to surrender. The city of Metz was reported to be entirely clear at 1435 hours on November 22, 1944!

The fall of Metz was a major milestone in the history of the XX Corps. The loss of Metz and its encircling forts and the breaching of the Moselle River during one of the highest flood stages in its history was a major disaster for the German Wehrmacht. In losing Metz, the German armies lost a major anchor of defenses in the western front. The bridging of the swollen Moselle River under tremendous fire power from the guns of the forts was a major engineering feat. The sweeping encirclement of the forts and their systematic reduction was a triumph of the highest magnitude for all the troops commanded by the XX Corps. The XX Corps had lived up to its popular slogan, "In Spite of Hell and High Water." These words were very appropriate at this juncture. The Battle of France was nearly over, and the Battle of Germany was ready to begin.

The liberation of Metz was an extremely emotional event for the French citizens of this ancient city. People who were huddled in their homes with great fear during the battle that lasted several weeks, now poured out into the streets in spite of the rubble lying all around them.

Many of them were crying with great joy and relief. A group of young girls, dressed in their native Lorraine costumes, burst into singing the "Marseillaise," and the townspeople joined in repeating the French national anthem. These were the emotions of liberation from tyranny.

General Walton H. Walker and his top aides entered the conquered city of Metz to participate in the celebration that these French people had prepared for its liberators. Joining General Walker were the commanders of the infantry divisions that entered Metz: Major General Stafford L. Irwin of the 5th Infantry Division and Major General Harry L. Twaddle of the 95th Infantry Division. American troops stood in formation in front of the Hotel de Ville in the centrum of Metz, while General Walker turned over the administration of the control of Metz to Major General Dody, the military governor of the city. General Walker made the following statement to the leaders and citizens of Metz:

GENERAL DODY, MONSIEUR PREFECT:

It is with supreme pride and pleasure that I return to your hands the ancient and courageous fortress CITY OF METZ, which has been liberated by assault by soldiers of the 95th and 5th Divisions of the XX Corps, Third United States Army.

During the infancy of our Republic, France aided America with materiel, money, and men. Every American soldier feels it a privilege that he is able to assist to some extent in repaying the debt owed to France. It is my hope and belief that the city of Metz will forever be a symbol of the friendly relationship that has always existed between our two countries. The City of Metz is yours.

General Dody then responded with these words:

My General Walker:
You have been willing in the midst of the battle now raging in front of the American and French troops to formally turn over to us the city which you have delivered. This gesture goes straight to the heart.

Soon, the head of the French government, General DeGaulle, will come here to our old city of Metz to express the joy that France has on this historical occasion.

Since the glorious days of the Battle of Normandy the Third Army under the command of General Patton has literally flown from city to city and from victory to victory.

Yesterday—LeMans, Chartres, Reims, Verdun: much history is recalled by each of these names. From now on, connected in our memory of them will be the XX Corps of the American Army, and the name of its commander, General Walker.

Today—it is Metz, whose military post is so heavy with glory. Tomorrow—Germany, and the liberation of our brothers who are prisoners or who have been deported from our land. On this square, in the heart of the city from whence Lafayette left for America, it has brought at this moment a new bond in the Franco-American friendship.

General, permit me as one soldier speaking to another

soldier to extend to you in the name of all the authorities and for the population of Metz, and of Lorraine, our gratitude, and give you the accolade in testimony of our fraternity.

Monsieur M. Rebourset was the Prefect of Metz, the highest administrative official of the city government. He made this response to General Walker and the XX Corps.

General Walker, Commander of the XX Corps, American Army:

Today you are giving Metz the great honor of visiting its leaders, its municipality, and its citizens. May we be allowed to express our feelings on this great occasion. This will always be a day of heartfelt remembrance.

The citizens of Metz today end a four-year period of enemy occupation. The people of Lorraine have always been of firm heart, but it has been necessary to hold on and hope. We were never able to speak freely—not even to express our feelings or our own personalities. The language of France was forbidden us. Our people were forced to take part in the formation of an enemy dictatorial party. We were conscripted with bleeding hearts in an enemy army. We were deported, displaced, evacuated, and there was no suffering which we have not known or felt.

From all this, General Walker, you, the leader of admirable troops from your great country and our allies have freed us. No word of human speech can adequately express our thanks. And, another glorious note is that Metz, one of the most powerful fortress cities of Europe, has been taken by you, my General. It is not too much to predict that your name will go down in history with the illustrious title of "Conqueror of Metz."

These are but a few words to be said in such a glorious moment before we return to our many material tasks and resume our normal life. May we hope that the end of the war is very near.

Long live General Walker.

Long live his glorious XX Corps D'Armee.

Long live the United States of America and our Allies.

General George S. Patton sent this letter of commendation to General Walker:

HEADQUARTERS
THIRD UNITED STATES ARMY
Office of the Commanding General
APO 403

21 November 1944

SUBJECT: Commendation
TO: Commanding General, XX Corps
            APO 340, U. S. Army

1. The workmanlike manner in which your Corps accomplished the capture of the heretofore impregnable city of Metz is an outstanding military achievement.

2. Please accept for yourself and pass on to the officers and men of the XX Corps my high commendation for the superior manner in which you accomplished your difficult mission.

G. S. PATTON, JR.
Lieutenant General, U.S. Army
Commanding

Shortly after the liberation of Metz, I visited several of the forts for an inspection of these gigantic fortresses. A couple of my buddies accompanied me in my jeep as we drove to the first fortification called Fort Plapperville, a huge complex in the inner ring. It was just a few miles west of Metz on the west side of the Moselle. As we drove up a winding road that led to the top of the hill, we came across the carcasses of more than a dozen horses. I had to navigate the jeep carefully between the dead animals. The German Army had used these horses to pull their artillery wagons because of their shortage of mechanized vehicles to do that job. These horses had been killed because

German horses killed at Fortress
Metz, France (1944)

of the enormous concussion of air resulting from the bombardment from American shells.

The fortress stood on top of the hill, and it looked like a castle with a large central courtyard. I drove my jeep into this plaza. Various kinds of abandoned vehicles were parked in this upper level, and when I walked down some steps to the lower level I found scores of boxes containing ammunition, as well as stacks of shells for the large millimeter guns. The German defenders never got to use them. The concrete walls that surrounded the buildings were tall and very thick, with steel tines and a fence of barbed wire imbedded along the top of the wall. A moat which was wide and deep surrounded the main building. The gigantic size of Fort Plapperville truly appeared as an impenetrable fortress. As I looked upon this awesome sight, I marveled at the courage and determination of our American infantry soldiers who finally conquered this hill as well as the other forts. The Almighty God was surely on our side during this ferocious battle, as men could not have accomplished this mission on their own. Praise be to God!

Author at Fort Plapperville, Fortress Metz, France (1944)

We jumped into the jeep and drove to another fort a few miles away. This was Fort St. Quentin, which was located closer to the city of Metz. Here the Germans had built some structures into the hillside with a courtyard in front of it. Tunnels inside the hill connected many underground rooms containing communications and quarters for the soldiers. On top of the hill, steel picket fences and barbed wire protected the courtyard and the entrances below. It was another heavily fortified bastion in the vast defenses surrounding Metz.

Fort St. Quentin at Fortress Metz, France, US 105mm gun (1944)

All of the German defenses in the outer and inner rings around Metz were now defunct, silent, and abandoned. The Nazi Wehrmacht had suffered a major defeat. God certainly was there, guiding and protecting our soldiers with legions of invisible angels stationed on all the ridges, hillsides, and valleys of the Moselle River. To God be the glory and thanks for showing his mighty power through our soldiers who victoriously conquered this mighty redoubt, which had not been captured since the Huns did it in AD 451. My buddies joined me in the jeep as we returned to the Corps' CP, deep in our thoughts of what we had just seen and experienced.

C'est la Guerre!

CHAPTER 17

The Liberation of Thionville

Command Post No. 18

Thionville, France
(The Lycee Gymnastique pour Jeunes Filles)
(A High School for Girls)
November 21, 1944–March 18, 1945

THE DAY BEFORE METZ WAS captured, November 21, 1944, the XX Corps Headquarters moved to the city of Thionville, fifteen miles north of Metz. During November, the major action in the war had occurred in the area around Metz and its many forts. During these same days, our Corps troops continued their forward drive on the north flank of the XX Corps zone of action with their mission to enlarge the Koenigsmacher bridgehead and move forward to the Saar river. Thionville had been liberated and cleared of all enemy troops, so General Walker ordered Corps Headquarters to move forward closer to the front.

We moved into a large school for girls of middle-school age which was located in the center of the city of Thionville. The buildings were built in the form of a quadrangle, with the four sides enclosing an inner courtyard. A chapel was connected to one of the sides. Our new quarters were roomy, dry, warm, and very welcome at this time of the year because of the oncoming winter. The classrooms provided adequate office space for each of the Corps' departments, and all personnel had private quarters in other rooms where we lived and slept on army cots. The school auditorium was adequate in size to accommodate meetings and assemblies as well as entertainment by traveling USO Shows. Our cooks loved the kitchen facilities that included stoves, kettles, and utensils in the roomy school cafeteria. The inner court was excellent for our daily calisthenics and conditioning exercises. All in all, we were ready for our winter stay, but we had no idea of how long this would be.

Lycee Gymnastique, (High School for girls), the XX Corps
Headquarters, Thionville, France (Photo dated 2010)

After the collapse of Metz, the 90th and 95th Infantry Divisions were available for the next phase of the war, which was to move east of the Moselle River to the Saar River. The enemy barrier that stood between these two rivers was the Maginot Line. Its ponderous forts were situated on commanding ground. They had originally been built by the French facing Germany as their protection from invasion, but they now were occupied by German defenders facing west toward France.

The next mission of XX Corps troops began on December 2, which was to seize Saarlautern and its vital bridge across the Saar River. This town was heavily defended by pillboxes and bunkers sandwiched between houses. The assault troops abandoned the plan to engage in street fighting, so they devised a new one. On the morning of December 4, in complete darkness, an entire battalion of the 95th Infantry Division paddled across the Saar River into Saarlautern. Outposts were quickly captured as the German defenders were taken by complete surprise. The battalion reached the vital bridge where they eliminated the startled guards before they were able to react. Another patrol of infantry and engineers seized the other end of the bridge on the west bank of the river. All wires leading to the bridge were cut and mines and demolitions were cleared from the structure. The men found four five hundred-pound American aerial bombs laid end-to-end in the center of the span. They were disarmed and hauled off the bridge. This stone bridge was captured intact!

The intact bridge enabled infantry and tanks to move into Germany to establish a small bridgehead. By December 6, two more bridgeheads were obtained, and our troops were now up against the formidable Siegfried Line, the German West Wall. The belt of this line in front of our troops was about three miles deep, including anti-tank obstacles. The Germans had built a second line of obstacles ten to fifteen miles to the rear of this belt.

Meanwhile, during the first two weeks of December, many of the Metz forts still held remnants of the German defenders but these holdouts eventually surrendered as they faced isolation and starvation. Hundreds of German officers and enlisted men exited from the forts and were sent to POW compounds. Troops of the American divisions were tired and weary, and were rotated to the XX Corps rest camp in the city of Metz, while others regrouped with their units.

December 12, 1944: Liberation Day in Thionville

Thionville, France was a small, strategically located town with a population of perhaps six thousand to seven thousand on the west side of the Moselle River, about fifteen miles north of Metz. In early September, the 90th Infantry Division was fighting on the north flank of the XX Corps zone of action, and on September 12, the Division's 358th Combat Team liberated the city of Thionville. The German defenders fled across the river to Fort Yutz which was one of the fortifications of the Maginot Line. It wasn't until two months later, after the floods which had ravaged the Moselle River had receded, that troops of the 90th Division successfully built a Bailey Bridge from Thionville to Fort Yutz on the east side of the river. This enabled the 358th Combat Team to capture the German defenders of the Fort on November 11, 1944.

The citizens of Thionville decided to celebrate their liberation from Nazi occupation during the preceding five years. City government was again in the hands of French officials, and the townsfolk were happy once more. Therefore, the city fathers declared December 12, 1944, as "Liberation Day," and the XX Corps was at the center of the celebration because we were the American liberators of their beloved city. All the personnel of the XX Corps Headquarters Company were involved in the celebration, and we dressed in our parade uniforms, shined our shoes, and polished the brass buckles of our belts. We too were ready to celebrate!

Hotel de Ville, Thionville, France on Liberation Day (December 12, 1944)

The Hotel de Ville was several blocks from our quarters in the Lycee Gymnastique. At mid-morning, we marched in formation to the town square and joined the thousands of people who were lining the streets. It was a tremendously happy scene. I was with my buddies while we were standing in front of the main entrance to the Hotel de Ville. A wide sidewalk connected the door to the street. A big banner was stretched across the front of the city hall at the third floor level of the four-story building. On it were painted these words in large letters: *"Vive La France."* Over a hundred schoolgirls, from elementary school age to teenagers, stood in two groups which flanked the pathway into city hall. They were dressed in their gala native Lorraine costumes of colorful dresses and decorative aprons, long white stockings, and lacy cloth head scarves.

After these official ceremonies were completed, all the citizens dispersed and found a place to stand along the main street in central Thionville to watch the big parade that was about to begin. Our XX Corps personnel mingled with the French citizens along the street where we experienced the same joy of freedom that these liberated people felt at this moment. The big parade

General Walker (left) with the Thionville Mayor on Liberation Day, December 12, 1944.

began with a band of French army musicians dressed in their uniforms and wearing steel helmets. Several companies of French troops followed the band, dressed in uniforms with black berets and rifles on their shoulders. They were followed by groups of French citizens who carried flags and banners which identified various clubs and civic organizations. Then there were groups of children in Lorraine costumes followed by women who were dressed in colorful long dresses, long white stockings, neck scarves, head scarves, and lace caps on their heads. There were also groups of marching men who were dressed in their own native Lorraine costumes of black jackets that were buttoned up from the belt line to their necks, with wide-brimmed black felt hats on their heads.

Thionville citizens watching parade on Liberation Day (December 12, 1944)

The parade concluded with the vehicles of the Thionville fire department. A huge truck that obviously was pre-war vintage carried several firemen sitting next to reels of hoses, with ladders stretched across the top of the truck. I couldn't help but notice the two sleek, shiny air horns mounted on the hood, which seemed a little out of place. Another fire truck pulled an old-fashioned wagon with ladders and reels of hoses, and firemen stood on the rear running board.

When the parade ended, my buddies and I mingled with the citizens of Thionville, as they thanked us as their liberators with numerous samples of wonderful Moselle wine, and accompanied with countless toasts to America and American soldiers. It was truly a joyous and memorable day for everyone.

Vive la France!

Thionville Liberation Day parade (December 12, 1944)

Thionville Liberation Day parade (December 12, 1944)

Thionville Liberation Day parade (December 12, 1944)

Thionville Liberation Day parade (December 12, 1944)

Thionville Liberation Day parade (December 12, 1944)

Thionville Liberation Day parade (December 12, 1944)

* * * * * * *

Fifty Years After the Liberation of Thionville

October 13, 1994

In the autumn of 1994, I returned to Europe to trace the military steps that I had taken fifty years earlier while I served in the XX Corps between 1944 and 1945. My wife Eleanore went with me. We rented a French car in Paris, a very nice four-door Renault, and drove to Normandy. We began our odyssey at Utah beach and the XX Corps Command Post No. 1 in the Normandy apple orchard. During the four weeks that we roamed across Northern France and across Germany into Austria, we were fortunate to find and visit every one of the thirty-four Command Posts that the XX Corps occupied during the war.

We spent a day in Bastogne, Belgium looking at the museum displays that replayed the "Battle of the Bulge." Bastogne is just a few miles outside the northwest border of the Duchy of Luxembourg, and Thionville is twenty miles south of Luxembourg City. On October 13, 1994, we drove on a new four-lane highway from Bastogne through the city of Luxembourg to Thionville, which took about an hour. We arrived at the Tourist Bureau in Centre Ville where I told the receptionist that I had lived in Thionville as an American soldier for four months in 1944–1945 with the XX Corps Headquarters and that I wished to speak to someone who might know about the history of our unit's stay in Thionville fifty years ago. She made a telephone call, speaking in French, about my inquiry, and then handed me the phone. The man on the line spoke English and said to wait a few minutes because he wanted to see me.

Within three minutes, a man of short stature walked into the Tourist Office and introduced himself as Mr. Dominique Laglasse. He said that he was the head of the Municipal Archives of Thionville, and his excitement in meeting me was obvious. He was in the process of preparing a pictorial book for the 50th Anniversary celebration that the people of Thionville were planning to celebrate in one month on November 11. He showed me many photos of the XX Corps and General Walker from the city's liberation day fifty years ago. He told us that General Walker's son, who currently was a general in the US Army was planning to come to Thionville to participate in the festivities, because the city was planning to rename a street in honor of his father, "Boulevard de General Walton Walker."

Mr. Laglasse took us on a walk in the centrum and showed us a street sign with the name "Rue de XX Corps." It was a thrill to see the XX Corps name in so many places in Thionville. He showed us the building which in 1944 was the

Hotel de Ville where the ceremony had taken place with General Walker and the City Mayor. The big liberation parade had occurred on this same street.

The large girl's school in which the XX Corps Headquarters personnel had lived in was only a block away from the Hotel de Ville, and Mr. Laglasse escorted us there. I recognized it immediately. He spoke to the school receptionist about the reason for our visit. Soon we were greeted by a lady who was wearing a large cross on a heavy chain around her neck. She was the principal of the school and was dressed in street clothing rather than in the habit of a Nun, since this was a Catholic school. After Mr. Laglasse explained to her that I was an American soldier and a member of the XX Corps which had occupied this school building during the war, she was very eager to take us on a tour of the school. Originally, this was an all-girls high school serving students from grades ten to twelve, but the principal told us that the present enrollment was eighteen hundred students from kindergarten to grade twelve.

The principal showed us the school chapel, and I clearly remembered how it was when I had attended Sunday worship services there. Our Corps Chaplains held both Protestant and Catholic worship services for all corps personnel here fifty years ago. I got goose bumps while I stood here and remembered how I had worshipped here under completely different circumstances. It was in these same pews where we soldiers heard God's Word of forgiveness of our sins and salvation through the merits of Jesus Christ, our Savior. We were reassured that we had complete protection from our guardian angels during those days of constant danger, and we had given thanks for all of God's great goodness to us. These pews were filled with soldiers during those wartime days, and our faith kept us going.

My thoughts returned to the present as the principal showed us other phases of education at this school. We entered the inner courtyard which was crowded with students engaged in recess games and having lots of fun, yelling and shouting and playing on the playground. We were introduced to some of the teachers who were on playground duty.

As we walked along the main corridor inside the building, the principal stopped at a large plaque that was fastened to the wall. I noticed a small American flag on one side of the plaque and a French flag on the other side. She proudly explained that this plaque was a prominent display of French gratitude to the XX Corps of the US Army and its commander, General Walton H. Walker. I was flabbergasted, and my emotions took over with tears welling up in my eyes. This was an honor to my beloved XX Corps, and then I realized that this commemoration included me too, because I had lived in this very building at that time as a member of the army staff. I was truly humbled!

The following words were engraved on the marble slab that hung on the wall in this school as a constant reminder to the French students of the liberators of Thionville during those dark days of the great war in 1944:

**Ici à l' Institut
Notre-Dame de la Providence
du 21 Novembre 1944 an 18 Mars 1945,
etait installe´ le quartier general
du XXe Corps de l' Armee Americaine
sous les orders du General Walker
et de son Chief of Staff General Collier.
Merci à nos liberateurs**

The plaque in the Lycee Gymnastique in Thionville, France,
dedicated to the XX Corps (Photo dated 1994)

The final stop on the tour of the school was the dining hall. A large group of students were eating lunch, and the principal interrupted them and announced that we were visitors from America, and that I was an American soldier who served with the US XX Corps that liberated the city of Thionville. She told them that I had actually lived in this school building during the winter of 1944–1945, and how grateful the townsfolk of Thionville were toward us. Immediately, all these students smiled and cheered, and shouted "Merci," "Merci," as they clapped their hands very exuberantly. I could no longer contain my emotions, and my tears flowed. This moment was thrilling, and it is etched permanently in my memory.

Our wonderful tour of the Lycee Gymnastique came to an end. We said good-bye to the school's principal in the French style of a kiss on each cheek, saying the word "merci" many times. As we said "au revoir" to Mr. Laglasse and thanked him for his kind attention he also thanked us for our visit to Thionville, which he said would increase his enthusiasm for the upcoming 50th Anniversary Celebration of the Liberation of Thionville.

Street in Thionville, France, named in honor of the XX Corps (Photo dated 1994)

During the drive back to our hotel for the night, I continued to be on a huge high from the wonderful day I had enjoyed in Thionville. My heart was full of joy from our reception at the school and the Tourist Bureau, and my memories of the actual Liberation Day on December 12, 1944, came to life as I relived that happy day.

CHAPTER 18

The Battle of the Bulge

AFTER THE FALL OF FORTRESS Metz, the Third Army and the XX Corps began planning the next phase of the war, namely, to cross into Germany itself, then cross the Rhine River to seize the city of Frankfurt. Field Order No. 14, dated December 16, called for the XX Corps to advance east to penetrate the Siegfried Line, also known as the German West Wall. A few attacks were launched at Saarlautern and some small bridgeheads were established across the Saar River.

These plans came to a sudden end on December 16 when the Nazi High Command launched its mammoth counter-offensive in the forests of the Ardennes. At this time, the front lines of the Allied advance were roughly along the borders of Germany with Luxembourg and Belgium. On the German side of this border, running in a north–south direction, the Germans had built the venerable Siegfried Line of defenses. This was the area where the German Army penetrated deeply through the American forces, and this ferocious battle came to be known as the "Battle of the Bulge."

The Ardennes is a large area of more than 2.7 million acres located in southeastern Belgium, northern Luxembourg, and northeastern France. It consists of extensive forests, rolling hills, and old mountains that average approximately fifteen hundred feet in height. The region is typified by steep-sided valleys that were carved by fast-flowing rivers. The most important river is the Meuse. The Ardennes are sparsely settled, except for the cities of Bastogne, Houffalize, St. Vith, Malmedy, and Verviers, all located in Belgium. These towns played prominent roles in the Battle of the Bulge.

The German attack on the 16th was officially known as the Ardennes Offensive. The plan was for the Nazis to advance through the forest to reach the Meuse River, and then turn northwest to capture Antwerp and Brussels. Hitler himself chose this plan as it seemed to be the most doable for the Wehrmacht to make a blitzkrieg attack through the weakly defended Ardennes Mountains. If he succeeded in capturing the port of Antwerp, four complete armies would be trapped behind German lines without supplies. They were America's First and Ninth Armies, Canada's First Army, and Britain's Second Army. Hitler chose his brilliant Field Marshall Gerd von Rundstedt as the commander of the Ardennes Offensive.

The German Sixth SS Panzer Army, led by Sepp Dietrich, was the northernmost attack force, with its objective to capture Antwerp. The Fifth Panzer Army under Hasso von Manteuffel took the middle route in order to capture Brussels. The German Seventh Army led by Erich Brandenberger took the southern route to protect the flank of the Fifth Panzer Army. A few days before the initial attack began, a task force of English-speaking German soldiers dressed in American uniforms went behind the allied lines to create havoc. The uniforms and dog tags were taken from corpses and POWs. Their mission was to go behind American lines and cause disruption by changing signposts, misdirecting traffic, cutting telephone lines, and seizing bridges across the Meuse River. The weather during this time placed the Allies at a major disadvantage because of fog, low clouds, and snow, which prevented the US Air Force from flying reconnaissance and bombing missions.

The German attack began at 5:30 a.m. on the morning of December 16 with a massive artillery barrage by the Sixth SS Panzer Army, and by eight o'clock, all three German armies were attacking in the Ardennes. A snowstorm was in progress in the forests as well, and the poor road conditions and traffic control led to massive traffic jams and fuel shortages. However, in spite of American resistance, the German armies made progress by overcoming defenses which were thinly spread out. Many allied soldiers were killed or captured, and there were substantial losses in arms and equipment. On the first day, the Germans made deep penetrations at several spots of the allied lines, with the possibility of breaking out into the clear.

This huge offensive operation by the German Wehrmacht had caught the Allies by complete surprise. Their intelligence had no inkling that this attack was on the verge of happening. On December 17, the second day of the offensive, General Eisenhower met with his principal commanders at SHAEF Headquarters in Versailles. They now realized that the fighting in the Ardennes was a major offensive and not a local counterattack, so they ordered immediate reinforcements to the Ardennes.

On December 17, Eisenhower had only two divisions available in reserve: the 82nd and 101st Airborne Divisions. After their parachute drop in Holland these two divisions were recovering and re-equipping in camps near Reims, France. Artillery and anti-tank units were attached to them, and the 101st Airborne was rushed to Bastogne, Belgium, in trucks, a distance of one hundred miles. The 82nd Airborne went further north to St. Vith, Belgium, thirty-two miles beyond Bastogne.

Two days later, on December 19, German troops reached the outskirts of the town of Bastogne, where there was a major network of eleven hard-topped roads that were built through the mountainous terrain of the Ardennes region. Two separate westbound German divisions had bypassed Bastogne on the north and south. The only corridor that was open into Bastogne was to the southeast, and the Germans had finally closed it, thereby completely surrounding the town. The allied situation was extremely serious because the Germans had trapped a large number of American troops from several divisions.

On the 19th, General Eisenhower and his top aides hastily traveled from SHAEF Headquarters in Versailles to a bunker in Verdun, about thirty miles from the front. Present at this meeting were General Omar Bradley of the 12th Army Group, General George Patton of the Third Army, and General Jacob Devers of the 6th Army Group. An agreement for an immediate counterattack was quickly decided, but how would this be accomplished?

Patton's Third Army troops were in place at this time along a sixty-mile front that was south of the bulge area that stretched from Luxembourg to the city of Nancy. His army was a large and powerful force of four Corps, each having three divisions, and they were already scheduled to drive east to crack the German West Wall. However, these plans were changed and put on hold, and instead, several divisions of the Third Army were diverted north to hit the Germans on their southern flank in the Ardennes.

The challenge that Patton faced was to turn his Third Army divisions, with all the men, tanks, vehicles, and supplies in a 90 degree direction to the north and to attack at right angles to the axis of attack that his forces had been pursuing. This was an extremely difficult and complex maneuver to execute, especially in the Ardennes, where there was a limited road network. For this new plan to be successful, Patton wanted an adequate amount of POL (petroleum, oil, and lubricants), ammunition, ordnance, transport, replacements, rations, etc., to be available. To accomplish this task, he requested one of General Bradley's aides to find a freight train which Patton could borrow temporarily, and to find one by any means—fair or foul. Patton's wish was granted as that officer managed to "steal" a freight train somewhere in France.

By December 21, Bastogne was surrounded by German forces, and an unthinkable situation had occurred, because many of the American troops were trapped in the city. They included combat commands from both the 9th and 10th Armored Divisions and the *entire* 101st Airborne Division under the command of Brigadier General Anthony C. McAuliffe. Patton's assignment was to rescue these trapped units. The general put together a striking force whose objective was to move up from the south of the bulge through Luxembourg and northeastern France. His new army consisted of three corps: the III Corps commanded by General Milliken; VIII Corps led by General Middleton; and the XII Corps led by General Eddy. My own XX Corps was not included in this task force, as Patton assigned us to stay put in our present location east and south of the Moselle River. Our job was to protect the recent hard-won gains, but we were spread out very thinly for the difficult days ahead. We remained in our Corps Headquarters in Thionville.

General Weyland of the XIX Tactical Air Command moved his headquarters to Luxembourg to be closer to the bulge area. The bad weather prevented his pilots from flying their missions, but during this lull in the air war, three fighter groups were transferred from the IX to the XIX TAC, and the Eighth Air Force in England sent a P-51 fighter-bomber group.

On December 22, the weary troops of the 101st Airborne were barely holding their ground around Bastogne, when four German couriers arrived at the American lines while carrying a white flag of truce. They handed the American guards a written document that demanded their surrender in two hours or face annihilation. General McAuliffe then sent his famous reply, when he scribbled these words on a piece of paper:

> *To the German Commander:*
> *Nuts!*
> *The American Commander*

The German soldiers were puzzled about the cryptic one-word reply, so one of McAuliffe's officers explained to them that "nuts" meant the same thing as "go to hell." [Note: during these years the word "nuts" was a very common reply that many people, including myself, used in everyday conversation. It was a short version of such expressions as "au shucks," "not interested," "disgusting," or "what the hell."]

On December 23, the weather improved dramatically, and General Weyland wasted no time in getting his planes into the air. He sent out seven groups of fighter-bombers and eleven groups of medium bombers to conduct massive bombing missions on German supply depots in the rear, while P-47 Thunderbolts attacked German troops in the Ardennes. Cargo planes dropped much-needed supplies to the defenders of Bastogne, which included medicine, food, blankets, and ammunition. A team of surgeons landed in the city by glider to care for the seriously wounded.

Patton then moved his headquarters to Luxembourg City, just a few miles from the trapped troops in Bastogne. The plan to move his army for a rescue operation was enormously complicated. About one hundred thousand troops turned north, along with thousands of tons of equipment and supplies. Thousands of jeeps, trucks, tanks, and howitzers sped north toward Bastogne, 125 miles away, over roads that were covered with snow and ice. At night, the drivers ignored blackout rules and traveled at full speed with their lights on. Signal battalions set up a new communication network after laying 19,500 miles of telephone wire.

Christmas Eve had arrived, and the news from the Ardennes front was grim. The weather was cold and miserable, and our spirits were depressed, not only because of the bad news from the Bulge, but also because it was Christmas Eve, which had had so many happy memories for me. Life was very tense at XX Corps Headquarters in Thionville because we were on high alert. Our lines that faced the German defenders were spread pretty thin because Patton had picked the 10th Armored Division and the 5th Infantry Division to be part of his "rescue army" at Bastogne. These two units had just won the Battle of Metz a few weeks earlier.

A couple of our guys had been in contact with their friends who were stationed in Luxembourg City, and they were told that a winery in the city was "discovered and appropriated" by a combat team from the armored division. So two of the mechanics in our motor pool loaded about six five-gallon empty water cans into the back of a jeep and drove there. In late afternoon, they returned to Corps Headquarters with a supply of newly liberated and wonderful-tasting Moselle wine.

After supper on Christmas Eve, we gathered in the day room at our school headquarters, and my mood, as well as the mood of my buddies, was depressed. I became very sad when my thoughts turned

The XX Corps' 1944 Christmas Card

to my family at home, and I knew that on this night they were celebrating the birth of my Savior Jesus Christ by attending the worship service at my church in Clintonville. The children of St. Martin Lutheran School were presenting their joyful program of songs and recitations, just as I had participated in barely more than five or six years ago. After the service, Mom and Dad would visit briefly with relatives and friends outside the church, before heading to their warm home. My brother and sister-in-law would be with the folks, and then they would gather in front of our Christmas tree which always stood in front of the three-pane bay window in the living room and exchange presents. I was quite sure that their conversation in front of the Christmas tree revolved around me, and if they wondered where I was and if I was OK, or even alive. I was glad that they didn't know that I was a mere forty miles from the battlefields of the Bulge, which certainly was the big news back home. After opening their presents, Mom would have served the schnecken, stollen, and cookies that she had probably baked that morning, along with wonderful hot chocolate, as we were a chocoholic family. That was our tradition at home, and on this Christmas Eve, I was extremely homesick.

There were many homesick guys sitting around in the day room, and as the evening hours passed by, each soldier related how he celebrated Christmas Eve with his family. The motor pool guys brought a five-gallon water can into the room which contained the Moselle wine. We drank it from our aluminum canteen cups as we did not need a fancy crystal wine glass to enjoy this elegant fruit of the vine. Our story-telling and wine party continued until midnight—and this evening turned out to be a completely different way of observing Christmas Eve for each one of us who were so far away from our families.

I got up in late morning on Christmas Day (a Monday) and went to the chapel for the eleven o'clock Christmas service that was conducted by the Corps Chaplain, a Methodist pastor. It was so good to sing some of the familiar hymns and carols, and it lifted my spirits. The Corps' cooks did a marvelous job of preparing a sumptuous turkey dinner with all the trimmings. It was way too much food for me, and I felt sad and guilty when I heard that the battered troops who were trapped in the Bulge ate K-rations for their "Christmas Dinner."

Patton's Third Army was engaged in severe fighting on the outskirts of Bastogne, and finally, during the afternoon of December 26, a regiment of the 4th Armored Division reached the town of Bastogne, which ended the German siege. That night forty trucks filled with supplies entered the city along with many ambulances that finally were able to evacuate 652 wounded Americans. The defenders of Bastogne demonstrated a heroic defense against tremendous odds. During four days of improved weather conditions that began on December 23, over eight hundred C-47 cargo planes dropped supplies to the trapped soldiers, and fifty gliders landed within the encircled town of Bastogne with medical personnel. General Weyland took advantage of the good weather and sent the full force of his fighter-bomber aircraft over the German forces, inflicting huge losses on the enemy's transport and fuel depots.

On Christmas Day, Gen. Alfred Jodl told Hitler the devastating news that the German Army was at a standstill just four miles short of the Meuse River and that the objective of crossing the river must be abandoned. From the 26th to the 29th, the Panzer divisions failed to make any advances, and the fifty-mile-wide spearhead through the Ardennes had to be shrunk into a narrower front. The reason for this was that even though the German forces in the middle thrust through the Ardennes were moving rapidly, the columns on the north and south flanks were lagging behind, and therefore left unprotected.

* * * * * * *

During the bitterly cold and snowy days of the Battle of the Bulge, a soldier in the 101st US Airborne Division (the "Screaming Eagles") was on guard duty at an advance command post close to the German lines near Bastogne, Belgium. His guard post was outside of an old school house where his officers were holding their planning sessions during the height of the fighting during the Bulge.

The intensely cold temperature during that night caused severe frostbite to this soldier's feet. His feet became swollen and numb, so he was taken to an army field hospital in the city of Thionville, France. This facility was a mere five blocks from where I was living in the Lycee Gymnastique pour Jeunes Filles.

I did not know this soldier, but it was interesting that he spent several months in the hospital that was just "down the street" from me. After medical treatment in Thionville, this soldier was sent to southern France for rehabilitation.

The surprising twist to this story is that I met this soldier five years later. It was then that I learned his name was Arthur J. Schmitz, when I married his sister, Eleanore, in Milwaukee in 1949.

* * * * * * *

The month of January 1945 began with extremely cold and bitter temperatures. It was labeled as the coldest and snowiest that was experienced in this part of Europe in many years. Weapons froze up; the casualties from frostbite were enormous, and trucks, jeeps, and other vehicles had to be run every half hour or so to keep the oil from freezing. Snow in some places was waist deep. Roads were icy and slippery, and they were cluttered with burned-out and abandoned equipment that was left behind by the German armies. The Wehrmacht, however, continued to fight.

The American soldiers in Bastogne did not have any camouflage for their uniforms, and they stood out as prominent targets with their olive-drab color. The women in the city of Bastogne came up with a remarkable idea to fix this problem. They asked all the women in the city to give up their white bed sheets, and they sewed them into a cape that the GIs slipped over their heads. This camouflage blended with the snow, and was a unique gift of love for our soldiers from the women of Bastogne.

New Year's Eve was a non-event at XX Corps Headquarters, as General Patton's special troops were engaged in fierce battles in the Bulge. We were continually at high alert because our front lines were extremely thin, and there was a high risk that German troops might infiltrate and launch an attack in the XX Corps sector that stretched from Thionville south to Metz and Nancy. The first week in January was bitterly cold, and the deep snow was all around us. It was very quiet at Corps Headquarters, with not much going on besides our daily work schedule. On Friday morning, January 5, my boss in G-3 Air, Col. John Huckins, informed me that he had decided to go to Nancy for the weekend. The American Red Cross Center in Nancy was hosting a big party and dance to welcome the New Year, and my boss was invited.

Colonel Huckins said that he was going to fly to Nancy in a Stinson L-4, single-engine liaison plane whose pilot was attached to our G-3 Air division. The Colonel asked me to drive his jeep to Nancy where I could also stay for the weekend, and on Sunday, I should drive the Colonel back to Thionville. I hesitated and felt a tinge of disappointment when he told me his plan. I told the Colonel that I had my heart set on attending the big USO show that was performing that evening at Corps Headquarters in the Thionville school where we lived. The big star of this show was Mickey Rooney, my very favorite Hollywood actor. Colonel Huckins assured me that it would not be a problem but that I should attend the show and drive to Nancy after the show ended, and he would have someone watch for me at the Red Cross Club later that night. I was very happy with this decision.

After lunch, I drove Colonel Huckins to the airstrip at the edge of Thionville and watched the small plane take off and head south to Nancy. During the rest of the afternoon, I was excited for the evening show.

Mickey Rooney was the stage name of Joe Yule Jr., a young actor who was born in 1920, so he was only three years older than I was. I had seen many movies that featured Mickey as the leading actor, and I loved his acting and antics. He was very short, which was funny when he performed in movies with such women as Lana Turner and Judy Garland, who were much taller than he was. He starred in the films of "Boys Town," "Babes in Arms," the "Andy Hardy" series, and many others. Mickey was the number one box office actor during the war years.

The USO troupe consisted of several musicians, a female singer, and the humor and antics of Mickey Rooney. The two-hour performance was everything I had expected, and the show ended too soon as all the guys in the auditorium were thrilled to enjoy this respite from the boredom of winter. My spirits were riding high after the show as I prepared for my long drive to Nancy that night.

It was past ten o'clock, and I prepared myself for the bitterly cold night by putting on layers of warm clothes, like long-johns, two pair of wool socks, boots, a sweater under my jacket, the heavy wool overcoat that hung down to my boots, and my wool cap that fit snugly under my steel helmet. I enjoyed a mug of hot chocolate and a half-dozen cookies as I went through this elaborate dressing procedure.

During the winter months, my normally "open-sided" jeep was enclosed with canvas and plastic windows, and a canvas roof was attached to the windshield. It had no heater, but I felt I was adequately dressed for this cold night in January. I started the engine for a warm-up and placed my carbine upright into the gun bracket that was attached to the middle of the dash area.

I drove through the quiet streets of Thionville and headed south onto the two-lane road that led to Metz, eighteen miles away. The distance from Metz to Nancy was another thirty-four miles, so I figured that my total trip of fifty-two miles would bring me to Nancy and a warm bed by midnight. The jeep's headlights were fitted with narrow slits for blackout driving because our orders prohibited night driving with full-beam ones. This January night was dark and cold, with no moon, and I was out there all alone. I was uneasy and scared, and I thought to myself that perhaps I was very foolish to be on this adventure. I remembered that this front of the XX Corps sector from Luxembourg to Nancy was thinly occupied by our troops because many units had been sent north to The Bulge. I also had heard about various reports of infiltrations of German patrols into this sector behind our front lines. I began to feel more tense and nervous as I strained to follow the dim light that was filtered through my slitted headlights. The narrow lane of the blacktop road was pitted with many pot holes caused by shells and tank traffic left over from the Battle of Fortress Metz. The shoulders along this beat-up road were covered with high drifts of snow, and fortunately I met no other vehicles, so I could keep driving in the center of the road.

As I rounded a sharp left hand curve, my faint headlights revealed a huge object immediately ahead of me. It was standing partially on the edge of the road, and I slammed on my brakes as adrenalin surged through my body. I was terribly scared. I stopped my jeep just a few feet in front of this huge thing. Then I recognized that it was a huge Panzer Mark IV German tank that was destroyed and burned in a previous battle during the siege of Fortress Metz. The 70mm gun in the turret was still in firing position, and it jutted out over the road, but it now stood silent and dead. My heart was racing, and it felt like it would jump out of my body as I reached for my carbine and removed it from its storage rack. I slammed a bullet into the chamber and turned off the safety, and I laid the gun across my lap. What seemed like a long time was perhaps only a couple of minutes as I continued my trip toward the city of Metz.

My nervousness about this adventure increased, and I began to have regrets of why I decided to take this risky trip. My spirits improved as I reached the city of Metz and drove through the deserted streets that had no street lights to guide me since the city was in blackout. There still were many piles of rubble and bombed-out buildings as the Battle of Metz had ended only six weeks earlier. On the road south of Metz, I drove past many German vehicles including trucks, tanks, and weapons carriers that were destroyed during the siege, but now I was able to take it all in stride. I drove through the small French town of Pont-a-Mousson and soon arrived in Nancy.

Nancy is a large city, but I followed the directions that Colonel Huckins gave me, and I easily found the building that the American Red Cross Center occupied in the downtown area. It was just past midnight when I walked into the lobby and introduced myself to the lady at the desk. She spoke excellent English, and then I realized that she was an American. Wow! It was a great feeling of joy to be here safely. Word of my arrival got to Colonel Huckins immediately, and within a few minutes, he came from the party to greet me. Lots of American girls were around me, and I felt like I was at home. I shed some of the layers of warm clothing, and someone handed me a large mug of hot chocolate. There was food galore, real American food, not powdered or dried or fake stuff. Wonderful desserts tempted me, and I indulged eagerly. I related to my boss the exciting trip I had just completed while the people around me listened with great interest. It was a wonderful way for me to unwind.

I had a nice bedroom and a very soft bed, and I quickly fell asleep under a wonderfully warm quilt. I slept late Saturday morning and had a sumptuous American breakfast. Later I enjoyed the amenities at the center, and I wrote letters in the reading room, read magazines, and relaxed. The party had included only American officers, and I was the only NCO there, but I was treated extremely well because my boss made sure of it.

It was about three o'clock on Saturday afternoon when Colonel Huckins and I gassed up the jeep at the Red Cross motor pool and prepared to drive back to Corps Headquarters in Thionville. We wanted to get back before dark because it wasn't any fun to drive on these damaged roads under blackout conditions. We found that traffic was nearly non-existent, and we made good time. We found the German Mark IV tank on the road north of Metz, and we stopped to look at it in daylight. It really was huge, and Colonel Huckins agreed that it must have been very scary for me to meet this monster in the dark. There was no doubt that one of our fighter-bombers from the XIX Tactical Air squadron, which was attached to Colonel Huckins' G-3 Air division, had knocked out this Nazi tank. It had been peppered with .50 caliber machine gun bullets; the tank's tracks were blasted off, and the body was charred from fire. It was ironic that this enemy tank was one that a fighter pilot destroyed who was directed to this target by our own G-3 Air command post. The Colonel and I arrived in Thionville as dusk was approaching, and our Corps CP was a welcome sight. This had been an unforgettable weekend for me.

Meanwhile, the fighting in the Battle of the Bulge began to tip in favor of the Allies. Finally, on January 7, Hitler gave his troops the order to withdraw from the Ardennes, and this move ended all of the German offensive operations. The Third Army's Bastogne operations ended officially on January 16, 1945, when Patton's 11th Armored Division met General Hodge's troops of his 2nd Armored Division.

The Battle of the Bulge was the bloodiest battle encountered by American troops in World War II, with 19,000 dead. The official US count was 80,987 casualties of all kinds, meaning dead, wounded, and missing. The official figure given by the German High Command counted a total of 84,834 casualties on their side. In London, Winston Churchill spoke these words in the House of Commons: "This is undoubtedly the greatest American battle of the war and will, I believe, be regarded as an ever-famous American victory."

CHAPTER 19

Entry into Germany

WHEN THE BATTLE OF THE Bulge officially ended, the special forces that General Patton commanded in the Ardennes returned to their former commands, and the plans to enter Germany itself that had been on hold became top priority again. The German losses in terms of troops and equipment were enormous; their reserves were gone. The Luftwaffe was broken, and the German Army in the west had been pushed back across their own border into the Fatherland. In addition, the Russian Army was heading toward Germany in the east, and their offensive had already entered Poland and East Prussia.

The XX Corps was back to full strength, and General Walker's new orders were to attack the German Army in what was known as "The Saar-Moselle Triangle," an area of land lying between the Saar and Moselle rivers on the eastern and western lines, respectively. The base of the triangle consisted of high ridges that were rugged and heavily wooded, with few roads usable for armored vehicles. The triangle stretched nineteen miles from top to bottom and ten miles wide at the base. It was heavily defended by three Nazi divisions: an Infantry Division, a Panzer Grenadier Division, and a Volks Grenadier Division.

Between 1939 and 1940, Adolf Hitler planned and ordered the building of an extensive defense system called the "Siegfried Line." It was constructed along the western border of Germany that faced the Netherlands, Belgium, Luxembourg, and France, and ended at the border with Switzerland. Along its total length of four hundred miles, there were more than eighteen thousand bunkers, tunnels, and tank traps. The bunkers had walls and ceilings that were five feet thick and could accommodate up to a dozen men. The tank traps in the Siegfried Line were known as "dragon's teeth" because of their shape. These blocks of reinforced concrete were several feet high and stood in several rows on a single foundation. There were four or five rows of dragon's teeth built in irregular lines with the teeth rising higher toward the back. In some places, water-filled ditches were dug instead of building traps.

XX Corps troops were now up against the section of the Siegfried Line that was built in the Saar–Moselle Triangle. At the base of this triangle, the Germans had built a switch line which was two kilometers deep. There were many rows of dragon's teeth and anti-tank ditches along with pillboxes (bunkers) along this switch line. This extra depth of defenses and fortifications was built in this triangle because the large German city of Trier was situated above the triangle. Trier was an important communications center that guarded the Moselle River corridor, which extended to the Rhine River at Koblenz.

The word "weather" was perhaps one of the most frequently used terms that described the months of December, January, and the Battle of the Bulge. Heavy snowfalls and bitter cold temperatures plagued the land and the troops. Snow depths were one to two feet deep everywhere, and drifts were waist high. During these difficult days, XX Corps divisions were limited to patrols and probes in the Saar–Moselle Triangle, and a full-scale attack was still on hold. The winter ended abruptly on February 1, when the weather turned unseasonably mild and the deep blanket of snow melted rapidly. By February 4, the Moselle River had risen over twelve feet, thereby dislodging the floating bridges that XX Corps engineers had secured at several places. The river's current reached twelve miles an hour and doubled its normal width. One of the divisions lost about sixty men by drowning when they tried to cross the raging river in inflatable rubber boats that had been found in a Luftwaffe storehouse.

The swollen rivers and flooded lands gradually receded in the following days, and the 94th Division, which was attached to the XX Corps, waited patiently for its order to crack the Siegfried Line. General Walker issued the order to attack the Saar–Moselle Triangle on February 19. At 0400 hours, three regiments of the 94th jumped off and simultaneously the Corps Artillery unleashed 15,000 rounds of shellfire at the German defenders. The Germans were startled by this surprise assault of extraordinary intensity.

By the end of the day, the switch line had been breached, and XX Corps troops swept through mine fields and the wreckage of the pillboxes, bunkers, and dragon's teeth of the elaborate fortifications. The next day, the 10th Armored Division received orders to move through the breach, and two armored columns advanced quickly to capture Saarburg on February 21. This was the largest city in the triangle as well as the wine capital of this region. Huge stores of wine were found in the wine cellars and warehouses.

The next objective was to cross the Saar River and move on to capture Trier. Two floating treadway bridges were built across the river and tanks and supply trucks rolled across to secure a bridgehead. Corps troops fought their way into a number of towns in the triangle during the following days. On March 2, the city of Trier was cleared of Nazi defenders. The main bridge over the Moselle River was captured intact, and eight hundred prisoners were rounded up. Trier was Germany's oldest city, dating back to 14 BC. The old Roman wall still existed with its Porta Nigra which had been built by Augustus Caesar, but the Nazis had renamed it the Adolf Hitler Platz. Now, American troops occupied Trier, which was a huge railroad and highway network that was the doorway to the Palatinate and the route to the Rhine River. The Siegfried Line was broken and the Saar–Moselle Triangle was clear.

Colonel John Huckins, my G-3 Air boss, had a friend who was a worker and hostess at a Red Cross Canteen in a town in Belgium west of the Luxembourg border. This Belgian lady was in Thionville for a couple of days for meetings with the Red Cross people at the Thionville Rest Center. The Colonel spent a little time with her during off-hours while she was in town, and when she had finished her business, Colonel Huckins asked me to drive her back to her headquarters in Belgium. On this nice February day with clear but cold weather, we got into my jeep and took off for Belgium. My lady passenger and I breezed along the various roads without encountering much traffic. There was no fear of driving in this territory because we were far behind the front, and these Belgium towns were occupied by US troops.

I drove into one of these Belgium towns and did not slow down because there was no traffic. However, to my surprise, I was abruptly stopped by the US Army MPs. The Military Police said that I had exceeded the speed limit, but when they discovered that I had a civilian woman with me, and that she was a Belgian citizen, they got suspicious. It turned out to be a big interrogation for both of us, as we tried to explain everything. Finally, the MPs let us go, but I got a citation for speeding. I finally brought her back to her headquarters and immediately drove back to Thionville. I told Colonel Huckins about our adventures, and he asked me for the speeding ticket. He told me not to worry about it, and he would take care of the citation. I was "off the hook," and I never heard what happened about my citation, as it was never mentioned again.

When the XX Corps troops captured and occupied Trier, they were confronted with a new problem. Now that the Allies were in enemy territory, and there were civilians living in the ruins, it was necessary to have a government authority to take care of the needs of the people who were still living in the captured cities. Therefore, the US Army brought a civil affairs' detachment known as G-5, or Military Government, into these liberated cities and towns. The helpless victims of war and refugees who lost their homes and were hungry looked to their liberators to fulfill their needs for food, clothing, and shelter.

On March 3, 1945, a XX Corps G-5 detachment moved into Trier under the leadership of Colonel John W. Libcke, who had joined the Corps in England. Most of the eighty thousand citizens of Trier had fled or been killed, as 95% of the city had been destroyed. Approximately two thousand of the city's original population returned while Trier was administered by the XX Corps. All inhabitants were required to appear before Military Government G-5 personnel for a thorough check of their past lives under the Nazis and whether they were sympathetic to the former German government. It was imperative to ferret out Nazi collaborators and those people who might be dangerous to the community. During these interviews, the qualifications and occupational skills of each person were listed and workers with trades were put to work. Bakeries were inspected for capacity to produce and distribute bread, which was rationed. All foodstuffs and fuels were controlled. Normal city government was again restored in order to provide electricity, water, sanitation, and police and fire protection. All German civilians had to carry clearance papers as they moved about, and they even needed advance permission to go out of the city to a farm field. G-5 had set up road blocks and control points where passes were checked and violators of travel regulations were fined.

During previous years, the Nazi government rounded up and arrested German civilians who opposed the regime and sent them to concentration or work camps. In addition, many people in countries that were overrun by the German armies were deported to these same work camps. These people were forced to work long hours in forestry, road building, mining, manufacturing, and farming projects. Their living conditions were pitiable, with inadequate housing and barely enough food to sustain life. The German Army also maintained camps or "stalags" for prisoners of war at various locations within Germany.

As XX Corps troops advanced through the German lands they overran these camps, and the German guards ran away, thus permitting the prisoners to flee. Prisoners of war clamored to leave the POW camps and get back to their homes. These people were accommodated in some of the captured towns that had not been damaged until they could be evacuated to their homes. Army camps in Germany were used to house and feed DPs (displaced persons). American troops captured warehouses and trains that were stocked with food and clothing that was given to the refugees. There was a problem of severe looting because of a shortage of guards. Each American truck that returned to rear areas carried a capacity load of people heading to G-5 camps. Many other people, old and young, walked across the land, carrying baskets and bags containing all of their worldly possessions and heading to wherever their home was. At one of the Corps' displaced persons center, a former prisoner of war, an Italian doctor, was placed in charge of giving medical aid to the people with medical supplies provided by the US Army. As our XX Corps Headquarters advanced through Germany, we encountered many of these people as they traveled to assembly camps or to their home towns. Their faces revealed the suffering they had endured under the iron rule of the Nazi government.

By March 12, the Saar–Moselle Triangle was in the hands of XX Corps Infantry and Armored Divisions, and they were poised for an all-out clearing of the Siegfried Line that was in its zone of action. The next objective was to move into a region of Germany known as the Palatinate or the Pfalz in the German language.

The western and northern part of the Palatinate is densely forested and mountainous with deeply eroded river valleys. The Rhine River forms the eastern border of the Palatinate. More than one-third of the region contains the largest forest in Germany. The eastern part of the Palatinate consists of vineyards and winemaking and contains the famous German Wine Route (Deutsche Weinstrasse). The most important cities there are Mainz, Ludwigshafen, Koblenz, Trier, Kaiserslautern, and Worms.

From March 14 to 17, XX Corps troops battered the defenses of the Siegfried Line, and they succeeded in punching holes through the dragon's teeth of tetrahedrons, bunkers, barbed wire, and land mines. (A tetrahedron is a polyhedron with four faces.) The German defenders in the pillboxes fought back for a while but eventually they were captured, killed, or fled. Armored and Infantry troops fought their way across the difficult terrain of the Palatinate after constructing eleven floating Bailey bridges across the Saar river. Town after town was captured, some with fierce fighting and others that were abandoned. During this four-day period, our GIs had killed 2,300 enemy troops and captured 6,719. The defenses of the impregnable Siegfried Line were shattered.

Command Post No. 19

Saarburg, Germany
A hoch schule (High School)
March 18–20, 1945

After spending nearly four months (119 days) and the entire winter of 1944–1945 in the girl's high school in Thionville, our XX Corps Headquarters moved its CP into Germany. It was very exciting when we got the order to pack up and move into the country of the enemy, but we felt a little sad to leave Thionville because of all the experiences and memories we had from our long stay there during the bitter winter.

As the front lines spread across the Palatinate, General Walker needed to be closer to the action, so we moved twenty-five miles from Thionville to the German city of Saarburg on the Saar River. We occupied another building which had been used as a high school but now was abandoned. As American troops headed to Saarburg, teachers and students moved out. It was interesting to browse through the books and lessons we found in the classrooms as well as the propaganda posters and filmstrips. I found a copy of the book *Mein Kampf*, written by Adolf Hitler, which I took home as a souvenir.

The German situation in the Palatinate became more and more disorganized. General Walker laid out his strategy for clearing the Germans out of the Palatinate and pushing them across the Rhine River. The 12th Armored Division and the 94th and 80th Infantry Divisions headed toward the Rhine city of Worms. The Germans continued to flee in long columns of motor vehicles east from Kaiserslautern. Allied planes firing rockets and machine guns strafed and bombed the retreating forces.

Command Post No. 20

St. Wendel, Germany
A former Monastery
March 20–22, 1945

The sweep through the Palatinate turned the fighting into a rout for the German armies, and our XX Corps Headquarters moved to the city of St. Wendel. We set up our offices and quarters in a beautiful church building which originally had been a monastery, but the Nazis turned it into an advanced school for SS troopers. It was ironic to find that this church building with its large stained glass rose window and elegant interior that was originally built to the glory of God had been turned into a school for teaching SS soldiers how to kill, maim, and torture humankind.

Our stay at the St. Wendel monastery lasted only two nights and a full day, so we moved our CP again to a place in the Palatinate called Weiherhof, where we settled into a large school building.

Command Post No. 21

Weiherhof near Meisenheim
A School for Hitler Youth
March 22–29, 1945

This school building was on a hill in the countryside near the small village of Meisenheim. We now were only thirty-five miles from the large city of Mainz on the Rhine River. This school was used by children who were ten to fourteen years old who were members of the elite "Hitler Jugend" or Hitler Youth Organization. Propaganda material was visible in every classroom.

The twelve-day sweep across the Palatinate was accomplished by the Third Army's XII Corps on the north and the XX Corps in the center. The south of the Palatinate was overrun by the US Seventh Army. It was a crushing defeat of the German armies, with 42,888 soldiers imprisoned, 4,000 killed, and 7,300 wounded for a total of 54,188 casualties. A twenty-five-mile stretch of the Siegfried Line was destroyed and overrun, and four thousand square miles of rich coal deposits and important industrial sites were captured. On March 24, the entire left bank of the Rhine in the Palatinate was in the hands of the Americans. Here we were at the last great barrier, the wide surging waters that the XX Corps needed to conquer, and beyond it lay the rich heart of North Germany and the great cities of Wiesbaden, Frankfurt, Hanover, Hamburg, and Berlin.

General Patton sent a directive to General Walker that our XX Corps's assignment was to cross the Rhine at Mainz. This was one of the widest points in the entire length of the river, with a bank-to-bank distance of almost two thousand feet. The timing in March was fortunate because the water level was not expected to rise because the snow in the river's source in the Alps would not bring high water until May. The banks of the Rhine at Mainz were relatively flat which would ease the launching and landing of assault boats. The direction of the river at Mainz ran from southeast to northwest, and it was deep with a strong current. Also, the Main River joined the Rhine at the city of Mainz as it flowed straight west; however, it was narrower and slower than the Rhine.

The Third Army's Field Order No. 19 directed that Rhine crossings would be made by the VIII Corps on the left at St. Goar; the XX Corps in the middle at Mainz, and the XII Corps on the right at Oppenheim. The US Navy arrived to assist in the Rhine crossing. They came from the ocean six hundred miles away and brought assault boats and landing craft, LCMs and LCVPs which were manned by the Navy. On the night of March 27, the first assault waves paddled across in assault boats, and they were followed by motor-propelled assault and storm boats. German resistance was scattered and disorganized, and two bridgeheads were established.

The city of Mainz was on the left bank of the Rhine and directly across the river was the city of Wiesbaden. The Corps of Engineers started to build a treadway bridge at Mainz on the morning of the 28th by attaching fifty-four floats together and laying treadway tracks across the pontoons. They named it the "Sunday Punch Bridge." ("Sunday Punch" was the name of the XX Corps weekly newspaper.) This was the longest treadway bridge ever built in the European Theater of Operations, a distance of 1,896 feet. It was completed in twenty-five hours under combat conditions, which was a superior achievement. A smoke screen was laid down, and anti-aircraft protection was provided. The enemy was badly demoralized, and six thousand prisoners were taken. At the town of Friedberg, a thousand German soldiers put down their arms and refused to fight.

Command Post No. 22

Wiesbaden, Germany
Hotel Rose
March 29–31, 1945

The quick success of crossing the Rhine and clearing the city of Wiesbaden a day after the initial assault prompted our XX Corps Commander to order our move to a new CP. On March 29, I gingerly crossed the mighty Rhine River over the "Sunday Punch Treadway Bridge," driving the G-3 Air jeep with Colonel Huckins by my side. This was an awesome moment for both of us, to see and cross this famous river on the long floating bridge. We reached the opposite shore in the big city of Wiesbaden and drove directly to the centrum. Our new home was in the famous and elegant Hotel Rose. During our two-night stay, we felt pretty important in our fancy hotel rooms and eating in the big dining rooms. Our cooks had fun using the hotel's elaborate kitchen and dining facilities.

General Patton was extremely pleased when he got the news about the XX Corps' successful crossing of the Rhine, and he decided to use this occasion by heading for the river, along with several members of his staff. A reporter described this event with these words: "Patton drove to the river and crossed it on the pontoon bridge, stopping in the middle to take a piss in the Rhine. Then he picked up some dirt on the far side as an act of taking possession of the land in emulation of William the Conqueror.

The Main River enters the Rhine where the cities of Wiesbaden and Frankfurt are located. An engineering battalion of the 5th Infantry Division constructed a Bailey bridge across the Main into Frankfurt-am-Main. This city had been heavily shelled earlier, and there was some street fighting, but in two days the city was held by the Americans. Warehouses were found that were filled with tanks, half tracks, guns, and ammunition, as well as stores of food. Many civilians were found hiding in cellars, and when they emerged following their liberation, wide-spread looting began. Six hundred German wounded soldiers were found in a military hospital. Former Wehrmacht members or deserters were ordered to turn themselves in at the City Hall. The tasks were overwhelming, and it was urgent to establish Military Government in Mainz, Wiesbaden, and Frankfurt-am-Main.

Military Government officers had the daunting task of establishing an orderly government to maintain peace and to develop a new economy. In Frankfurt, a former editor of the "Frankfurter Zeitung" was thoroughly screened by counter-intelligence and then was appointed as acting burgomeister for the city. A long-time member of the police force, who had been dismissed by the Nazis for giving out information against them, was appointed acting chief of police. Many former policemen were screened and put on the force. Centers were established for displaced persons, and food for them was obtained from warehouses because looting had become serious. Former community officials who had been removed from office by the Nazis were reinstalled in their former offices or other jobs. Since communication media were destroyed, loudspeaker units traveled around the city to broadcast orders and instructions to the civilian population. Proclamations were posted and broadcast which required the surrender of firearms, weapons such as swords and daggers, radio transmitters, cameras, and binoculars.

During our stay at the Hotel Rose in downtown Wiesbaden, we watched the German civilians come to the central plaza, bringing their weapons as ordered by the military government. The pile of contraband grew into an enormous heap of entangled stuff. Now it was our turn to obtain "souvenirs," and the GIs came to this pile of the spoils of war. I found some fancy ceremonial swords there that dated back to the times of Kaiser Wilhelm and the Prussians. I did not find the highly prized, long-barreled automatic Nazi Luger pistol or the well-known Leica camera with its fantastic Zeiss Icon lens, the best in the world at that time. Some guys did find a limited number of those items, and I was very jealous of them. However, I brought home several Nazi daggers with blades made of the high-quality Solingen stainless steel and fastened into gorgeous, colorful, ornamental handles styled in a spiral swirl and displaying the Nazi swastika.

Command Post No. 23

Alsfeld, Germany
Postamt (Post Office Building)
March 31–April 3, 1945

The divisions of the XX Corps moved swiftly through enemy territory, encountering feeble resistance. The Fulda river, which flowed north, went through the large manufacturing city of Kassel, which was the next big target. There was only moderate resistance from other towns along the Fulda, and our troops found many bridges intact, so the river was crossed with little effort.

General Walker decided it was imperative to move the Corps Headquarters closer to the fast-moving front, so on March 31, we moved to the city of Alsfeld, about fifty miles south of Kassel. For the first time, we traveled on the German Autobahn which went through the cities of Wiesbaden and Frankfurt-am-Main in the direction of Alsfeld. This was our first sight of the superhighways that Hitler had built all across Germany during the 1930s and 1940s using slave labor.

These marvels of engineering were impressive because no highways as elaborate as these were found in America. They were constructed of concrete with two lanes in each direction separated by a wide median strip. No surface roads entered the Autobahn directly but instead crossed on overpasses and underpasses. There were fantastic bridges that crossed ravines and gorges as well as sweeping exit and entry ramps. Hitler's plan for building these superhighways was primarily for military reasons. Now our American Armies were speeding over these same roadways even though our vehicles had to detour around the destroyed bridges and overpasses. No mines or other obstacles were encountered, and the German armies were in retreat.

We saw some incredible sights as we advanced along the Autobahn. There were groups of refugees and forced laborers standing along the roadside, waving joyfully as we passed by. Some of these people were liberated from worker's camps, and they were dirty, unkempt, ragged, and hungry, but they stood and sat by the roadside and waved and cheered as the Americans drove past them. When we drove through German towns, white flags were flying from virtually all buildings, and people were leaning out of windows and waving at us. Captured Nazi army officers and soldiers were guarded as they sat on the banks of the Autobahn and watched in disbelief as the American tanks, half-tracks, and trucks whizzed by them into the heart of their Fatherland.

In Alsfeld, we moved into a large building that housed the Postamt, or post office, where we stayed for three nights. The building had been abandoned for some time, so all postal equipment and stamps had been removed. By April 4, the XX Corps's troops had again spread out over an extensive area, and they met only scattered enemy resistance. Airfields were overrun and partially assembled fighter planes were captured. In the liberated towns, citizens looted the warehouses which contained crates of shoes, food, clothing, and other commodities.

After the fall of Kassel, XX Corps divisions continued their drive east toward the cities of Eisenach, Gotha, Erfurt, and Weimar. They were all connected with Autobahns. It was time for us to move east too to be closer to the fluid front lines. On April 3, we set up our next CP in the small dorf of Falkenberg, about ten miles south of Kassel.

Command Post No. 24

Falkenberg, Germany
Schloss Falkenberg
April 3–10, 1945

The large German manufacturing company called Henschel und Sohn was located in Kassel. It was established in the early 1800s by Georg Christian Carl Henschel and his son Carl Anton Henschel when they started manufacturing locomotives, and later expanded into building other transportation equipment such as trucks, buses, and trolleybuses. Prior to World War I, the Henschel engineering works began building armored fighting vehicles, known as tanks, or "panzerkampfwagen." During World War II, the company had eight thousand workers working in two shifts, with extensive use of slave laborers.

The tanks that were manufactured were the Panzer, Panther, and, later in the war, the most dreaded Tiger tanks. The King Tiger (Konigstiger II) tanks were huge armored vehicles built on a Porsche chassis and protected on the front of the tank with a steel plate that was 150mm thick. The main gun on the turret of the tank was twenty feet long and was a variation of the 88mm anti-aircraft gun. Each round it fired weighed forty pounds. This 45-ton behemoth was an awesome fighting machine that was greatly feared and respected by the Allies.

The chief engineer and designer of the tank program at Henschel was Dr. Erwin Aders. He lived with his family in the huge Schloss Falkenberg, located a few kilometers south of Kassel in Falkenberg. We arrived at the Schloss Falkenberg in early afternoon of April 3. The Aders family had fled, but all the elegant furnishings were still in place. The three-story building had the typical German half-timber decorations and many windows. It was built in the shape of a quadrangle surrounding a courtyard with one opening to the outside. There was sufficient room in this complex to house our entire headquarters staff of 120 men.

We set up our offices in various rooms located on the ground level on the courtyard side of the building. We set up our sleeping cots in rooms in the upper floors. It was late afternoon on April 3 when I left the G-3 Air office to go on an errand to another office across the inner court. I was the only person in the courtyard, and I heard the sound of an approaching vehicle, so I turned to see who it might be. To my great surprise, I noticed that the plate on the front bumper of the command jeep displayed four shiny red stars. I knew immediately that it was General George S. Patton Jr.! The General's driver drove directly to where I was standing and stopped next to me. The top of the jeep was folded down into an open position, and the commander of the US Third Army grabbed the top of the windshield with both hands as he stood up. His six foot two inch frame towered above the vehicle, and my eyes focused on his glossy helmet, which reportedly was covered with thirty-two layers of lacquer. In its center was a cluster of four silver stars, the rank of a "full general." On his right hip, his leather belt held his pearl-handled pistol which protruded from the leather holster. It was a beauty which media reporters loved to write about.

As I froze into position in front of the general, he said, "Hello, Sergeant." I answered, "Yes, sir, General," and I saluted crisply and clicked my heels together. General Patton saluted back and then asked me "Sergeant, where in the goddamn hell can I find your fucking General Walker?" I then said, "Sir, General Walker's office is inside the first door on the ground level" as I pointed in that direction. Patton said, "Thank you, Sergeant," and we both saluted each other as the driver headed toward Walker's office door. Having these brief words with General Patton was an awesome event for me, and I heard directly some of the vulgar and foul terms that he was known for using when he spoke. Aside from this, General Patton was one of the greatest American generals of World War II, and I greatly respected the man.

Events were moving very rapidly as XX Corps infantry and armored divisions captured town after town. Enemy resistance was weak and sporadic, and their armies were retreating eastward. As American troops entered these cities, they liberated American, British, and French prisoners of war from their camps as well as slave laborers from their concentration camps. German cities in the XX Corps zone had the familiar names of Eisenach (the birthplace of Johann Sebastian Bach and where Martin Luther lived), Erfurt (where Luther lived as a student and a monk), Gotha (a large insurance and publishing center), Weimar (the former headquarters of the Weimar Republic), and the city of Jena, the headquarters of the huge optical factory, Carl Zeiss, manufacturer of the highest quality optics and lenses for Leica cameras, telescopes, and microscopes. I was not able to make any side trips to Eisenach and Erfurt because we were moving through Germany so swiftly.

Command Post No. 25

Treffurt, Germany
Dorfschule
April 10–11, 1945

We lived in the Schloss Falkenberg for seven nights where we enjoyed elegant living with all the amenities found in these fine quarters. The Corps' divisions were moving rapidly and with little resistance in the state of Thuringia, so we moved again, this time to Treffurt, ten miles north of Eisenach. We stayed only one night in Treffurt in the only school house in this small dorf or town. The stone building was undamaged and consisted of three stories with high gables and high windows. Its architecture was very nice.

Command Post No. 26

Gotha, Germany
Insurance Company Office
April 11–13, 1945

The city of Gotha lies midway between Eisenach and Erfurt, a short distance of twenty-eight miles, and we moved there on April 11. Our new CP was set up in a large insurance company office building in downtown Gotha called Versicherungs Gesellschaft. It was an elegant structure built with marble blocks, with tall windows and pillars at the front entrance. This office had been evacuated by its employees on short notice as American troops entered the city, so all the desks and files were left in the condition that the employees had been working on when they departed. We set up our offices in the employee work areas and used other offices to sleep in. The Corps' kitchen was set up in the Company's parking lot. The Corps Commander issued strict orders to all personnel that we should not tamper with, disturb, displace, or examine any insurance documents or records that were in desk drawers or in files. Since this was an insurance company, it would have caused a horrible business disaster if anyone would have done this, so nothing in this office was touched by Corps personnel.

On Friday morning, April 13, reveille was sounded at 0600 hours. My cot was placed next to a large mahogany desk that belonged to an insurance executive. My buddies had also set their cots in various places around the large rooms that held many desks for office workers. When we awoke, the first words we heard from the OD (officer of the day) were: "President Roosevelt is dead." It was shocking news, and we were surprised because we hadn't heard any news about his recent health. At the hour we heard this news it was late evening the night before on April 12 back in the States when he died.

Franklin Delano Roosevelt was born on January 30, 1882, and died at the age of sixty-three years in Warm Springs, Georgia. He had acquired the disease of infantile paralysis, later called polio, when he was a young man, and became paralyzed from his waist down to his feet. He could not walk or stand, but only sat in a wheelchair. During his entire presidency, the American people only saw pictures of him from the waist up. Journalists and news photographers had orders to never speak about his paralysis or to photograph him in the wheelchair. In official photographs with world leaders during the war, such as with Churchill and Stalin, the group picture always showed them sitting, and without Roosevelt's wheelchair.

Roosevelt left Washington a few days before he died and traveled by train to Georgia, where he had frequently spent time in the past to enjoy the healing effects of the mineral baths at Warm Springs. On April 12, he suffered a massive stroke and died a few hours later. FDR set a new precedent in American politics because he was re-elected president for a third and then a fourth term. The excuse given by his Democrat Party was that the war was going on, and it was not wise to "change horses in mid-stream," as the popular phrase was used during the months of electioneering before the votes were cast. Thus, in 1941 Roosevelt won his third term, and in November of 1944 he won an unprecedented fourth term, having served the country for a total of twelve years. (I did not vote for Roosevelt in that election, which was the very first time in my life that I could vote. I had cast my absentee ballot on October 6, 1944 in Jarny, France.)

Harry S. Truman was the vice president, and now took over the leadership of the United States as our new president. We discussed politics with each other that April morning in Gotha, and we wondered what would happen next in the war and in our lives. We all felt that the end of the war was imminent because Germany was collapsing all around us. We also felt a little sad that President Roosevelt missed our great American victory in Europe that occurred just twenty-two days after his death.

Command Post No. 27

Weimar, Germany
Fritz Sauckel's Residence
April 13–18, 1945

On Friday afternoon on April 13 in Gotha, we received orders to move again; this time to the large city of Weimar, thirty miles east of Gotha. The reason was that Corps' infantry and armor were continuing to chase the fleeing German troops with very little resistance. Weimar was the city where the short-lived Weimar Republic was founded in 1919 following the end of the First World War, and which dissolved fourteen years later in 1933. This city was known for its culture and some of its notable residents included Johann von Goethe, Friedrich von Schiller, Franz Liszt, and Johann Sebastian Bach.

Our new CP was in the mansion owned by one of Hitler's high-ranking Nazi henchmen, Fritz Sauckel. It was an enormous building set on top of a small hill with a semi-circular driveway leading to the front entrance of the house. The furnishings were elegant and were left in place after the family fled. Fritz Sauckel held various positions in the Nazi Party, and in 1942, Hitler appointed him to the position of General Plenipotentiary for Labor Development. He reported directly to Hitler. His job was directing and controlling German labor needs, and when labor was in short supply in Germany, Sauckel filled these manpower needs by using harsh methods, deporting approximately five million workers from Eastern-occupied countries and forcing them to work in the German military industrial complex. Sauckel ordered these slave laborers to be exploited "to the highest degree possible at the lowest conceivable degree of expenditure." He was responsible for the death of thousands of Jewish workers in Poland.

At the Nuremberg War Trials, Fritz Sauckel was found guilty of war crimes and crimes against humanity. He was hanged on October 16, 1946. His last words were: "I die innocent, my sentence is unjust. God protect Germany!" It was an awesome experience that my buddies and I lived in the elegant home of this Nazi war criminal for five days.

Upon our arrival in Weimar, we heard the disturbing news about the discoveries of several Nazi concentration camps. The next day, we were ordered to visit one of these horrible death camps that had been found only a few miles from our CP in Weimar. The horrors that I saw and experienced there were the most unbelievable and nauseating sights that I had ever witnessed, and they made a very profound impression on my mind that has stayed with me for my entire life. That dreadful place was called the Ohrdruf Concentration Camp.

CHAPTER 20

Ohrdruf: A Nazi Death Camp

THE SMALL TOWN OF OHRDRUF, Germany, is located ten miles south of Gotha in the state of Thuringia. The local residents delighted in its history because it was in this town where Johann Sebastian Bach composed some of his music. It also appeared like any other ordinary, unimpressive town that the American military troops had passed through on their sweep through Germany, except this time it was different following a horrible discovery. The 80th Infantry Division and the 4th Armored Division, both attached to the XX Corps, liberated the local townsfolk; however, when they came to the outskirts of the city, they discovered a Nazi concentration camp that had been abandoned by its commanders just hours before the American patrols arrived. Inside the camp they found piles of human bodies, some covered with lime and others partially incinerated, and still other corpses lying in a field ready to be buried in open trenches.

This was the Ohrdruf Concentration Camp, a Nazi forced labor and extermination camp located twenty-five miles southwest of Erfurt. The Ohrdruf camp was created in November 1944 and supplied slave labor for the construction of a railway to a new communications center in Weimar. Ohrdruf was a sub-camp of the major concentration camp network of Buchenwald, which was located four miles from Weimar. The Buchenwald network had 174 sub-camps and external commandos, or members, and Ohrdruf was one of them. External commando means a "work team."

On April 4, 1945, Ohrdruf was the first Nazi concentration camp liberated by the US Army. One month before its discovery, Ohrdruf had a prisoner population of some 11,700, but during the days prior to its liberation, the German SS evacuated nearly all of the prisoners on death marches to Buchenwald. The prisoners who were too ill to walk were killed by the SS guards.

When Gen. Dwight D. Eisenhower, Supreme Commander of Allied Forces in Europe, was informed about this gruesome discovery, he went to the camp on April 12 with Gen. Omar Bradley and Gen. George S. Patton, whose 4th Armored Division discovered this holocaust. Eisenhower was appalled at "the visual evidence and verbal testimony of starvation, cruelty, and bestiality which were so overpowering as to leave me a bit sick." Eisenhower said, "I made the visit deliberately, in order to be in a position to give first hand evidence of these things if ever, in the future, there develops a tendency to charge these allegations merely to 'propaganda.'"

General Patton could not bring himself to enter a shed that contained the naked bodies of prisoners which were stacked into piles. He got sick and vomited because of the horrible sight and smell of death. This made a powerful impression on Patton, and he wrote the following entry in his diary that evening:

> "In a shed was a pile of about 40 completely naked human bodies in the last stages of emaciation. These bodies were lightly sprinkled with lime, not for the purposes of destroying them, but for the purpose of removing the stench. When the shed was full—I presume its capacity to be about 200, the bodies were taken to a pit a mile from the camp where they were buried. The inmates claimed that 3,000 men, who had been either shot in the head or who had died of starvation, had been so buried since the 1st of January. When we began to approach with our troops, the Germans thought it expedient to remove the evidence of their crime. Therefore, they had some of the slaves exhume the bodies and place them on a mammoth griddle composed of 60-centimeter railway tracks laid on brick foundations. They poured pitch on the bodies and then built a fire of pinewood and coal under them. They were not very successful in their operations because there was a pile of human bones, skulls, charred torsos on or under the griddle which must have accounted for many hundreds."

When General Eisenhower returned to his headquarters after his visit to Ohrdruf, he sent an order to his generals that every American soldier who was stationed in the vicinity of the Ohrdruf camp was to go there to see these atrocities because Ike wanted numerous eye witnesses who would corroborate the truth of this horrendous event to the world. On April 19, Eisenhower sent a cable to Gen. George C. Marshall in Washington with a request to bring members of Congress and journalists to see the newly liberated concentration camps, since more camps, like Buchenwald, had been found after Ohrdruf. He felt that the American public needed to know the truth about these Nazi atrocities. Immediate permission was given for various delegations to visit the camps by President Truman and Secretary of War Henry L. Stimson. We received this top priority order to go to the Ohrdruf camp to see for ourselves the startling discoveries of crimes to humanity as well.

The following morning, Saturday, April 14, 1945, I warmed up the motor of my G-3 Air Department jeep and my boss, Col. John Huckins, joined me along with two other guys. We traveled southwest on the Autobahn from Weimar to Ohrdruf, a distance of thirty-three miles. There were many American soldiers at the camp when we arrived.

This is my eyewitness story

Ohrdruf Concentration Camp was located in a partially cleared forest of pine trees with several open areas that contained various camp buildings. The entire camp was enclosed with two rows of twelve-foot high barbed wire fences set a few feet apart. A wooden guard tower was built about fifteen feet above the ground on a platform set upon four poles. The guard booth was enclosed on three sides with boards and a roof. A sloping wooden ladder led up to the platform.

I walked through the open gate leading to the camp's main street. This main gate consisted of two parts that swung into the middle when it was closed. Each ten-foot-high section was covered with criss-crossed barbed wire. The main street was an unpaved, dirt road.

Drab, one-story barracks buildings stood on both sides of the street. Several were painted green,

Ohrdruf Concentration Camp, Ohrdruf, Germany (April 14, 1945)

but most of them badly needed fresh coats of paint. These barracks contained windows that were tall and narrow and had tube-like metal chimneys protruding from the roofs. Living conditions within these barracks were very dismal for the prisoners. Their bunks were four tiers in height and their "mattresses" were straw, like farmers provide for cows to lie on; they had no blankets but merely slept in flimsy, ragged, and torn clothes.

The stench from urine, feces, and filthy, unwashed clothing was so overpowering that it took my breath away. I covered my nose and mouth with my hand in a vain attempt to ease the nauseating feeling I had in my stomach. The men who had lived in this inhuman place were not here when I looked at their bunks—I would find them later in a shed or laid on the ground next to an open trench in a nearby field.

Ohrdruf Concentration Camp, Ohrdruf, Germany (April 14, 1945)

What I had just seen left me in a daze as I left the barracks and resumed my walk on the main street. At the end of the rows of barracks, the street widened into a courtyard large enough to hold a large group of men. They probably stood here to hear orders and announcements.

In the yard I noticed a contraption which I immediately recognized as a gallows, because there were two vertical rough-hewn beams that were bolted to supporting braces on the ground. A horizontal board was placed between the vertical poles about two feet above the ground. It served as a platform on which prisoners stood. A cross beam at the top connected the two vertical poles, and two iron fasteners hung down from it. The prisoners stood on this gallows with their arms raised and their wrists shackled to the fasteners above them. This horrible device was evidently used frequently by the SS guards to whip and beat the inmates, probably until they died.

A few yards beyond the gallows, in the center of the square, I came upon a pile of dead men lying in disarray. Each one had a bullet hole in his head. They had been murdered by SS guards just hours before American troops had entered the camp. Camp officials had been moving some Ohrdruf inmates to the Buchenwald camp by forced marches in order to avoid the approaching US Army, but these poor men lying at my feet were evidently too weak to make the march, so they were hastily exterminated. These men were dressed in shabby, striped, prisoner clothes; some wore boots and others were barefooted.

There were approximately thirty bodies lying in various positions as they collapsed from the bullets in their heads. I felt sick and stunned as I looked into their faces, and my thoughts turned to the families of these men who lived back in their home countries, who mercifully would not see this horrible death of their loved ones. These men at Ohrdruf were Slavic

Ohrdruf Concentration Camp, Ohrdruf, Germany (April 14, 1945)

people from nations in Eastern Europe and were brought to Germany to live in this slave labor camp while they worked on the railroad construction project.

Ohrdruf Concentration Camp, Ohrdruf, Germany (April 14, 1945)

Several one-story administrative buildings stood on one side of this compound, which contained the offices of the commandant and his officers as well as the quarters for the SS guards. When I entered this office, I noticed that the desks and work areas were hastily abandoned by the officers when they fled before American troops arrived. It soon became evident that this office was a weird place, and the men who ran this camp engaged in ghoulish fetishes of collecting "human souvenirs."

The book lying on the desk had a cover made of human skin. The lamp shades on the desk lamps were made from human skin, and there were picture frames that contained skin showing tattoos. There were various ornaments strewn around the office made from the skin of the slaves who were killed, but the most grisly object was a coin purse with its open end tied with a draw string. To my great horror, I discovered that this was made from the external sac of skin from a man's scrotum. This truly was a lurid place which jostled my stunned brain into total disbelief.

My head kept spinning as I walked on a path between buildings that led to some storage sheds. The horror became worse when I looked through the open door of this dilapidated building. I looked upon a huge pile of naked corpses, one on top of another and stacked in alternate directions with the head of one body next to the feet of another. It was a pile of human beings that resembled a stack of cordwood in a wood shed. I felt much too sick to count

Ohrdruf Concentration Camp, Ohrdruf, Germany (April 14, 1945)

the number of corpses, but there were probably fifty to sixty dead men. I noticed their protruding ribs, barely covered with skin, thighs about the size of my wrists, and arms without muscles but only the bone wrapped in skin. Heads were shaved. All of these emaciated bodies were covered with quicklime in an attempt to hasten the decay of the corpses. (Quicklime is a white caustic powder, calcium oxide, made from crushed limestone. It is used in manufacturing, waste treatment, and in other industrial processes. I remember my Dad sprinkling quicklime into our outdoor privy on the farm where I grew up.)

The odor of decaying flesh that permeated this shed filled my nostrils with an overpowering stench, and as I turned away, I could barely stifle my urgent feeling to vomit. My eyes became blurred, and I was in a daze as I walked past several storage buildings that brought me to an open field. The horrific scenes of human torture, suffering, and death did not end... there was more to witness.

In this field, the Germans had laid some railroad ties criss-crossed with rails, forming a grate over a fire pit. Firewood was placed between the rails, and the bodies of dead prisoners were laid across the rails on top of the wood... like a human sacrifice. As I looked on this scene, the feeling of numbness in my body and soul reached its utmost, and my eyes were blurred from the tears that I couldn't hold back. Here were the charred remains of these poor slaves, whose emaciated bodies were totally burned or partially charred. The blackened faces and sunken eyes showed the agony they suffered in the final minutes of their lives. Now a new sensation overcame me; it was the smell—the very nauseating odor of burned flesh. My nose absorbed this unfamiliar odor, and it hit my brain with a jolt. The burned flesh had a very sweet and nauseating smell which reminded me of the smell of a gardenia, a flower that smells so sweet that your stomach feels nausea.

(Note: The sweet, nauseating smell that I experienced that day at Ohrdruf had burned so deeply into my senses in my brain that I "smelled" it every day for some three or four months following this horrendous encounter with death.)

A little further on in this field, I came upon scores of corpses laid in rows on this grassy slope. The naked bodies were spaced a couple of feet apart and all faced in one direction. Their feet were crossed at the ankles, and a narrow board the same length of their bodies, laid on top of each corpse. There were more rows of dead men, but their bodies were

Ohrdruf Concentration Camp, Ohrdruf, Germany (April 14, 1945)

covered with white sheets. Nearby, long trenches had been dug, and it looked like the German administrators had planned to bury these slaves in the trenches but were unable to complete the job when US troops overran the camp.

After spending several hours at the Orhdruf Concentration Camp, Colonel Huckins and I agreed we had endured enough horror, so I got the jeep and we drove back to our CP in Weimar. Two other guys rode with us, and on the trip back, there was complete silence, but we all knew the thoughts that were racing through each other's minds. I don't remember eating any meals the rest of that day. The nauseating, foul smell of burned human flesh was extremely powerful in my nostrils and brain, and it wouldn't go away.

Ohrdruf Concentration Camp, Ohrdruf, Germany (April 14, 1945)

That evening I wrote a letter home, but I didn't think I should send it to my parents and upset them with this horrible, unbelievable news. Instead, I sent it to my brother Amos, and I asked him to decide whether our parents should read it. However, as it turned out, the horrific news of the discoveries of several more Nazi concentration camps in Germany had already spread across the United States as well as the world. Their names were *Ohrdruf, Buchenwald,* and *Dachau!*

Author's letter to his brother published in
FWD Company newspaper (May 1945)

By the time Mom and Dad read my letter to Amie, they had already heard
about these terrible discoveries over the radio. My brother also took my letter to
the hometown newspaper, the *Clintonville Tribune Gazette,* and they published
it immediately. The Four Wheel Drive Auto Company (FWD), where I had
worked before entering the service, had a Company newspaper called *"The
Drive News,"* and they published my letter on its front page in the May 23,
1945 issue, with this heading and introductory paragraph:

"FWD Boy Tells of German Atrocities."

"In a letter to his brother, Amos Schulz of the Purchasing Department and Amos' wife, Sgt. Eugene Schulz, Amos' brother, formerly of the FWD Sales Department, gives his eye witness account of the horrible atrocities found by Americans in a German prison camp. So that we may all read, from the pen of one of our own boys, the deeds of these mad men, his letter is reprinted in part below."

This is my eye witness letter that I sent home..........

Saturday, April 14, 1945

Dear Amie,

I want to tell you of an experience that I had and one which I never want to see again—ever. When I tell you this story you will actually tell me I'm a liar. You will say that nothing like that could ever happen. I didn't believe it—but I do now.

I visited and went through a German Concentration Camp not long after it was liberated. It was a sight of horror and terror like the world has never seen. When I read stories of Nazi atrocities and torture in these camps, I took it with a grain of salt. It was unbelievable and a story that a reporter thought up, like an Edgar Allen Poe story. I know different now and it's much more gruesome than papers stated.

I went to this Concentration Camp, and it consisted of barracks in rows with wide streets between. And there before me in the street were about 30 bodies lying in a heap. The men in this camp were Slavic people used for slave labor and deliberately starved until they died. Many were shot. They were without food until all that remained was a skeleton covered with skin. Their thighs were no larger than my wrist.

After a number of men had died, the fanatical Nazis stacked the corpses in a room, one on top of the other, like cordwood, and had sprinkled the naked, stinking bodies with lime, until they had time to bury them. It was a horrible, gruesome, spine-chilling sight and made anybody sick. This is the honest truth and I swear it.

247

While the men were still alive, they were crowded into small rooms to sleep. Their filthy beds were of lousy straw with no blankets or covering. They had to eat their measly food, if any, out of dog dishes, and used the corner of the room for a toilet.

Can you begin to imagine a human being living worse than a hog like these unfortunate men did? No, you can't imagine it, but I **saw** it. In the street was a platform with a cross pole up high on which was a noose and chains. Here they were tied and whipped and beaten before the other prisoners, then shot through the head. All these corpses had been dead for eight days when I was there, and the stench of decayed flesh was unbearable and stifling. The living prisoners had to endure this constantly.

The Nazis also had an oven where they roasted and cremated the bodies; some were charred and half burned when I was there. These are some of the horrible atrocities that I actually saw, the true, cold facts about Nazi brutality. That is what we are fighting against, and what every American should know. I know now.

Just think of the excruciating suffering these innocent people had to suffer. And you think, "Why did God let such things go on?" Humans with souls and minds being treated a thousand times worse than beasts. We walked silently away, and we began to burn with anger; I'm sure each man prayed a prayer to God that the guilty criminals responsible for this would be brought to the awful justice which God Himself will administer. This camp is but one example, and there are many more in Germany where thousands die daily from disease, starvation, torture, and murder.

This is the awful truth, and I hope it hasn't made you sick. But I want you to know it, and read this to anyone else whom you think might want to hear it. If they won't believe this, tell them that when I come home, I'll tell you more, and I have proof too, because I have pictures of it. This was the most horrible experience I've ever had, but yet in a way, I guess it did me some good; perhaps not now, but later. Such is war and how Germany hoped to conquer the world, but God intervened.

Love, Your Brother Eugene

There were countless articles written by journalists and eyewitness individuals about Ohrdruf and the other newly discovered concentration camps. *The Stars and Stripes* published the following account written by its staff correspondent, James Cannon, who reported about the reaction of the citizens of Ohrdruf when they were ordered to visit the camp by an American military officer.

THE STARS AND STRIPES

April 10, 1945
We Weren't to Blame, They Said, When Slaves Died
By James Cannon, Staff Correspondent

OHRDRUF, GERMANY, April 9, 1945 (Delayed)
The mayor of Ohrdruf did not come back today to the concentration camp on the hill above his town. He had seen what was behind the vines of barbed wire yesterday. Last night he hanged himself. But all those who became big and rich under Fascism today stood in the filthy street between the shacks of this community of pain. All those who had found Nazism a profitable faith came in their well-cut suits.

At the end of the street lay the 30 bodies of the murdered labor slaves. Behind the barracks stacked in a shed were forty more lime-devoured corpses. Around the bend of the road was the pyre of railroad ties where the fire-blackened bones and ashes lay in the sprinkling rain. Beyond the grill was a great pit where 2,000 lay buried after being beaten, starved, and shot to death by their Nazi conquerors.

One was said by escaped inmates to be an American paratrooper, an American flyer or an American-born Pole civilian. No one was certain. But in that horrible bivouac sprawled German political prisoners, German-Jews, and citizens from all the countries the Nazis have invaded.

Col. Hayden Sears, of Boston, commander of CCB 4th Armored Division told them why they were here on the hill. "While you spoke of your culture this was going on in your country," said Sears, a great-shouldered man with a big voice he made deliberately small. "You people supported a government that supported this kind of business. Out of decency we shall leave the women here."

They trudged up the street, their women in a whispering knot behind them, and now there was mud on their shiny shoes. They came to a tangle of bodies. The living looked at the dead and the dead stared back at them and there was no sound on the hill. The open-eyed dead were wasted by starvation. Their thighs were sticks and the flesh was as thin and flabby as muslin. You wondered why it had been necessary to shoot them. They would have died from malnutrition in a few days. It seemed impossible that this wasted cluster of corpses could have ever been considered enemies of these well-flashed people from the town at the bottom of the hill.

"Hitler would not have this," said an old man with a disease-withered profile. He was the rich man in Ohrdruf, while only the prisoners of the camp knew want. Above the camp on another hill, a symbol of his loyalty to the party was the castle he had built since he had been rewarded with war contracts for his paint factory.

Two SS guards of the camp screamed as three Russian inmates charged them. The MPs stopped the brawl. One of the guards wept. His nose bled. They were told to go into the stinking shed and they did, walking by the lime-eaten bodies, moving with the fascinated slowness of sightseers at this curious wake. The SS guards proclaimed their innocence as though they had rehearsed the speech and the hysteria of their plea sounded comical. A pain-hunched Belgian prisoner, hobbling on broomstick legs and speaking in a voice that seemed lost in his rope-thin throat, said he had watched them club two men to death.

At the grill in the field, the citizens of Ohrdruf examined the mechanism which turned the burning bodies over the spruce logs. They journeyed to the vast pit where a log stuck out of a rain watered lagoon of blood. They listened while Col. Sears told them they were members of the party who had sanctioned this. War criminals must be tried for those murders, the Colonel said.

But this was not their guilt, the citizens of Ohrdruf explained. They had never shot a man or burned one or used a club. Yes, they were of the same political faith as the executioners. They prospered from the work of these slaves. This camp was in their town, but they had never come here before this day. Therefore, the citizens said, they were blameless.

But were they?

* * * * * * *

On April 11, 1945, US Army troops liberated the Buchenwald Concentration Camp, located only four miles west of the famous city of Weimar. It was ironic that this Nazi death camp was established next to this German city known far and wide for its cultural life. Famous personalities who spent parts of their lives in Weimar were Goethe, Shiller, Franz Liszt, and Johann Sebastian Bach. The poet Goethe used to spend time writing under a beech tree in the quietness of a woods on a large hill known as the Ettersberg. It was at this place that the Nazis built the concentration camp called Buchenwald, which means Beechwood.

At the time of its discovery by American troops, Buchenwald had a population of over 80,000 prisoners. There were also 174 sub-camps (including Ohrdruf) and other external commandos at various other locations in Germany. The official goal of Buchenwald was the destruction of the prisoners by work. Thousands were murdered by work, torture, beatings, starvation, and lack of hygiene. Thousands of other inmates were murdered in the infirmary by lethal injections, medical experiments, and contamination by typhus bacillus. Buchenwald also had cremations and performed the "harvesting" of human skin.

Reuter's News Bureau published the following account in London newspapers:

GERMAN CIVILIANS SEE FOR THEMSELVES

LONDON, April 19, 1945 (Reuter)---
Allied armies are taking steps to insure that German civilians shall see something of the horrors of their concentration and POW camps.

"Germans you meet scoff unbelievingly when you tell them about atrocities committed in their midst and in their time," a News Chronicle correspondent reported from Weimar.

German civilians, he wrote, are now being conducted on tours of these camps, where they see the unburied corpses and the wasted bodies of the dying but not yet dead.

One thousand Weimar citizens toured the Buchenwald camp in groups of 100. They saw blackened skeletons and skulls in the ovens of the crematorium. In the yard outside, they saw a heap of white human ashes and bones.

Men, including uniformed German policemen, were white-faced and shocked. Some of them broke toward the end of the inspection, and several women fainted.

A United Press correspondent reported a liberated British commando told him the Buchenwald camp was a "human experimental station" where Germans injected prisoners with typhus germs and used them to find a cure for phosphorus burns.

A *Stars and Stripes* correspondent with the US First Army wrote these words about the use of human skin made into gruesome "ornaments":

NAZIS' ORNAMENTS MADE FROM SKIN OF THEIR VICTIMS

WITH THE FIRST ARMY, April 21, 1945 (AP)---
Lampshades, bookbindings, and other ornaments made from the skin of Nazi victims who died in the notorious Buchenwald concentration camp were found near Weimar.

Capt. Dabney Penick, of Montclair, New Jersey, and Maj. M. C. Goodwin of Atlanta, found Germans had these hideous souvenirs. "They were sort of a fad which was started by the wife of the prison commandant," Penick said.

There was one piece of skin from a man's chest mounted on a board and covered with cellophane. Some German had seen the figure of a nude woman tattooed on a prisoner's chest. The section was mounted on a board apparently for wall decoration, Capt. Penick said.

* * * * * * *

One of the most notorious camps was surrendered to the American Seventh Army on the 29th of April, 1945. It was the infamous Dachau Concentration Camp located ten miles northwest of Munich. It was the first such camp established by the Nazi leaders, as early as 1933, and served as a prototype and model for other concentration camps that followed. Almost every community in Germany had citizens that were taken away to the Dachau camp, which resulted in a popular jingle spoken by the people which said:

"Dear God, make me dumb,
that I may not to Dachau come."

A total of more than 200,000 prisoners from thirty countries were housed at Dachau from its inception, with two-thirds being political prisoners and one-third being Jews. It was estimated that over 25,000 prisoners died at Dachau plus another 10,000 in its sub-camps, primarily from disease, malnutrition, and suicide. A typhus epidemic swept through the camp in early 1945 which killed many of the weaker prisoners. US troops rounded up the citizens of nearby towns and brought them to the Dachau camp to see for themselves the horrors that these Nazi commanders and SS guards had subjected the prisoners to. Then the local townspeople were ordered to clean up the camp's facilities.

The liberation of these German concentration camps revealed to the world the horrible reality of Nazi brutality to humanity. The proof of the truth of these discoveries of the deeds committed by the leaders of the Nazi regime was reinforced by firsthand journalist accounts, as well as by many eyewitnesses.

I was an eyewitness to this awful truth!

CHAPTER 21

Victory in Europe

FROM THE 4TH OF APRIL through the 13th, the XX Corps Headquarters moved as rapidly as the divisional troops who were attached to it. We remained in Weimar for five days because of the stay-put orders we received from Eisenhower's Supreme Headquarters. Our Ghost Corps had made a lightning advance during the first half of April; some of Germany's largest industrial cities had been captured and eight major rivers had been crossed under enemy fire. The Corps' infantry and armored units had advanced over three hundred miles in nineteen days.

Our advancing troops had found many camps for displaced persons, totaling about a quarter of a million people. This put a huge burden on Military Government personnel. Looting was a large issue which required extra troops to maintain order and guard warehouses and other installations. City officials needed to be screened for Nazi sympathizers; weapons had to be turned in. Travel was stopped, and curfews and people controls were set up.

During the rapid advances of our troops, supplies became a serious problem. The five-gallon gasoline can became a scarce item because supply dumps were widely scattered. The bridging material used for Bailey bridges was scarce when new rivers needed crossing because they were still in place over rivers in back areas. In those rear areas, permanent bridges were built as rapidly as possible so that the Bailey bridge materials could be sent to forward areas. The very hard usage left their marks on our trucks, and the older vehicles were no longer repairable so they were abandoned.

It was during this time that Third Army authorities heard some disturbing news that huge quantities of money and art stolen by the Nazis was buried in a deep salt mine in the State of Thuringer in the newly liberated combat zone. General Patton's troops occupied the land where the salt mine was found, and Patton summoned Generals Eisenhower and Bradley to join him for the descent into the old mine. A German citizen took them down the elevator shaft on a rickety wooden platform that served as an elevator. At the bottom of the mine, the Generals were astounded to find stacks of gold bars and gold coins. There were boxes which contained about three billion reichs-marks. Various valises were bulging with loot, jewelry, and personal items that were confiscated by the Nazis from prisoners who were sent to concentration camps. The art treasures were stolen from French art museums and from collections found in private homes.

General Eisenhower, upon seeing this unbelievable stash of stolen gold and art treasures, told Patton to immediately save them and remove them to the Reichsbank in Frankfurt before the Russian Army arrived on the scene. Patton wasted no time and arranged for cargo trucks, tanks, and air cover along with a battalion of Rangers to move the loot to Frankfurt. The move to safety was successful.

Our Corps' location at Weimar was the limit of our advance to the east and farther east than any other unit in the European Theater of Operations. We were advancing in a northeasterly direction toward Berlin, and from Weimar we were only 150 miles away from the greatest prize of all… the capital city of the enemy, where the tyrant Adolf Hitler was now directing the war from his underground bunker. Now a new order from SHAEF came to General Patton that required him to change directions for his Third Army. Berlin was not our new objective, but instead, our Corps and its divisions were directed to turn southeast and drive down the Danube Valley toward Vienna, the capital of Austria. The plan was to meet the Russian Army, which was steadily pressing westward through Czechoslovakia into eastern Austria. This new development was a bitter disappointment to Patton, who had been extremely eager to liberate Berlin. He had experienced the same frustration when he was denied bringing his Third Army into Paris. Needless to say, all of us at Corps Headquarters had the same reaction. We had hoped to capture Berlin too!

On the 18th of April, Corps Headquarters moved from Weimar to its new Command Post at Pommersfeldon, a distance of 120 miles. This new CP was near the Autobahn, twelve miles south of Bamberg and twenty miles north of Nurnberg. The XX Corps was selected to be the center of a Third Army wedge to head into the heart of Austria, with the III Corps on our right flank, and the XII Corps on our left.

Command Post No. 28

Pommersfelden, Germany
Schloss Weissenstein
April 18–22, 1945

We were extremely impressed with our new CP in the Schloss Weissenstein because it was a real palace. For five great days, we lived in splendor in the elegant rooms of this sprawling baroque-style architectural gem. There was artwork on all the walls and ceilings, enormous chandeliers, statues, and sculptures everywhere. The elegant furniture had been removed and placed in storage somewhere, but we didn't mind when we set up our cots in these fabulous quarters. Our cooks used the kitchen facilities, and when we went to pick up our chow, we wound through endless halls that were beautifully decorated. Not long after we moved on into Austria, General Patton moved his Third Army Headquarters into Schloss Weissenstein.

All XX Corps troops jumped off on April 20 and fought their way through the hilly and wooded terrain of the Danube Valley. German soldiers were surrendering in droves, and our infantry divisions advanced very quickly as they found roadblocks that were undefended and towns that showed little or no resistance from enemy troops.

Command Post No. 29

Reichenswand, Germany
Jacobean Chateau
April 22–26, 1945

On April 22, we loaded up our trucks with all our equipment and supplies and moved again. We drove through the large city of Nurnberg where we saw the tremendous destruction from Allied bombing. There was not one building that was undamaged. Piles of rubble lay in the streets, and in some places, we drove over these heaps of bricks, stone, and wood that our bulldozers had not yet plowed a drivable path through. Most of the city of Nurnberg lay in utter ruin.

Destruction in Nurnberg, Germany (April 1945)

Destruction in Nurnberg, Germany (April 1945)

XX Corps Headquarters set up its CP in the small village of Reichenswand, located about five miles east of Nurnberg. This chateau had a design of a box-like building that had two round towers at its front which looked like they belonged on a castle. The chateau was surrounded by trees and shrubs, and there was a large garden of flowers in the rear. The setting was very nice. The owners had evacuated earlier, so we had access to the entire complex.

The 65th and 71st Infantry Divisions reached the Danube River on April 25. The great industrial city of Regensburg had been built on the Danube at the point where the river makes an abrupt turn from an east–west direction to the southeast. Corps infantry made assault crossings of the Danube on pontoon bridges and surrounded the city. Preparations for attack were in progress when an offer of surrender was sent to both the 65th and 71st Divisions by the German Major General Leythauser. His unconditional surrender was accepted on April 27. Thus, the XX Corps of the US Third Army completed the siege of Regensburg in record time, the city which had been the Castra Regina of the Roman Empire in ages past.

[Castra Regina, which means "fortress by the River Regan," was originally a Roman fortified camp at the very edge of the empire, founded around AD 90 It is located in today's Alt Stadt, or the Old Town section of Regensburg. It is a maze of medieval streets. During its turbulent history, it served as the capital of Bavaria, free city of the Holy Roman Empire, launch pad of three major Crusades, a prize for Charlemagne and Napoleon, the birthplace of Don Juan, and the death place of Johannes Kepler.]

Command Post No. 30

Burglengenfeld, Germany
Portlandsementwerk
April 26–28, 1945

On April 26, we moved to a town called Burglengenfeld, fifteen miles north of Regensburg. We set up our CP in the office buildings of a huge Portland cement factory that was set in the middle of some farmland, next to some huge hills that were being mined for the limestone used in making cement. This manufacturing facility was in good working condition, as it had not been damaged by bombing or shelling.

On April 27, Corps personnel observed a big event, which was the promotion of our Corps Commander, Major General Walton H. Walker, to Lieutenant General. At mid-morning we all assembled on the lawn in front of the Cement Works' main office building. Spring had arrived as we stood in formation under a grove of flowering fruit trees where we enjoyed the wonderful sweet fragrance of spring flowers. We were quite surprised when General Patton arrived in his command vehicle. He was dressed in a short jacket and high combat boots. He wore his ultra-shiny helmet with its many coats of lacquer; and the four silver stars denoting his rank as full general glittered in the sunlight. A wide, leather belt held his signature weapon in its holster—the white pearl-handled revolver.

At the designated moment during the ceremony, General Patton personally pinned the three stars of the rank of Lieutenant General on General Walker. These same stars had been worn by General Patton who had received them in like manner from General Eisenhower, Supreme Commander of the Allied Forces. This was a joyful day for all of us at Corps Headquarters.

The Author (left with sunglasses) with buddy, Bob Reim, at
American Red Cross Donut Wagon, Germany (1945)

Command Post No. 31

Regensburg, Germany
Palace of the Duke of Thurn and Taxis
April 28—May 2, 1945

The day after General Patton's visit, we moved into the city of Regensburg, where we occupied the palace that belonged to the Duke of Thurn and Taxis. It was built on a high ridge from which we could look down onto the city of Regensburg and the Danube Valley.

"Thurn und Taxis" was a German family that was a big player in the postal services of Europe in the sixteenth century. Ruggiero de Tassis (the name was later changed simply to Taxis) founded the postal service in Innsbruck, and the family held this business for centuries. The service was based in Brussels and reached destinations in Rome, Naples, Spain, Germany, and France by courier. The company lasted until the eighteenth century, but the wealthy family still exists and resides in Regensburg. The palace was unoccupied by the owners, but all of its furnishings were still in place, and we enjoyed our four-day stay in these elegant quarters.

On the morning of May 1, we heard this astounding news: **"Adolf Hitler is dead."**

This news was electrifying as it signaled to all of us that the end of the war was imminent. We knew that the German Wehrmacht was collapsing on all fronts, and enemy soldiers were laying down their arms by the thousands. The Russian Army, which was approaching from the east, had already entered the suburbs of Berlin. The following details of Hitler's death were soon revealed by news outlets.

During the month of April of 1945, Hitler and his staff moved into the Führerbunker, located fifty feet below the Reich Chancellery building in Berlin. This was a huge underground complex containing thirty rooms on two floors. It was bomb-proof and had its own air recycling plant. Here Hitler held daily briefings with his generals and where he issued frantic orders to defend Berlin at all costs.

On April 20, Hitler celebrated his 56th birthday in the bunker. During the day, he emerged from the bunker to meet a group of boys from the Hitler Youth organization and presented them with the German Iron Cross. In honor of his birthday, Hitler asked his aides to distribute chocolates to the troops.

Hitler held a long military conference in the bunker on April 22, where he exclaimed that the end of his Third Reich had come, but that he would stay in Berlin to the end, despite the urging from his staff that he should escape to the mountains and the National Redoubt at Berchtesgaden. Herman Göring, who was Commander of the Luftwaffe and second in command of the Third Reich, sent Hitler a telegram, offering his service to take over leadership of the Reich since Hitler had decided to remain in Berlin to the end. This infuriated Hitler, and he ordered that Göring was to be arrested and jailed. He actually was locked up on April 25.

A couple days later, Hitler received word that Joseph Goebbels' Propaganda Ministry had reported that Hitler's trusted and loyal staff officer, Heinrich Himmler, the SS Reichführer, had tried to contact the Allies to offer Germany's surrender to Eisenhower. When this news was confirmed, Hitler flew into a rage, according to witnesses, and for immediate revenge, he ordered Himmler's personal representative, SS Lt. General Hermann Fegelein, who was in the bunker, and also the husband of Eva Braun's sister, to be taken to the Chancellery garden above the bunker to be shot.

More devastating news from the outside world came into the bunker on April 28, when Hitler was informed of the violent death of his Italian ally, Benito Mussolini. The dictator, along with his mistress, Clara Pettachi, had been shot, and their bodies were hung upside down in a square in Milan. Hitler vowed that he would not have such humiliation, so he considered taking poison and having his body burned.

At midnight on April 28, Hitler married Eva Braun, his long-time mistress. The brief civil ceremony was held in the bunker in Hitler's private sitting room, with a Nazi official performing the job. The small group held a wedding celebration in the bunker's conference room with a champagne breakfast. The wedding couple was joined by Joseph and Magda Goebbels, Martin Bormann, Hitler's top aide, and his two secretaries, Gerda Christian and Traudl Junge.

After breakfast, Hitler and Junge went into an adjacent office where he dictated his Last Will, dated April 29, 1945, 4:00 a.m. It was signed A. Hitler and witnessed by Dr. Joseph Goebbels, Martin Bormann, and Colonel Nicholaus von Below. Hitler also dictated a long document called a "Political Statement," in which he made accusations against the individuals who had betrayed him and blamed the war on international Jewish interests.

Hitler spent the rest of Sunday preparing for his end. He feared that the cyanide capsules that he had ordered might be fake, so he gave the poison to his dog Blondi. The dog died, so he was satisfied. The news that day was dire, as the Russian Army was within the city of Berlin, engaged in street-to-street combat, and exploding shells were shaking the Chancellery.

Early on Monday morning, April 30, Hitler emerged from his private quarters and said farewell to his staff members, military aides, and the inner circle of his closest advisors. Then Hitler and Eva ate their final meal, a vegetarian lunch. He ordered his chauffer to deliver 200 liters of gasoline to the Chancellery garden. The couple then went into their private sitting room to be alone. At 3:30 p.m., after hearing a gunshot, Bormann and Goebbels entered the room and found two bodies. Hitler and Eva both had swallowed cyanide capsules, and Hitler had also shot himself in the right temple. Their marriage lasted less than forty hours.

As they had been instructed, Bormann and Goebbels carried the bodies from the bunker to the Chancellery garden where they doused them with the gasoline that Hitler had ordered earlier. Their bodies were burned completely by repeatedly adding gasoline until nothing remained except bones, which were swept into a canvas and buried in a deep shell crater. The next day, May 1, Goebbels and his wife poisoned their six young children in the bunker, then went to the Chancellery garden where they were shot by their orders to a SS guard, and their bodies were burned. Martin Bormann disappeared, and his body was never found.

The Stars and Stripes, the US Armed Forces newspaper, published a special issue with the headline in 3 ¼ inch bold type. It contained these two words: **"Hitler Dead."** In a subtle and humorous twist, there was a single word enclosed in a box in the top corner of the newspaper. It simply read: **"Kaputt."**

Stars and Stripes newspaper headline, May 2, 1945

Meanwhile, XX Corps' divisions moved toward the Inn River, which formed the border between Germany and Austria. The 13th Armored Division along with three infantry companies entered the city of Braunau, Austria on May 2. This city by the river was the birthplace of Adolf Hitler.

Command Post No. 32

Adldorf, Germany
Schloss Adldorf
May 2–4, 1945

XX Corps Headquarters moved forward again, opening its 32nd Command Post (the 14th in Germany), at the Schloss Adldorf. This castle was located in the German countryside about forty miles from the Inn river. Reports showed that the disorganization of the German Army was complete, and all American units pushed forward more and more rapidly. The rapid moves of our unit often occurred even before towns were cleared of the enemy. Adldorf was still being cleared when Chief of Staff Collier requisitioned a house in the town. It was a schloss that was owned by a countess who lived there. When she learned that it was to be used by the Commanding General of the XX Corps, she asked for "a few honest soldiers" to help dig the family silver service from its burial place in order to serve the General's table properly. Military Police provided the detail, and several chests of old family silver were dug up in the backyard.

Convoy of Hungarian soldiers after surrender,
Adldorf, Germany (May 3, 1945)

Convoy of Hungarian soldiers and refugees after
surrender, Adldorf, Germany (May 3, 1945)

Convoy of Hungarian soldiers and refugees after
surrender, Adldorf, Germany (May 3, 1945)

New orders were received to move Corps Headquarters from Germany
into Austria, across the Inn river. We traveled on the Autobahn to the city of
Passau, a town built where the Danube and Inn Rivers join together. This was
a pretty town where the St. Stephen's Cathedral held a prominent position on

the high rock outcropping astride the two rivers. This beautiful Baroque church was built in 1688, and the city residents boasted that it held Europe's largest organ, with 17,774 pipes and 233 registers. The great Austrian composer, Anton Brückner, who was born in the town of St. Florian near Linz, gave concerts on the Passau organ. The bridges across the Danube were destroyed, but we crossed the rushing river on the Bailey bridge that was hastily built by the engineers. This was the largest Bailey bridge built in the entire European Theater of Operations.

Command Post No. 33

St. Martin, Austria
Schloss of Count Arco Ferdinand and Valle
May 4–June 10, 1945

We moved into our new quarters in the small dorf of St. Martin, Austria, which added a new entry to my list of countries visited in the world. This small town was in a lovely rural area where there were small dairy farms nestled in the foothills of the Austrian Alps. St. Martin was about forty-five miles north of Salzburg and fifty miles west of Linz.

The Schloss of Count Arco Ferdinand and Valle was our home for the next thirty-eight days, and our final Command Post during combat in the ETO. The owners of this schloss had vacated it, and its size accommodated all personnel of Corps Headquarters. The history of this residence was vague, but it apparently belonged to heirs of the Archduke Franz Ferdinand of Austria, who was a prominent political and social person in the early history of Austria.

The Schloss was built in a wooded area on the north side of the town. It consisted of three stories, and the outside walls were covered with ivy vines. Two bronze statues of lions lying on platforms were placed on either side of the shaded pathway that led to the wide gate and doorway, which opened into a large quadrangle. In the center of the quadrangle was a huge fountain with statuary. There were enough rooms that I had my own private one. We began to feel excited that the war would end very quickly when we arrived in Austria.

On May 5, the day after our arrival in St. Martin, the XX Corps received the order from SHAEF (Supreme Headquarters Allied Expeditionary Forces) that the River Enns would be the farthest point of advance of all units attached to the XX Corps because the Russian Army was approaching it from the east. On May 6, General Walker sent a tactical detachment to a command post at Kremsmünster, which was only ten miles west of the River Enns, and seventeen miles south of Linz. The Kremsmünster CP was in a beautiful Benedictine Abbey, which was an ideal location for American military VIP's to assemble for the upcoming formal festivities that were planned when meeting the Russians. All Corps' fighting units consolidated their positions while many units of the German Army were surrendering. The enemy asked where to surrender, but there were so many German units that they were told to pass through American lines to the rear areas.

The 71st Infantry Division sent two platoons to the Inn river on the 5th of May to reconnoiter and make contact with the Russians. On the way, they encountered a German SS Major who asked to surrender his troops to Lt. Samuels of the 71st Division. His corporal, who was designated to be the interpreter, was blindfolded and taken to the German Headquarters which was located in a large castle, along with Lt. Samuels. He spoke with Major General von Gyldenfeld, the Chief of Staff of German Army Group South. There the Germans pointed out on a situation map where the Russian Army was located—thirty-eight miles away at Hofstetten, Austria. The German General seemed anxious to surrender to the Americans rather than to the Russians.

Lt. Samuels' platoon then began their return trip to XX Corps Headquarters, bringing the German General and his staff along with a caravan of SS military police. The formal surrender occurred at 1800 hours on May 7th before General Walker, but it only applied to those German troops who could reach the west bank of the Enns river by midnight on May 8. By the deadline, 90,000 German soldiers surrendered to the XX Corps!

On May 8, another event was taking place at our advanced CP at Kremsmünster. Our Corps' Chief of Staff, General Collier, was present to accept an unconditional surrender of the Slovakian Government, represented by their Prime Minister, Dr. Stephen Tizo, along with the Ministers of Finance, Economy, Education, and Banking of Slovakia.

The time had arrived to contact the Russians, and Collier was assigned the task by Walker. Collier left Corps Headquarters at St. Martin with a small entourage and headed for the Enns river. After crossing the river, they proceeded along the Autobahn, which was littered with burned out Tiger tanks, abandoned half-tracks, huge artillery guns, and a large amount of German equipment on both sides of the highway. No enemy personnel were seen because they had dispersed into the woods for fear of discovery. Soon the detachment came to the top of a hill where they spied a column of machines and men, but were they the Russian Army? A red flare was fired into the air, and after a long wait, an answer was given in the form of a red star shell burst in the sky, whereupon Collier and his staff moved ahead.

When the contact was made, Russian and American soldiers hugged each other while there was much incoherent babbling and shouting. Every Russian soldier had at least a gallon of vodka which was eagerly passed around. Many pictures were taken and cigarettes exchanged. The Russian detachment belonged to the Russian XX Corps, and they provided an escort to Russian Corps Headquarters in Melk, a city located fifty miles west of Vienna. The Russian column was on its way to the Enns river, which was the demarcation line that separated the forces of the United States and the Union of Soviet Socialist Republics (USSR).

Collier and his party, under Russian escort, slowly headed for Melk on the Autobahn. They encountered numerous lend-lease trucks and jeeps which America had sent to Russia before entering the war. There were huge Stalin tanks, tractor-towed canon, horses, mules, oxen, and nearly every type of locomotive. Upon their arrival in Melk, they found the city engaged in wild celebration, with Russian soldiers marching and singing.

Finally, Collier reached the headquarters of the Russian XX Guards Infantry Budapest Corps. Russian guards led them to an upper floor where they were introduced to Major General Michail Ivanovitch Zobelin, who was the Chief of Staff to Lieutenant General Birokoff. Zobelin then called for vodka, and they promptly celebrated the destruction of Der Fuehrer's Wehrmacht. An abundance of food was set before them, including potato salad, caviar, breads, pickled herring, brandy, champagne, and wine.

Someone called "Attention," and General Birokoff, the commander of the Russian XX Guards Infantry Budapest Corps, entered the room. He was a typical Russian: short, squat, steely-blue eyed, and with a shiny shaved head. But his eyes twinkled, and he had a happy face, for this was a great day. The American and Russian generals agreed on a plan for the two armies to meet on a bridge over the Enns River at 1800 hours on that day, May 8, 1945. Colonel Meehan, who was the XX Corps G-1 and Assistant Chief of Staff, was sent back to Corps Headquarters in Kremsmünster to inform Walker about the plans to meet at the river.

After the impromptu party in Melk, Collier and Birokoff traveled in a convoy through the city while they were showered with flowers and kisses. The column moved so slowly that it took three hours to reach the east bank of the Enns River, where a Russian guard of honor was waiting. A similar guard of honor was in place on the American side.

The American and Russian Commanding Generals and their aides marched toward the center of the bridge. Walker and Birokoff saluted each other and shook hands. Walker, in the name of the United States of America, decorated Birokoff with the Legion of Merit, Commander Class. Then he awarded Major General Zobelin, the Russian Chief of Staff, with the Legion of Merit, Officer Class.

After this ceremony on the bridge, the American and Russian delegations drove to a country club near the city of Enns where the Russians hosted their own ceremony. Birokoff, in the name of the Union of Soviet Socialist Republics, decorated Walker with the Order of the War for the Fatherland, First Class. Collier received the Order of the War for the Fatherland, Second Class. The flags of the two Corps' were exchanged as mementos of the occasion, as well as the personal flags of the Commanding Generals. A sumptuous banquet was enjoyed by the two armies, which together had defeated the notorious enemy, Nazi socialism, which now lay in ashes after its attempt to conquer the world.

May 8, 1945—THE WAR IS OVER!

Tuesday, May 8, 1945, General Dwight D. Eisenhower dispatched the following order to General Walker.

FROM: SHAEF FORWARD
TO: CG, XX CORPS

1. A representative of the German High Command signed the unconditional surrender of all German land, sea, and air forces in Europe to the Allied Expeditionary Force and simultaneously to the Soviet High Command at 0141 hours central European time, May 7, under which all forces will cease active operations at 0001 hours May 9.

2. Effective immediately all offensive operations by Allied Expeditionary Forces will cease and troops will remain in present positions. Moves involved in occupational duties will continue. Due to difficulties of communication there may be some delay in similar orders reaching enemy troops so full defensive precautions will be taken.

3. All informed down to and including Division, Tactical Air Commands and Groups, Base Sections, and equivalent. No release will be made to the press pending an announcement by the Heads of the three Governments.

There was a tremendous outpouring of joy and happiness, as well as relief at the XX Corps Headquarters on this V-E Day. Every GI displayed a never-ending smile, and back-slapping and laughing was the rule of the day. Loud whoops and yelling interspersed every conversation. The thoughts of many guys immediately turned to home, and we all began to think about the point system of counting the days until we could return home. But as for me, I would have to wait another seven months before my day of departure would arrive.

The Southern Germany edition of *The Stars and Stripes* on May 8 displayed this headline: "ETO War Ends." In the Paris extra edition, the three-inch headline consisted of only one word: "VICTORY." Celebrations broke out in the world's greatest cities—in Times Square in New York; in Trafalgar Square and Piccadilly Circus in London; and along the Champs-Élysées in Paris.

Stars and Stripes, Paris edition (May 8, 1945)

In New York, Wall Street's ticker tapes and shredded telephone books poured out of office windows into the streets below. Times Square was jammed with office workers, waving, shouting, and screaming with great joy. People crowded churches everywhere for prayers and thanksgiving. Flags were waving and complete strangers kissed pretty girls. Radio stations dropped regular programming and instead they broadcast a constant stream of the good news of the victory of the Allied Forces in Europe.

In London, Britons thronged the streets waving flags and shouting, while many people visited Westminster Abbey for their own prayers of thanksgiving. Loudspeakers carrying the latest victory news were placed in Trafalgar Square, Piccadilly Circus, and other public places. Batteries of powerful electric lights were erected at Buckingham Palace to once again illuminate the King's home, which had been in total blackout for many years. The English pubs had already received adequate stocks of liquor for celebration. RAF bombers roared over London and dipped their wings in a salute of victory and joy.

A warm sun was bathing Paris, where the news of victory was greeted with people embracing and kissing each other and offering numerous toasts with cognac and champagne along the Champs Élysées, Place de l'Opera, and the Place de la Concorde by the Louvre. Workers had hastily erected floodlights at the Place de la Concorde, the Arc de Triomphe, and the Cathedral of Notre Dame. Flags of the Allied Nations were displayed on the main streets.

At XX Corps Headquarters, all personnel were given the day off by Walker. On this day, I resumed writing daily in my diary. We were prohibited from keeping a diary from the day we left New York until today, which covered the entire period that we were in the combat zone. This was my first entry:

"Tuesday, May 8, 1945, St. Martin, Austria, V-E DAY

The day dawned bright and sunny, and it was a very warm and beautiful day. Everyone was happy at the news of the war's end. Right after dinner, Major Unwin, Lt. Dykes, Lt. Petrow and I went on a trip to the lake country. I drove the G-3 Air jeep. We traveled south to the Atter See which is about 20 km long, and surrounded by evergreen and pine-covered cliffs and the snow-covered Alps. The water was blue-green and so clear, and the cool breezes so refreshing.

It was the most beautiful sight I've ever seen.

This is all high-class resort district, and the lake shore is built up with pretty cottages, and every so often high-class resort towns. There are four lakes grouped together, and we drove around them, over mountains and through dense pine and fir forests. Then we drove on to the beautiful Austrian city of Salzburg, surrounded by the towering and white-capped Alps."

I enjoyed this Alpine trip immensely, and it was difficult to describe my inner joy, happiness, and relief that the war was over and that my combat days would now become only a memory. The immersion into the forests, lakes, and mountains of God's beautiful creation was refreshing and good for my soul. I basked in joy and thanksgiving during supper that day with all of my buddies because all of us had safely survived the war.

Spring had arrived, and the days were getting longer, so after supper, Lt. Dykes and I jumped into the jeep and took a ride into the countryside surrounding St. Martin. Suddenly, we saw a large German transport plane flying at a low altitude, apparently looking for a place to land. It was a three-motored JU-52 transport aircraft with the German cross painted on the wings and fuselage. Our G-3 Air pilots used an airstrip near St. Martin where this plane was heading for a landing. I immediately accelerated the jeep, and we sped to the airstrip, where I drove right up to the aircraft just as it was coming to a stop and turning off its engines.

After the noisy motors were shut down, the door at the right side of the fuselage opened up and four German airmen jumped out and surrendered, holding their arms high over their heads. They were dressed in their Luftwaffe uniforms, and each man had a .32 caliber pistol strapped around his waist. Dykes and I quickly grabbed the leather holsters containing the pistols, and after we had disarmed them, I interrogated them in German, since I was raised in a German-speaking family. My partner didn't know any German.

The Luftwaffe captain told me that there were fifteen women and children inside the plane, who were the wives and children of these four air force officers. These German airmen had confiscated this old tri-motored aircraft and placed their families on board, and had escaped from a German military airport in Prague, Czechoslovakia. The Russian Army was on the doorstep of their homes, and they had decided to fly into American territory where they would surrender to our forces rather than be POWs under the Russians. They believed they would get better treatment from the Americans.

I told the pilots to ask their families to leave the plane, and the women, with their young children, emerged one by one. They were a pathetic-looking group, the women dressed in long, dull-colored dresses, with shawls around their shoulders and scarves covering their heads. Each one carried personal items tied in a bundle, and the children were also dressed in worn clothing and carrying small baskets containing personal items. It could be said that these people escaped from the Russians "with only the clothes on their backs."

As Dykes and I looked at this group, I think we both felt as nervous as they did. It was an odd feeling that this group of people who had been our enemy now stood there facing us, who were the victors in this conflict. Now they were asking us for mercy and no doubt felt apprehensive about their future lives as our prisoners.

As I continued to converse with these people, I found that my knowledge of German returned to me. They were pleased to tell about their plight to an

American who could understand them in their own language. It was less than a half-hour after their surrender that several XX Corps officers, including G-5 Military Government personnel as well as Military Police, arrived at the airstrip, because they also had watched the big plane flying around the town of St. Martin and hurried to the airstrip to investigate. After I had briefed our Corps officers about what I had learned from these German air force defectors, the G-5 officers took the women and children back to town for processing, and the MPs took the fliers to the PW cage.

V-E Day, May 8, 1945, turned out to be a quintessential day in my life. The fantastic emotions and events of this day included the tremendous joy and happiness of the war's end; the foremost thought of soon returning home to my family; the trip of motoring through the glorious scenery of God's creation in the Alpine mountains and lakes; celebrating the victory with my closest buddies, with whom I had traveled through the dangers of combat; and finally, the unexpected event of the surrender of the German fliers and their families who escaped from the threat of their capture by the Russians by flying in the old, dilapidated aircraft to our zone of safety. (I also had obtained a nice souvenir which was the .32 caliber pistol that I had taken from the German Luftwaffe captain when he surrendered to me.)

As I lay in bed that night, all these thoughts raced through my mind over and over again, and it took a long time to fall asleep. Above all, I said a prayer of thanks to God and fell asleep with this song on my lips: "Praise to the Lord for He has done marvelous things."

The achievements of the XX Corps, the Ghost Corps, as a gallant fighting machine of the US Third Army, were outstanding and noteworthy. Here is a brief summary of the combat activities of the XX Corps, beginning with the first day in combat, August 1, 1944, at Avranches, France, until its meeting with the Russian Army's XX Corps on the bridge over the Enns river in Austria on May 8, 1945.

Days in Action: 279
Distance: 1,300 miles against the enemy
Prisoners of War: 431,419 (forty-three German divisions)
Accomplishments:
1. Spearheaded the Third Army's drive across France to the Moselle River (600 miles in twenty-eight days). Swept through Germany in twenty-one days, and drove into Austria in twenty days.
2. Captured Metz (First assault capture of it in 1,500 years).
3. Pierced the Siegfried Line in the Saar–Moselle Triangle and captured Trier.

4. Opened the Saar Valley and Palatinate.
5. Assisted in the destruction of German Army Group G.
6. Built longest tactical bridge over the Rhine River at Mainz (1,896 feet).
7. Cut behind the enemy in a one hundred-mile, two-day drive to Kassel.
8. Led the way across Central Germany to Chemnitz, going farther east than any other ground unit.
9. Turned south to attack through the Danube River Valley.
10. Captured German Army Group South.
11. Captured fleeing government officials of Slovakia.
12. Contacted Russian XX Corps, which had driven straight west from Sevastopol.
13. Crossed nearly all of the principal rivers of western Europe.

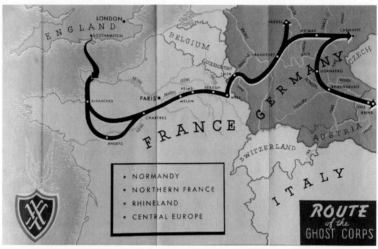

The route of the XX Corps from Normandy to Austria (1944-1945)

Our lives quieted down following V-E Day because with no more combat and the work connected with it we didn't have much to do. We spent the next few days writing letters, reading, cleaning out files, seeing a Hollywood movie almost every night, and just relaxing.

In my G-3 Air Section, there were only three people now, and I had a new boss, Major Norman Linden, who was from Boston. I was chief clerk and my assistant was Bob Reim, who was from Philadelphia. My former boss, Colonel Huckins, left Corps Headquarters and returned home to New Hampshire.

On the weekend of May 20, Linden and I drove to Regensburg, a 150-mile trip that took six hours. We passed through the cities of Braunau (Hitler's home town), Muhldorf, and Landshut. We stayed in a zimmer in Regensburg for the night and explored this beautiful city on the Danube. With the war now ended, citizens were beginning to clean up their city from the war damage, and small businesses were beginning to recover. It was fun to be tourists instead of soldiers.

On May 20, General Walker received orders from Washington that he would be relieved from his duties in Europe and return to the States for reassignment. This was emotional news for me because I knew Walker personally since the first day that I had arrived at Corps Headquarters in Camp Young, California. I was in the office with him for nearly three years. The next day, he left St. Martin and went to the airport in Linz, Austria, where he inspected an Honor Guard, after which he gave a farewell handshake to General Patton and a final salute. Walker wrote the following farewell letter to all of us at XX Corps Headquarters:

HEADQUARTERS XX CORPS
APO 340

20 May 1945

A FAREWELL MESSAGE TO ALL OFFICERS, WARRANT OFFICERS AND ENLISTED MEN OF THE XX CORPS

In relinquishing command of the XX Corps I desire to express to each of you my gratitude for the splendid job you have done.

From the hedgerows of Normandy, across France to Metz, through the SIEGFRIED LINE, across the RHINE and DANUBE RIVERS, on through Germany and into Austria we have served and fought together. You have done your part well, and I say without qualification that the Officers, Warrant Officers, and Enlisted Men of the XX Corps have no equals. Your conduct on the field of battle has proven that to me. Your individual deeds of heroism will remain forever in the hearts of our people.

Your cooperation has been complete and your application to duty continuous. No commander could have asked more. Your unqualified loyalty to me during these past months will hearten me in performing all my future duties.

/S/ WALTON H. WALKER
Lieutenant General, United States Army
Commanding

General George S. Patton Jr. sent the following letter of Commendation to General Walker and the personnel of the XX Corps:

HEADQUARTERS
THIRD UNITED STATES ARMY
Office of the Commanding General
APO 403

21 May1945

SUBJECT: Commendation
To: Lieutenant General Walton H. Walker

From the landing of the XX Corps in England until the termination of hostilities in Europe, you and your Corps have been outstanding for dash, drive, and audacity in pursuit and in exploitation.

Your determination and great tactical skill were evinced in your capture of Metz and subsequent advance to the Saar and capture of Saarlautern.

Your reduction of the Moselle–Saar Triangle and the capture of Trier was a brilliant feat of arms. The operation starting March 13 and terminating May 9, during which you turned the Siegfried Line, destroyed the center of enemy resistance, and crossed the Rhine, finally terminating your victorious advance in Austria, were in keeping with your previous exploits and standards.

Of all the Corps I have commanded, yours has always been the most eager to attack and the most reasonable and cooperative.

You and your Corps are hereby highly commended for your outstanding achievements.

/S/ G. S. Patton Jr.,
General

Copies to:
    Army Ground Forces
    Twelfth Army Group

276

The day that Walker departed, a new general arrived to take command of the XX Corps. He was Maj. Gen. Louis A. Craig, a fifty-four-year-old cavalry soldier who graduated from West Point. He was the Commanding General of the 97th and 9th Infantry Divisions in Europe before he took command of our corps.

After the cessation of hostilities, the work of the Military Government (G-5) increased tremendously. This meant the establishment of a permanent government in the towns and counties as well as civil activities pertaining to fire, police, water, sewage disposal, and debris clearing. Civilian responsibilities included rebuilding and repairs. Food supplies and stores were closely controlled and the immediate opening of bakeries, drug stores, butcher shops, and other food stores were allowed. This also included small factories and shops. Displaced persons constituted the largest problem facing the XX Corps. Camps were built for them, and they were housed according to their nationality. They were well-fed and clothed and received medical care until they could be returned to their homes.

It was a lovely spring day on which all XX Corps personnel received a copy of General Orders Number 75, dated 20 May 1945. The order stated that each of us would be awarded the Bronze Star Medal. This was fantastic news, and we were an elated bunch of guys. My citation read as follows:

Bronze Star Medal

Technician Fourth Grade, EUGENE G. SCHULZ, 36296972, INF, Headquarters XX Corps, for meritorious service in connection with military operations against the enemy in France, Germany, and Austria between 1August 1944 and 9 May 1945. Technician Schulz's services merit high praise. Entered Military Service from Wisconsin.

A few days later a memorandum from the G-1 Department specified the sequence of events for the big ceremony. Our excitement mounted as we polished our shoes, shined the brass buckles, and pressed our dress uniforms. Some guys got a quick haircut.

On Friday morning, May 25, the assembly time was 0800. We got into formation in front of the vine-covered Schloss of Count Arco Ferdinand and Valle in St. Martin. There were eighty men from headquarters company who stood in a line in front of the main entrance to the Schloss, where we faced the two lion statues that guarded it. A platoon of Military Police stood in formation at each flank of the row of men to be decorated. A military band from the 13th

Armored Division was assembled on the right flank of the MPs, and they provided the music for the ceremony. Flag-bearers holding the American flag and the XX Corps colors stood in front of the formation.

The Schloss in St. Martin, Austria, XX Corps Headquarters, (May-June 1945)

The Company's Commanding Officer (CO) yelled "Attention!" The band played two flourishes and the General's March during the arrival of General Louis Craig, Corps Commander, and General Collier, Chief of Staff, along with Colonel Meehan, G-1, and two tray bearers. The CO barked "Present Arms" and we saluted while the band played the national anthem. The CO yelled "Parade Rest," which meant separating our feet and holding our hands behind our backs. The CO read the citation for the Bronze Star Medal: "for meritorious service in connection with military operations against the enemy in France, Germany, and Austria between 1August 1944 and 9 May 1945."

General Craig, followed by a tray bearer, walked down the line of recipients and pinned the medal on each soldier, while the band played softly in the background. The General stopped in front of me while I stood at parade rest, took a Bronze Star from the tray bearer and pinned it to my shirt above the left pocket. He shook my hand and said, "Congratulations, Soldier." There was a lump in my throat, and I had an indescribable feeling of pride about receiving this great honor during my military service to my country. I sincerely wished that Mom and Dad could have been present for this stirring ceremony, and I'm sure they too would have felt an enormous sense of pride.

After General Craig had pinned the last soldier in the formation, he made a brief speech in which he said that we had earned this decoration "only by our initiative and untiring efforts to perform our duties for the successful victory of the Allies." The ceremony ended as the band played two flourishes and the

General's March while Generals Craig and Collier left the area followed by the colors. We were dismissed and had the rest of the day off. I wrote this comment in my diary: "Today was the greatest day in my army life because I was decorated with the Bronze Star Medal!" The medal is a five-pointed star of a bronze color which is suspended from a red ribbon that has a blue stripe running vertically in the middle.

During the following days, there wasn't much to do, so we had lots of time on our hands. Official duties were winding down, and my job now consisted of typing long reports written by G-1, G-2, G-3, and G-4 officers about combat experiences and

The Author's Bronze Star Medal (May 1945)

results of the XX Corps for the historical war records. I also went on frequent sightseeing trips in the jeep with my buddies and attended a movie nearly every night. I wrapped my Bronze Star Medal as well as several Nazi daggers and other souvenirs in boxes and sent them home. I wrote letters and spent much time reading.

One beautiful May day, I drove Major Linden to the town of Vocklabruck to visit the 80th Infantry Division. Our Corps officers had assignments to visit various units that were attached to the corps, for a final inspection before they were sent back to the States or deployed to the Far East because the war against Japan was still raging. Major Linden and I were thrilled at the beauty of the Alps and the Alpine lakes that we observed on our trip. When we arrived at the headquarters of an Engineer Battalion, we were welcomed to a big beer party that was in progress. We joined in the festivities and thoroughly enjoyed their hospitality with hamburgers, beer, and fun.

On June 1, Major Linden and I made another inspection trip to some XX Corps units that were stationed near the gorgeous Atter See in Austria. This lake looked like a jewel surrounded by towering mountains and crystal clear water. The Austrian farmers were cutting hay on the steep Alpine slopes. Women and children were using scythes and hand rakes instead of machinery as we used on my home farm in Wisconsin. I thought it was unusual that the hay was shocked onto posts with cross pieces to dry in the air rather than on the ground, whereas at home we raked the hay into windrows.

From the Atter See, we drove west through the beautiful city of Salzburg, then north to Passau on the Inn river where we took the Autobahn to

Regensburg. The highway was parallel to the Danube river, and we drove through picturesque Bavarian towns. We stopped to inspect a truck battalion that was camped on the estate of Fritz Thyssen, who had been the chief executive officer of the huge Skoda Munitions Works of Czechoslovakia. This unit was made up of black soldiers with white officers. After the inspection, Major Linden and I ate with these guys in their mess hall. This was a new experience for me because I had never been around black people before. (There were no black people in my home town of Clintonville.) These truck drivers were very comical and happy-go-lucky, and I had a lot of fun watching and interacting with them. Our two-day trip covered 210 miles.

Several days after this inspection trip, we received the order that the G-3 Air Section was liquidated, so Major Linden, Bob Reim, and I were transferred to G-3, my original department. Bob and I washed the jeep and returned it to the motor pool, which meant that we no longer had a personal vehicle at our disposal. I got an assigned job in G-3 and reported to two new officers: Captain Lull and Lieutenant Hicks. My job now consisted of typing numerous Status Reports of Alerted Units for Redeployment. With the war's end, it was a major job to redeploy units and deactivate soldiers going home for discharge.

Wednesday, June 6, 1945 was the one-year anniversary of D-Day, and General Eisenhower declared this day, D+366, a holiday for all the troops in the ETO. We thoroughly enjoyed this beautiful day of leisure.

XX Corps Headquarters received a new order from General Patton which stated that we would move from Austria to Germany. This would be our final CP in Europe. Our assignment was to be a major organization in the "Army of Occupation," and our new home was in Tutzing, Germany, next to a beautiful lake not far from Munich, with an enjoyable view of the Alps Mountains.

CHAPTER 22

Tutzing, Germany—A Summer of Fun

I MADE THE FOLLOWING ENTRY into my diary on Sunday, June 10, 1945:

"Dear Diary,

We moved today to our new CP at Tutzing, Germany, on the lake shore of Wurm See. It rained until two o'clock. Our half-track ran into the ditch and nearly tipped over. A truck pulled us out with a winch.

We went from St. Martin to Salzburg where we hit the Autobahn. The Autobahn to Munich is a most beautiful drive. The Bavarian Alps with snow-covered peaks were on the south. We came within thirty miles of Berchtesgaden (Hitler's "Eagle's Nest" retreat). We also passed the Chiem See which I think is the largest lake in Germany. It's much larger than Shawano Lake.

Munich is the fifth largest city in Germany and quite a bit beat up. The street cars were even running, and the city streets were crowded with people. Bomb damage was very great, but most of the debris in the streets has been cleaned up.

A beautiful macadam road, lined on both sides with trees, goes south to the lake. The resort city of Starnberg is at the north end of the lake, and Tutzing is midway down the west side of the lake. It's a wealthy resort town about the size of

Marion, Wisconsin, with many beautiful homes and cottages. The Headquarters General Staff is in a lavish office building right on the lake shore. The interior is luxurious, formerly some kind of office building. Our home is right across the street in a former nurses home. Bob Reim and I have a cozy room for two people. We have a bath tub, toilet, and running hot and cold water. We can also see the lake from our window. This is new luxury for us.

The lake is quite large, shaped like a lima bean. Looking across the lake on the east side are the Alps with snowy peaks. The view is magnificent. The Special Staff personnel live in the Seehof Hotel, a huge one by the shore. We eat in the large dining hall there. The kitchen is modernly equipped."

With the arrival of our XX Corps Headquarters in Tutzing, we began our new assignment as one of the major units in the "Army of Occupation" in Germany. The Corps' zone of activity was widely extended to the west to include the territory formerly occupied by the Seventh Army; from Ulm on the west, to Landshut on the northeast; to Salzburg on the southeast; and the German-Austrian border on the south. All the American troops who were stationed in this broad area were divided into four classifications: (1) those remaining in the European Theater of Operations; (2) those to the Pacific direct; (3) those to the Pacific via the United States; and (4) those to the United States for discharge.

Our location in Tutzing was a convenient place from which it was easy to travel all over Europe. This resort town was a mere twenty-five miles south of Munich and very close to the Autobahn. The beautiful Alpine town of Garmisch-Partenkirchen was nearby as well as the Austrian city of Innsbruck. On the first

The steamboat Starnberg on Wurm See, Tutzing, Germany (1945)

Sunday afternoon after our arrival in Tutzing, a bunch of us went for a boat ride on an old steamboat, named "Starnberg," that was fueled by coal. Its big chimney belched out thick black smoke as it sailed around the lake. It was 150 feet long and had a capacity of five hundred passengers. The lower deck consisted of a lounge and bar, and the open upper deck had benches. During the two-hour trip around Starnberger See, which was another name for Wurm See, several fräuleins served us free beer. The scenery was fantastic, and we saw many beautiful homes and cottages built along the shoreline.

Our mess hall was in the Seehof Hotel's dining room where we were served by German waiters who were dressed in white shirts, dark pants, black bow ties, and white jackets. They looked sharp and gave us excellent service during our stay here. White table cloths covered the tables, and we were now diners rather than GIs, so we packed away our aluminum mess kits and ate from real china. Our new status was thoroughly enjoyed, and we felt pretty important.

Our regular dress uniform consisted of a "blouse," or jacket, that was a long, loose-fitting garment that reached down past the hips. Early in the war, General Eisenhower began wearing a jacket that was form-fitting and short, reaching only to the belt line. We all loved that style when we saw photos of Ike wearing this new fashion. Then, to our pleasant surprise, we all received this new "Eisenhower Jacket" as an issue of clothing. We were very happy that we could now wear this "battle jacket," as it was called.

June 21st was a big day for me because I received a promotion to Staff Sergeant. For a long time, my rating was "Tec 4" which was the rating for the technical grade for Sergeant. According to the T/O (Table of Organization), my new job was Chief Clerk of the Air-Ground Liaison Section. My raise in pay was $18 per month, which brought my total monthly salary to $60.20. My buddy, Bob Reim, was also promoted, as he received my T/4 rating. After dinner, Bob and I took a long walk along the lake, and when we returned to our quarters, we sewed our new stripes onto our shirts and the new Ike jacket. It was a really good day.

Corps officers had their own Officer's Club in a large building on the lakeshore. There was also an "Enlisted Men's Club" in a huge mansion by the lake, only a short walk from our room. It had a front lawn that stretched to the lake, but there was no sandy beach here, only a low wall built along the water line from which one could jump into the lake. On June 22, the EM Club held its grand opening with a big party, where the 69th Signal Battalion dance band provided the music, and we enjoyed plenty of good beer called Munich Brau.

There were many travel opportunities for American troops in Europe who were waiting for deployment, and my first opportunity arrived on June 24. My name was pulled out of a hat for a four-day pass to Paris. I was elated that I would finally get to visit the "City of Lights" because our XX Corps, as well as Patton's Third Army, was denied the opportunity to liberate Paris in August 1944. My buddy Joe Messner and I were the lucky winners of the passes from G-3.

At 1300 on Sunday afternoon, eighteen EMs and two officers left the rear echelon motor pool in one 6x6 truck. Two drivers rode in the cab while the rest of us rode in the rear of the truck bed along with our duffle bags. We sat on benches on each side of the cargo bed under the shelter of the canvas tarpaulin that covered the whole truck. All bags were at our feet. Our first destination was the XX Corps Rest Center in Thionville, France. We traveled on the Autobahn through the cities of Munich, Augsburg, Stuttgart, Karlsruhe, Heidelberg, Ludvigshaven, Kaiserslautern, Saarbrucken, and Metz, finally arriving in Thionville at 3:00 a.m. after traveling four hundred miles in fourteen hours. This Rest Center was located in the same school building that we had occupied as our CP during the winter of 1944–1945. It was named after our XX Corps.

I slept late and missed breakfast, but we were served by pretty French waitresses at the noon lunch. In early afternoon, we drove the short distance to Luxembourg City, where we walked around Old Town and tried the local beers. After eating a big steak dinner in the Luxembourg railroad station that was provided for GI transients, we boarded a train at 9:00 p.m. It was a tiring overnight ride in an old train car, sitting on wooden seats and benches without cushions.

The train stopped in Reims, France, at 6 a.m. on Tuesday, where we had breakfast at the American Red Cross. The last leg of the trip took us to Paris' East Station, arriving at 11:00 a.m., and a bus took us to the Pavillion Hotel Red Cross Club. We had a lovely room at the hotel's annex three blocks away, where we reveled in our new luxury—soft beds and a private bath. We ate our meals in the elaborate dining room where we were served by petite French waitresses, while a string ensemble played music during the dining hour. This pampering was great, and we really "lived it up."

During the next four wonderful days in this beautiful city, Joe and I walked miles and did all the sightseeing we could manage. It was a thrill to see the enormous granite tomb of Napoleon in the high-domed Hotel des Invalides. We walked to the Eiffel Tower, the magnificent landmark that reached twelve hundred feet into the sky. The tower was still closed as it was during the war, so we couldn't see Paris from the top observation deck. We crossed the Seine River and visited the Trocadero and the Arc de Triomphe in the center of the huge intersection which contained about twelve streets. The Tomb of the Unknown with the Eternal Flame was under the Arch. We walked down the long, broad, tree-lined avenue called the Avenue des Champs Élysées, from the Arch to the Place de la Concorde at the Louvre. The famous art museum was closed, so we walked to the Church of St. Madeleine and then to the Paris

Opera House. Its interior was unbelievably beautiful, with the biggest crystal chandelier I had ever seen, and floors, walls, and columns of elegant marble.

The next day we took a bus trip to Versailles, Paris' residential suburb that contained fabulous homes. We went to the luxurious Palace of King Louis XIV, with its many rooms full of furniture, paintings, and statues. The gardens surrounding the palace were full of blooming flowers, and the manicured hedges were trimmed in geometric designs. The pools and fountains were shut down during the war and were not yet in operation. Joe and I returned to Paris in the afternoon and took a sightseeing trip by bus, revisiting many of the sights we had walked to the preceding day. In the evening, Joe and I attended a show at the world-famous Follies Bergere. It was a fabulous production of music and dancing with beautiful half-nude girls in gorgeous costumes.

We slept late the next morning, and after breakfast, we went shopping with a French girl from the Red Cross Center who spoke English. She took us to the big perfume houses of Paris, like Lucein Lelong, Schairperili, Coty, and Dana. Joe and I bought perfume, powder, and lipstick to take home to the women in our families. Later we took the Paris Metro to the Basilique du Sacré Coeur (Cathedral of the Sacred Heart), which was built on a hill in the Montmartre district of Paris. This was the most beautiful church I had ever seen, with a huge central altar and numerous side chapels and altars. The inside of the large dome was beautifully painted, and we climbed up the three hundred corkscrew steps to the cupola on top of the dome. The view of the entire city of Paris was breathtaking. From the very top of the cathedral, we went down into its depths to the crypt where we saw the tombs of important Roman Catholic clergy and church leaders.

Our wonderful week of sightseeing and enjoyment of the pleasures of Paris came to an end on Friday evening when we left the railroad station for the first leg of our trip home. We arrived in Reims at midnight where the ARC provided hot coffee, sandwiches, and doughnuts. We rode on the truck through Luxembourg to Thionville where we had a hot dinner at the XX Corps Rest Camp. Our trip continued on the Autobahn, and we finally arrived in Tutzing at 5:00 a.m. To our surprise, we learned that the enlisted men of the General Staff had been moved from the nurse's home into the large Park Simpson Hotel, two blocks from Headquarters. We had to find it in the dark, and after locating a bed, I zonked out until noon on Sunday, July1.

Bob Reim and I were very happy with our new room in the Park Simpson Hotel. It was on the third floor and had a balcony that faced south toward the lake. We had a fantastic view of the snow-covered Alps that formed the horizon beyond the southern end of Starnberger See. The hotel was built on a hill and evergreen trees covered the slope that led down to the lakeshore. We spent many hours on our balcony drinking in the beauty of this scene as we watched the changes in mood during all kinds of weather, sunrises, and sunsets.

Wurm See, Tutzing, Germany (view from Author's room at Park Simpson Hotel (July 1945)

My work load at XX Corps Headquarters dropped considerably during July. My only work consisted of typing a long troop list of the soldiers who were being moved or sent home for discharge. I was very interested in this procedure because I was anxious to go home too. My Adjusted Service Rating Score (ASR) stood at sixty-eight points because I had just received five more ASR points for receiving the "Battle Star for Central Europe," which was added to my military ribbons. Soldiers who had eighty-five points and higher were allowed to go home, and I was getting more and more anxious to be in that group.

We engaged in many recreational activities during our summer in Tutzing. We played volleyball nearly every day in the court next to our hotel, often with other military units that lived in our occupation area. This was our most enjoyable activity. The 3rd Cavalry group kept their horses in a stable outside of Tutzing. Some German civilians took care of these beautiful horses, and they saddled them for us whenever we went for a horse-back ride.

I attended Sunday church services at the Tutzing Evangelical Church, which had opened for services after having been closed during the war. This was a small, attractive church with pews that held about two hundred persons. A German organist played for services, and worshipping in a church, listening to a real pipe organ, and singing familiar hymns were very thrilling and fulfilling. Partaking of Holy Communion was a joy to receive after being absent during the long period of combat. Our army pastor was Chaplain Whittsett. Songs of praise and prayers of thanksgiving were sent to the Throne of Grace by GIs and German civilians, as God's church was once again open for worship after all the years of Nazi oppression.

New businesses were opening in Tutzing. A new PX was established, and I had a bottle of Coca-Cola which was a big treat—the first coke since leaving the States so long ago. The American Red Cross opened a "Doughnut-Drive-In" in a former café where we could get free coffee and doughnuts at any time of the day. We went to a movie every night in the service club's day room. They were 16mm films which frequently tore, and the picture was delayed while the projector operator spliced the film. My brother Amie sent me a few Kodachrome films which were hard to find back home because of the war effort, so I was able to use color film in my camera to capture the beauty of the Alps, lakes, and countryside. I wrote many letters during these days to family and friends.

One July day, we had an opportunity to see a traveling USO show in Augsburg. I was lucky to go when I pulled the right number out of a hat. After I ate an early steak supper at four o'clock, I climbed into the back of a truck with a bunch of other guys who had also won tickets, and we headed to the city of Augsburg, which was about sixty miles away. The traveling show was called "Billy Rose's Diamond Horseshoe" and we all enjoyed a variety of entertainment, including dancers, singers, comedians, clowns, and jugglers. It was a happy late-night trip back to Tutzing in the back of a 6x6.

The G-3 Section had its own rowboat at the Tutzing dock, and one evening two of my buddies and I rowed on the lake for an hour and a half. The Corps' MPs had a huge sailboat which they were preparing for an evening trip, and they invited us for a ride. The boat had two sails about forty feet high, and with a brisk wind, we sailed across the lake in a jiffy. It was a fun-filled evening on this beautiful, warm summer night. We thanked the MPs for the ride and went to the EM Club for some beers.

The day that American troops crossed the border into Germany, SHAEF issued orders that banned fraternization with German people. It was enforced until July 15, and we could now talk to and associate with German people. Some GIs were happy that they could date German fraüleins. I had fun using German to speak with the natives.

Several well-known dance orchestras from the States were on tour in the ETO to entertain the troops. Hal McIntyre came to Tutzing and performed in an open-air theater on a hill overlooking Starnberger See. We listened to a great concert of big band swing tunes that were popular during the war years.

July 22, 1945, was my twenty-second birthday. It was a Sunday, and I went to morning services at the Evangelical church. The day was sunny and terribly hot, and after the noon meal, we all went to the beach and donned our swimming trunks. Many of the guys went swimming, but I couldn't swim because I had never learned, so I stayed on the shore and got sun-burned. Part

The Author (right facing forward) with buddies at the beach in Tutzing, Germany (July 1945)

of the beach was filled-in with dirt, and it extended out into the lake a short distance where a concrete wall had been built where the water was deeper. This is where most of the guys dived or jumped into the lake. My buddies kept egging me on to do some swimming.

Finally, I got enough nerve and I jumped into the lake. I paddled with my feet and moved my arms, and I seemed to be making progress. I "swam" away from the wall for a while and then thought that I should go back to shore. When I turned around I noticed that I was farther than I realized, and I began to have doubts that I could make it back. In an instant, I lost confidence in myself, and I got scared. I stopped paddling, and then I began to sink. I held my breath for what seemed like a long time. As I went down, I still tried to use my arms and legs to get back up to the surface, and I was in great panic. Flash-back memories of my life raced through my brain, and I believed that this was the end of my life. I thought of my Mom and Dad and the sadness that my drowning would bring into their lives. I felt sorry about this foolish thing I had done and the shame I had brought to my family. I was scared to die this way, and I remembered that my own Grandpa Frederick Schulz had drowned in the Pigeon River in Clintonville, Wisconsin, in 1917. It was amazing that all these thoughts raced through my mind in a matter of split seconds.

After what seemed like an eternity, I suddenly felt the strong arms of my two buddies, Bob Reim and Ted Golineak, bringing me up to the surface. With my head above the water line, I took rapid new breaths of air, as my rescuers towed me to the shore and boosted me onto the pier. I was surrounded by a bunch of guys who were wishing me well, as my nerves began to settle down in the warm sun. The water in this Alpine lake was very cold, and I was chilled after this ordeal.

That evening, we had a delicious chicken dinner in the mess hall, after which we went to a movie. It was still early when the movie ended, so my buddies in the G-3 section decided to have a birthday party for me. It had been an exhausting and tiring day for me, and the party broke up, so that I could go to bed. As I lay in bed, I had a hard time getting to sleep. First and foremost, I prayed fervently to God to thank Him for preserving my life from my close encounter with death. The Lord had provided my two close friends to be nearby. I thought about Mom and Dad and the shock and grief that they would have suffered if I had drowned on my birthday, just a couple of months after I had survived the dangers of combat without a scratch. I felt shame about the foolish risk I had taken in thinking that I could swim and trying to show off to my friends. I had many such thoughts before I finally fell asleep.

The Feldafing Golf Course was located three miles north of Tutzing and Harry Pfeifer and I went golfing one afternoon. We rented a bag of clubs and four balls for 100 RM (Reichs-marks). There was a 10 RM fine for a lost ball because the war had caused a shortage of them. We played nine holes on a challenging course with plenty of obstacles, woods, and rough next to Starnberger lake. Par was thirty-five and I shot fifty-seven, but hey, I hadn't played golf for three years. I didn't lose any balls but found two for future use. After the game, we enjoyed a cold beer in the clubhouse. On August evenings, we played volleyball after dinner, usually with teams from other military units.

My friend, Joe Messner, decided to leave XX Corps Headquarters to attend school at the Army University in Biarritz, France, for two months of study, so I was chosen to take over his duties in the G-3 Section. During these days, there were many turnovers and changes among Corps personnel. On one Sunday afternoon, I had a surprise visit from Delbert Johannes, who was the brother of my best friend, Kenny. Del and Kenny lived only two houses from me in Clintonville, and it was amazing how many guys got together with their friends from home through letters written to their respective families telling them where they were stationed. Del and I spent a wonderful afternoon at the American Red Cross canteen in Starnberg.

Major Norman Linden, my G-3 Section boss, left for the States for discharge to his hometown of Boston. I was sad to see him go because we had become very close to each other as we traveled around Europe in our jeep. When I signed the payroll report I received the Good Conduct Medal and Ribbon. I also received the 4th Battle Star to place on my ribbon bar as well as the 3rd Hershey Bar for my lower left sleeve which signified that I had served eighteen months in overseas duties.

On August 15, 1945, Japan surrendered unconditionally, and this day became known as V-J Day (Victory in Japan). World War II was officially over, and under God's providence America and the Allies were the victors. Peace had come and what a joyous day this was. Going home couldn't come quickly enough and leaving soon was foremost in my mind as well as for all of the troops in Europe. The task of moving millions of soldiers out of Europe, the transport ships needed, and the logistics of it was mind-boggling. So we all waited patiently day-by-day, and the rumors of departure were numerous.

We celebrated V-J Day, which was a holiday for servicemen all over Europe, by going on a tour of the Alps. A XX Corps bus took fifteen of us on a trip to Oberammergau, a village near the Austrian border. This is the place where the famous Passion Play is held every ten years. However, its performances had been suspended during the war years. We had a tour of the theater, which sat six hundred people, and looked at the wardrobes of the players and the scenery for the play which included the wooden cross on which they hung Jesus for his crucifixion. A wonderful view of the Alps Mountains formed the backdrop of the stage, which was outdoors and without a roof. We continued our trip to see the Schloss Linderhof which was the summer home of King Ludvig II, the "Mad King" of Bavaria. This small but elegant schloss was modeled after the Palace in Versailles, and it was beautifully furnished. A large pool in front of the building was adorned with statues.

The next stop was in Garmisch-Partenkirchen which was the site of the 1936 Olympics. The big ski jump used in the games was built into the mountain, and it was a spectacular structure. The Zugspitze is the highest mountain in the German Alps with an elevation of 9,400 feet. We took a cable car to the top of Wank Peak where we enjoyed a breathtaking view of the scenery, and I could see the Starnberger See some sixty miles away. We spent an hour at the café on top of this mountain and enjoyed a stein of beer. It was a perfect day as we returned to Headquarters in time for supper.

August had ended, and I had enjoyed a wonderful summer of fun and travel, the traveling USO shows and movies, as well as sports and the many evenings spent at the Enlisted Men's Club enjoying the wonderful German beer. On September 5, we celebrated the third anniversary of the activation of the XX Corps, now known as "The Ghost Corps." As one of the youngest military organizations in the US Army, our corps had established an illustrious history of accomplishments, and now, with peace in the world, it was appropriate to celebrate. General Craig declared a two-day celebration to be held in Tutzing.

On the first day, the 65th Infantry Division band held a parade in Tutzing. At nine o'clock, we boarded the lake's excursion boat, the "Starnberg," for a cruise on the lake. The band provided music on board while we enjoyed the favorite German beverage—beer. When the boat reached the town of

Starnberg, my G-3 buddies and I got off the boat and spent several hours at the ARC, after which we hitch-hiked back to Tutzing. A group of thirty-six P-51 fighter planes flew in formation over the town and buzzed the lake. This was a neat sight to watch. The traveling USO show entertained us, and later we went to the EM Club for refreshment. Four big searchlights played games in the sky over the lake, with the powerful light beams playing tag with each other.

The celebration continued the next day with another parade, which started on Tutzing's main street and ended at the baseball field. The 65th Infantry Division band led the parade in which I marched along with our whole Headquarters Company. Patton arrived to engage in the festivities, and he gave an inspiring speech at the ball field in which he congratulated "his favorite Corps," as he put it, and then awarded decorations to a few individuals. In conclusion, we "passed in review" before Patton, Craig and other top brass. The Corps Artillery gave Patton a seventeen gun salute, a thrilling event to be sure.

XX Corps men enjoying a day by the lake, Tutzing, Germany
(1945) (Author third from left at table)

After a big dinner at noon at the ballpark, we went to the beach because it was a warm and sunny day. Later in the afternoon, the Corps' cooks prepared an elaborate buffet supper at the EM Club by the beach that included potato salad, cold roast beef, buns, vegetables, and cake. For the first time during our sojourn in Europe, we were treated to Coca-Cola, as much as we wanted, and this was a wonderful treat.

The evening entertainment at the EM Club was a traveling USO show, and the first act was four men who were comedian wrestlers; they performed very funny stunts that were not serious wrestling moves. The main event was a variety show from Munich which included dancing girls, singers, and a very fine German swing band. The evening culminated in a fantastic display of fireworks over the lake. Our two-day celebration of the XX Corps' third birthday was a very successful and memorable event.

On September 6, Sergeant Claude White, who was Chief Clerk of G-3, left us for his trip home and final discharge. General Craig designated me to be the temporary G-3 Chief Clerk until a new soldier arrived for this position, at which time my job was to train and brief him for these duties. I also received the good news that I had received an additional eight points to my discharge score, which now totaled seventy-six points. The army also announced that they had lowered the discharge score to eighty points, so I was within four points of going home. There were rumors that men with over seventy points would be home by Christmas. The waiting was hard!

During the next few days, I began to sift through all of my personal possessions so I would be ready to ship out when the day arrived. I threw away some junk and mailed all my collectables home, including my collections of *"The Stars and Stripes"* and *"Yank Magazine."* I planned to carry my uniforms and valuable items in my duffle bag. The exciting news that I had been patiently waiting for came on September 13, which stated that I was included in the next quota to go home. This group had ASR scores between sixty-five and seventy-six, and mine was seventy-six. The suspense was unbearable.

On Sunday, September 16, all of Europe returned to European Standard Time, so darkness came an hour earlier. On the next day, two important visitors arrived at XX Corps Headquarters, Generals Eisenhower and Patton, who dropped by to do some business with our top brass. It was nice to see them again.

The good news came to me at 5:00 p.m. on Tuesday the 18th. The order stated that I was shipping out tomorrow. My two buddies from G-3, Jim Maher and John Massa, were also going with me. Wow! We couldn't have been happier than we were at this moment. I spent the evening completing my final packing. I said good-bye to my G-3 Air associate, Bob Reim, who was also anxious to go to his home in Philadelphia, but he still lacked enough points. These were bittersweet moments because I was sad to leave my closest friends whom I might never see again in this life; however, the sweet part was the prospect of going home to enjoy a future life of freedom from this ferocious war that had destroyed so much human life and property.

The entry in my diary simply stated "Oh Happy Day!"

CHAPTER 23

My Journey Home

ON WEDNESDAY SEPTEMBER 19, 1945, I began my journey home for eventual discharge from military to civilian life. There were fifteen men from XX Corps Headquarters, including four guys from Wisconsin. Three of us were from G-3: Jim Maher from New Orleans, Louisiana; John Massa from Portsmouth, Ohio; and myself. We had no clue where we were going and all we could do was to check off the cities that we traveled through on the journey.

A 6x6 truck transported us to the 7th Armored Group Headquarters which was stationed in the Bavarian village of Siegsdorf, in a beautiful valley surrounded by mountains. This group headquarters consisted of only ninety-six men, and here we slept in a tourist home which was very comfortable and luxurious compared to what was to come. We had superb meals and lots of ice cream which was a great treat after not having it for such a long time. There were no duties here, so we did a lot of walking in this dorf's gorgeous scenery.

The next leg of our journey began at nine o'clock on the morning of Friday, September 21. We boarded a train at the local railroad station which was pulled by an electric engine. Our accommodations were in a *boxcar* because there were no passenger coaches available in this devastated country. Each of the dozen or so box cars in this train carried fourteen men, so we were quite crowded. I wrote the following words in my diary:

> "It was awfully hard sleeping on the floor of the boxcar, and the train jumped around considerably. My bones were so sore

I couldn't lie still. We had heated C-rations, hot coffee, and bread for meals."

Author (second from right) with buddies in box car of troop train. (September 1945)

Author (center holding cup) with buddies in box car of troop train. (September 1945)

Troop train of boxcars for trip to France (September 1945)

Our route across Germany passed through the cities of Munich, Augsburg, Ulm, and Strasbourg, where we crossed the Rhine River at noon on the second day of the trip. The train poked along, and eventually we crossed the German–French border and stopped in the French city of Sarrebourg, a distance of forty miles from Strasbourg, which took five hours. We jumped off the boxcar to get some exercise to recharge our weary muscles and partake in a hot meal at a large army transient mess hall that was located in this town. It was so wonderful to eat meat and potatoes and many side dishes and desserts instead of the C-rations heated over a sterno flame in the boxcar. After supper, we did some calisthenics before boarding our boxcar for the short trip to Nancy, France, where we arrived at 9:00 p.m. It was a short stop whose main purpose was to let us use the latrine at the station. When the train left, we again found a favorite spot on the floor of the boxcar to bed-down, covering ourselves with our army blankets and using our duffle bag as a hard pillow.

The third day of the journey was Sunday, September 23. The train stopped at the small town of Lerouville, France, at five o'clock in the morning. I jumped out of the boxcar after a restless night and used the facilities at the army camp located by the tracks. There were latrines available here and tables containing sinks and water, so everyone had a chance to clean up and shave. No shower for us though. We were treated to a great breakfast of bacon and eggs, schnecken, fruit, and coffee. This was a very enjoyable stop.

It was only ninety miles from this stop to the city of Reims, France, which we learned was our final destination, but it took forever to get there. We arrived in Reims at midnight. Trucks were waiting, and all the soldiers in the boxcars were transported to Camp Chicago, which was a huge wilderness of tents and nissen huts that were erected a few miles outside of the city. Six men were assigned to a tent. It was 3:00 a.m. when I plopped onto a cot and fell asleep quickly, completely exhausted.

For the next few days, there was nothing to do, and the weather was cold and rainy, so everyone tried to keep busy by playing cards, seeing movies at the camp theater, and spending time at the PX. I received an influenza shot which threw me for a loop with a very sore arm, a fever, and chills. I also had a complete physical and a dental exam that revealed a couple of cavities which the dentist filled. One night at the large Camp Chicago Theater, an orchestra from the AAF Air Transport Command presented a wonderful concert. I attended a football game at the Reims Municipal Stadium with the participating teams from the 101st Airborne and the OISE. After the game a group of us walked on the streets of downtown Reims.

I got a two-day pass to Brussels, Belgium, which was a popular destination for GIs who were waiting for their turn to go home. I traveled with four of my friends in an army truck for the four hour-trip on secondary roads. We stayed at the "November 11 Leave Club," which was operated by the American Red Cross. It was a large facility that had a lounge, dormitory, barber shop, photo studio, beer garden, and elaborate mess halls where Belgian mademoiselles served the meals. It was a treat to sleep in a bed with real sheets.

We went on a sightseeing walk of the city with an English-speaking guide. The Mannekin-Pis Fountain, we were told, was the mascot of Brussels. It is a small bronze statue of a little boy urinating, and it stands on a street corner a short distance from the Hotel de Ville. This must-see fountain was a little shocking at first sight, but it is a famous landmark. We visited the Bourse, the Tomb of the Unknown Warrior, the Palace of Justice, Hotel de Ville (city hall), the King's Palace, and the church of St. Gudule with its gorgeous altars, paintings, and statues. There was time for shopping before we saw the evening stage show in the breathtaking theater of the Opera House. The show was called "The Alhambra Follies" and had dancing girls and a good orchestra that played American songs. The third day, we shopped a little and later went to "GI Joe's Canteen," a great place where we enjoyed malted milks, sundaes, and cokes, which were luxuries that we had missed for a long, long time. We returned to Camp Chicago that evening with memories of a marvelous time in Brussels.

The days at Camp Chicago were cold, blustery and rainy, so we were given another blanket, and we got a coal stove for our tent. The coal smoke permeated our tent but our comfort improved. My name was pulled out of a hat, and I won a bottle of Three Feathers whiskey, so that also was a source of warmth for my tent mates and me.

When I signed the payroll for my September pay I got an extra 850 francs, equivalent to $17. Every soldier got the same amount of francs from the French government for being in the country for at least ten days. We all agreed it was a nice gesture.

The autumn days became warmer as the weather improved in France, and we engaged in a new form of recreation by playing touch football every day, resulting in aching muscles. Hollywood movies were shown every night, but in spite of all these activities, morale among the troops had its ups and downs based on the many rumors that continually spread throughout the camp. Of course, my morale always surged when I received lots of letters that eventually caught up with me because we moved so much lately. However, one day the news really depressed me because I heard that the longshoremen in New York City went on strike, so all troopships were tied up either in eastern United States ports or French and British ones until the strike was settled. Morale in Camp Chicago hit a new low! During these depressing days in October, I often wrote these words in my diary: "Another dull day. Nothing happened." I attended a lecture by an army colonel who spoke about the merits of reenlisting in the Regular US Army, but this did not interest me at all. The game "horse shoe" got popular, and I enjoyed this because I had played lots of matches of it during family outings back home.

On October 24, I received an unexpected two-day pass to Paris. A truck transported a bunch of us guys there. It was only ninety miles from Camp Chicago. We were dropped off at the Hotel des Invalides (Napoleon's tomb), and from there, we walked to the American Red Cross Club, one block away from the Champs Élysées, but its facilities were not that great. After a free dinner, I went on a search for my good friend from my high school days in Clintonville, Orvil Marquardt, whom I knew was somewhere in Paris because he had sent me a letter telling me this. (I had several dates with Orvil's younger sister, Bettie, when I was home on furlough before I shipped overseas.) I looked for Marky at an army unit that was housed near the Arc de Triomphe but was told that he had moved to Versailles.

Author (right) with Orvil Marquardt in Camp Satory, Versailles, France (October 1945)

I took the metro to Versailles and looked everywhere in Camp Satory, an old French Army camp that was now occupied with American troops. After a long search, I finally found Orvil in the 176th Field Artillery Battalion. It was a very happy reunion, and we had lots of news to share. After supper at his unit's mess hall, Marky and I went to Paris to a movie, and later we enjoyed a few beers at a café along the Champs Élysées. We returned to his camp, where I stayed overnight.

The next day, we stayed in his camp all day and returned to Paris for the evening where we walked up and down the Champs. Later, Marky returned to his camp, and I spent the night at the ARC Club in Paris. The next day, I walked many miles in the city, and when I got to the Eiffel Tower, I decided to take the elevator to the second landing, because it was now open to tourists. It had been closed on my last visit. The observation platform at the top, however, was still closed, as it had been during the war years. I visited the Trocadero and the aquarium and walked to the Louvre, which had reopened its exhibits. It was a thrill to see the famous Mona Lisa and Whistler's Mother, the paintings that I had heard about in high school. Marky came to Paris again, and after we had had supper, we enjoyed our final evening together over a few beers at the clubs along the Champs. After our good-byes, Orv returned to Versailles, and I went to the assembly point where our trucks were parked for the return trip to Camp Chicago. I got back to my tent and cot at 3:00 a.m., dead tired after having a wonderful time in Paris.

The final days of October were sunny and warm. There was nothing to do as we waited for the news about the dock workers strike, but there was still no settlement. On November 3, I got another three-day pass to Paris. This time I stayed at the plush Transatlantic ARC Club in the big hotel on Republique Square. I got a haircut, which I badly needed. After supper, I went with a group of guys to the Ensa Marigny Theater to see a play called "On Approval" which was performed by British actors.

The next day was Sunday, and I went with my buddy, Jim Maher, to Notre Dame, where Jim participated in the mass. The church was full of worshippers, and it was thrilling for me to hear the gorgeous organ music. After mass, Jim and I wandered throughout the cathedral, admiring the architecture, paintings, side chapels, and statuary, as this was the most magnificent place of worship I had ever seen.

In the afternoon, Jim and I were introduced to Grand Opera when we entered the Opera Garnier, a building of such beauty and furnishings like I had never seen in my life. The interior was built of marble and contained many paintings, sculptures, pillars, and lighting fixtures. The auditorium was huge, with five balconies and seats covered with maroon velvet. A gigantic chandelier hung down from the painted ceiling. A mademoiselle ushered us to our seats that were located on the main floor, five rows back from the orchestra pit, a perfect location. These seats cost 204 francs, which was an affordable price for GIs. The name of the opera was "Le Roi D'Y's," or "The King of Y's" in five acts. I was enthralled with the superb stage scenery, lighting, costumes, the singing of the actors and chorus, and the beautiful music of the opera orchestra. It was a thrilling and unforgettable experience in my young life.

On Sunday evening, Jim and I returned to the Champs Élysées to see a GI String Ensemble concert at the Ensa Marigny Theater, which was British. After the show, we stopped at a sidewalk café on the Champs for some beers and wonderful sandwiches made with delicious French bread and sausage. The next day, we went shopping at the Paris PX and then to a movie. After supper, we returned to the Ensa Marigny to see a GI show which was a parody of the opera "Carmen." There was an excellent swing band, and the actors were guys who were dressed as girls in elaborate costumes. It was hilarious and we laughed continuously. After the show and some refreshment at a café, we walked to the truck assembly point, and at midnight, we started the return trip back to Camp Chicago. I went to bed at 4:00 a.m., very tired but happy.

During the entire time that I spent in Camp Chicago, I was attached to the 7th Armored Group. On Monday, November 9, I got the wonderful news that our unit was scheduled to move to the staging area in two days. I packed my duffle bag with all my personal possessions, had a quick physical exam, and then I was ready to go.

The truck left Camp Chicago at 8:00 a.m. on Sunday, November 11, for the twenty-five mile trip to the town of Suippes. A train engine with a long line of box cars was standing at the station, and thirty-three men crowded into a 40&8 box car. We were headed for the French port of Le Harve. The weather was cold, rainy, and miserable as we endured the trip in the unfurnished box car, but we were glad to get a hot meal at ten o'clock that evening when the train stopped at a transient mess that the army had set up in a small town. The pokey train trip continued through the night, and at six o'clock in the morning, it pulled into the railroad station at Le Havre. We waited several hours for trucks to pick us up, and finally we were taken to Camp Philip Morris, located about two miles outside of Le Havre. This was our new home for the next few days.

Philip Morris was a huge, temporary army camp similar to Camp Chicago, with tents for sleeping and nissen huts for all other facilities. Water was scarce, being available for only two hours per day. The food was excellent, and it was cooked and served by German prisoners of war. The weather was miserable, cold, and rainy much of the time, but the camp had an excellent Service Club called "Club Tinsley." It was a swell place to hang out that had easy chairs, a library, and a snack bar. I passed the time by reading and playing a card game called "Casino."

On November 15, we received the wonderful news that we were hoping to hear for so long. An advance party from our Company was sent to the port to secure our quarters on a troop transport named *George Washington,* which was docked in the port of Le Havre and was scheduled to sail in two days. My excitement was rising, and it was hard to wait. I had a pleasant surprise when Orvil Marquardt came to see me. He was also in this camp, and his tent was only five blocks from mine. He was scheduled to sail the same day as I except on a different troop ship. Orvil and I had fun together, attended a movie, and the next day he visited me again. The next time we got together was several weeks later at home in Clintonville.

Embarkation Day: Saturday, November 17, 1945.

This was the day that all of us GIs had waited for since our first day of combat. We were going home—finally! At two o'clock in the morning I climbed into the big semitrailer truck that had no tarp to protect us from the cold rain as we traveled to the POE. We waited on the Le Havre dock until 6:30 a.m., and we got thoroughly soaked before we finally walked across the gangplank of the *George Washington.* This ship was built in Stettin, Germany, in 1909, and it sailed under the German flag as a passenger ship that provided transatlantic service between Bremerhaven and New York. The ship burned coal as fuel and had two smoke stacks. During World War I, it was interned in New York and finally was seized by the United States and renamed the USS *George Washington.* It was then refitted from a coal-burning, two-stack smokestack ship to an oil-burning one with one smokestack. It entered passenger service again between the United States and Europe. In 1940, it was refitted as a troopship and provided service between US East Coast ports and Great Britain and France.

This all-wooden ship weighed 25,570 tons, with dimensions of 725 feet long and 72 feet wide, and it carried 2,679 passengers, which was considerably smaller than the original *Queen Mary* that I sailed on nearly two years earlier. However, this day I embarked on this ship with 6,840 passengers including soldiers, nurses, WACS, and a few civilians. My quarters were on F Deck at the waterline. It was a stuffy and hot place with hardly enough room to turn around, but it was much more comfortable than traveling across Europe in a box car. Since the ship was built of wood, no smoking was permitted below the top outside deck, and the risk of fire was very high, so there were constant reminders to practice safety. We heard that our destination was Boston, Massachusetts.

We set sail at 9:30 a.m., and as we left the port of Le Havre, I noticed the tremendous destruction of the port facilities from Allied bombings and demolitions. This port was utterly destroyed. Later in the day, I converted my French francs into American currency which was truly a good feeling. I gradually settled in to my new surroundings on the crowded ship, and because the air was stuffy and the cabins so crowded, I spent as much time as possible on A Deck Aft. During daylight hours, the sun had trouble penetrating the fog of the Atlantic Ocean, and on clear nights, the moonlight glistened on the waves. I was fascinated to watch the phosphorescent minute ocean creatures that were churned up by the ship's propellers. The PA system on the top deck broadcast beautiful classical and popular music all day long. There were only two meals per day, a huge breakfast and a big dinner, and the food on this ship was delicious. The coffee was wonderful compared to the bad brew we had had during the preceding weeks. We had ice cream every night, the most desirable dessert that we had longed for during the past two years, and now we couldn't get enough of it, even though I had been able to get it several times before this. We encountered several days of stormy weather and heavy seas which caused the ship to pitch up and down like a yo-yo, which made many people sick, but I was OK. Each night we set back our watches by one hour, and several times by the half-hour.

Author (right) with buddies on deck of troop ship (November 1945)

Card game on deck of troop ship (November 1945)

GIs watching card game on troop ship (November 1945)

The sixth day at sea was Thursday, November 22, 1945—Thanksgiving Day. Every passenger on this ship was an American, and the Captain declared this day to be observed in the normal custom of the holiday. At 9:00 a.m., I attended the Protestant Thanksgiving worship service which was held on the open top deck. A choir sang several anthems. It was so thrilling to worship with a ship full of soldiers and nurses because we had so much to be thankful for to our God. We had survived the dangers of war and God gave us a successful victory, and now we were nearly home to our families and loved ones. What a joyous day!

The menu for our Thanksgiving dinner was elaborate: roast turkey, mashed potatoes and gravy, peas, cranberry sauce, bread and butter, ice cream, cookies, apples, and coffee and milk. It was a great feast. During the last two days at sea, everyone on board was in really high spirits, as we were getting closer to our beloved home in America. On the day of our arrival in Boston, I wrote the following entry in my diary:

USO tug in Boston harbor welcoming us home (November 1945)

"Dear Diary:

Sunday, November 25, 1945 "Good Old USA."

I got up at 0400, had breakfast, packed and went on deck. At seven o'clock we entered Boston Harbor, when a launch came out to meet us. On it was a sign reading "Welcome Home— Well Done," and on it were two bands and USO entertainers. Our ship's whistle and the whistles on all the other ships in the harbor began sounding off. Everyone was on deck cheering and waving, and it was really a thrill. We were home at last. We debarked at noon. The ARC served us doughnuts and a pint of fresh milk.

At 1330 we boarded a train in the terminal building, and in an hour, we were at Camp Miles Standish, thirty-five miles from Boston. We were assigned to a barracks, then took a long-needed bath, dressed in clean clothes, and had a good meal.

Tonight I made a phone call to home, and I finally located the entire family at Amie's house. I talked to Mom and Dad and my siblings for only fifteen minutes because all telephone circuits were so busy with soldiers calling their homes. This was a wonderful evening of hearing the voices of my loved ones again. At midnight, I went to bed on a wonderful mattress, springs, and sheets, but it was so soft that I couldn't get to sleep for an hour. Home at last, but I still can't believe it. I'm in a daze."

Deck of troopship jammed with GIs for glimse
of Boston. Home at last! (November 1945)

I had a wonderful night's sleep, and on Monday, my first day back in America, it was hard to convince myself that I was indeed back to my home country, where everything was so quiet and peaceful and no destruction of buildings and cities, no refugees and displaced persons, and no people begging for food and clothing. America truly was a country bountifully blessed by God, and returning soldiers and American citizens were thankful as churches were filled with worshippers. My thoughts all day were about my family at home in Clintonville, and I counted the few hours until I would see and hug them with tears of joy. I knew that today Mom would be on the telephone all day, calling her sisters and friends to say that she had talked to me by phone last night, and that I would be home by the weekend. Besides doing lots of happy talk with her friends, Mom would be planning the menu for my big homecoming dinner.

As all of my thoughts swirled about my reunion with my loved ones, I learned from my Captain that I was assigned the job of being a group leader in charge of eight men from Wisconsin who were headed to Fort Sheridan. I carried all their records and arranged for shipment of their baggage. On

November 27, I got up early in order to take the train to Chicago. We traveled through Rhode Island and Connecticut to New York City, then north along the Hudson river to Albany. The second day we traveled through New York state, Pennsylvania, Ohio, and Indiana, arriving in Chicago at 6:30 in the evening on November 28. We stopped in the Chicago freight yards, where we spent a sleepless night sitting in a seat in the day coach that we were assigned to.

At 5:00 a.m. on Thursday morning, November 29, the train left the freight yards and passed through the Chicago Loop to our final destination at Fort Sheridan, located in the northern suburb of Highland Park. Upon our arrival at the camp at 6:00 a.m., several hundred soldiers stepped off the train, and we all were ushered into a large hall where coffee and doughnuts were served followed by a welcome lecture. Later, we enjoyed a big breakfast in the mess hall after which we started our discharge processing. An officer took the records of the men that I was carrying, and I turned in most of my clothing and equipment to the supply department. I kept for myself one set of casual and one set of dress uniforms, including my Eisenhower jacket, which was adorned with patches, hash marks, and medals, and my wool overcoat and combat boots. Finally, we were assigned to a barracks, and I made a telephone call to Mom and Dad. It was a very happy conversation, and my reunion with my family was now only a few hours away, so the anticipation was overwhelming.

The next day was devoted to numerous activities concerning the final processing of our Separation Group, which numbered about a hundred soldiers. There was an orientation lecture about returning to civilian life, a final physical examination, counseling, listening to a talk about the GI Bill of Rights and the army life insurance coverage during our time of active duty, and the problems that we would encounter during our adjustment to civilian life.

Saturday, December 1, 1945: Honorable Discharge

The day I had longed for had finally arrived. There was a quick "show down" inspection of everyone's belongings during which the Army took away all unauthorized clothing and equipment. At ten o'clock I signed the final papers for my discharge and received my final pay, along with various ribbons that I had earned. A "homing pigeon" patch was sewed above the right pocket of my jacket, and I got two "ruptured duck" lapel buttons too. These were humorous items that were fun to talk about and were created to describe the final service of a soldier upon his discharge from the army.

At 11:30, there was a final ceremony conducted by the Camp's Chaplain, who gave a short talk after which we sang a hymn. Then, an Army Captain presented each of us with that most coveted document, the "Honorable Discharge." This was a very proud moment for me and a great satisfaction that I had had the privilege of having served honorably in the US Army for the greatest nation on earth. Then there was the final farewell to buddies with hugs and handshakes and slaps on the backs. At noon I walked out of the main gate at Fort Sheridan, Illinois—a very happy *civilian*!

At the train station in Highland Park, I bought a ticket at a soldier's discount. Along with my fully packed duffle bag that contained my souvenirs, Army clothing, and all my earthly possessions, I found a seat on the coach of the Chicago and Northwestern Railroad for the joyous trip north to Wisconsin. I changed trains in Milwaukee and took the local train that stopped in Oshkosh before I arrived in Clintonville at 9:00 p.m.

Dad and my brother Amie were waiting at the station, along with other families who were meeting their loved ones. We exchanged big hugs and tears on the platform. Fifteen minutes later, Amie was driving into the long driveway that led to our farmhouse on the north side of Clintonville. Mom was already on the porch and down the steps by the time I opened the car door. My sister-in-law Leone was right behind her. Hugs and tears lasted a long time, and this moment of endearment seemed more like a dream than a reality. Our family talked late into the night as I unpacked my duffle bag and showed off my army souvenirs. Mom set the table and put out freshly baked bread along with butter and strawberry jam, while Dad fetched some fresh milk from the milk house. I slept in my own bedroom, which overlooked the barn, sheds and the fields beyond, the room which Mom had kept as it was the day I entered service three years earlier. Home sweet home—at last! Oh, it was so good to be home, and I fell asleep with a prayer on my lips giving heartfelt thanks to my God for his unfathomable protection during my absence from my family, and for my safe return home to this wonderful reunion with my loving family that God had also kept in good health and safety.

The next morning I went to church with Mom and Dad, dressed in my regular suit with a white shirt and a tie, this being my first day as a civilian again. When Pastor Walter O. Speckhard noticed that I had returned home, he walked down the aisle and welcomed me back. After the service relatives and friends gathered around me, and everyone expressed their thankfulness and happiness for my safe return.

Sunday dinner was a big spread that Mom and Dad prepared. Mom made roast beef, mashed potatoes and gravy, and many vegetables. Dad served wine on this special day of homecoming. My brother Amie and his wife Leone, Uncle Paul and Aunt Hattie, Uncle Emil and Aunt Olga, and seven of my cousins were there too. There was much talk and my relatives asked many questions while joy and thankfulness reined in everyone's heart. God was good and to be praised for my safe return. The mantra that I had chosen at the beginning of my military service, "Be strong and courageous. Do not be terrified; do not be discouraged, for the LORD your God will be with you wherever you go," was fulfilled.

My new life, with its exciting dreams and plans, had just begun.

Acknowledgements

MY ORIGINAL PURPOSE FOR WRITING these memoirs was to share my legacy with my grandchildren. However, as more people heard about my plan, they expressed their own interest in reading them, so I decided to publish this book so all people could read about my military life.

These memoirs are principally the published history of the XX Corps of the United States Army in World War II and give details of my daily duties and life with the XX Corps Headquarters during the three years that I served with this unit. I also kept a daily diary in which I recorded my activities and experiences. The XX Corps was activated as a new military organization in late 1942. I joined the unit in February 1943 and remained with them until I was discharged after the war ended. The XX Corps Headquarters personnel were a closely knit group of soldiers, and the enlisted men and the officers, including the Commanding General, interacted with each other daily, which resulted in a smoothly running organization and a closely knit family.

These memoirs were written through the encouragement of my grandson, Benjamin Schulz, who as a teenager was interested in World War II history and loved to hear the "war stories" that I frequently told him. He urged me to write about my experiences in the U.S. Army and to document my training in army camps and my combat adventures in Europe, which eventually resulted in this manuscript. His frequent reminders to keep writing made me get the job done.

Ben majored in English in college, and he graciously volunteered to edit this book, for which I am eternally grateful. My granddaughter, Emily Schulz, who also majored in English, was very helpful in the final editing process.

I am indebted to one of the soldiers in our office, Jay Ottoson, who was a journalist at *The Miami Herald* before he entered the U.S. Army. His assignment was to gather the facts and the news of the XX Corps and its personnel and write the history of our unit, together with other Corps' personnel. Jay and I became good friends, and because he had close connections with the Third Army Headquarters, he took my exposed films to their photographic laboratory for processing. Many of the pictures which I took with my own camera are included in this book.

I thank my wife, Eleanore, who was very generous and patient with her time while I was doing the research and the writing of this manuscript. I am most grateful to her for doing the "first read" and making corrections and changes along with suggestions regarding its contents. She had heard many of these war stories during our married life, and her insight regarding my writing of the events was invaluable.

EGS

SELECTED BIBLIOGRAPHY

American History, Vol. XXIX, No. 2, Harrisburg, PA: Cowles Magazines, Inc., 1994.

Butler, D. A. *Warrior Queens, The Queen Mary and Queen Elizabeth in World War II*, South Yorkshire, UK: Leo Cooper, an imprint of Pen & Sword Books, Ltd., 2002.

D-Day and the Battle of Normandy, Cully, France: OREP Editions 2003.

Eisenhower, General Dwight D. *The Churchill I Knew*, National Geographic Magazine, August 1965.

Henley, Brig. General David C., *The Land That God Forgot: The Saga of Gen. George Patton's Desert Training Camps*, Fallon, NV: Lahontan Valley Printing, Inc., Western American History Series, 1989.

Hirshon, Stanley P., *General Patton, A Soldier's Life*, New York, NY: HarperCollins Publishers Inc., 2002.

LaFay, Howard, *Be Ye Men of Valour*, National Geographic Magazine, August 1965.

Lost Civilizations, *Early Europe: Mysteries in Stone*, Alexandria, Virginia: Time-Life Books, 1995.

Newsweek, May 23, 1994, D-Day Eyewitness to the Invasion, 1994.

Operational Terms and Graphics, Field Manual No. 101-5-1, Marine Corps Reference Publication No. MCRP 5-2A, Headquarters, Department of the Army, United States Marine Corps, Washington, D. C., 30 September 1997.

Reynolds, Quentin, *Winston Churchill*, New York, NY: Random House, 1963.

The Battle of Normandy: Official Guide of the D-Day Landings and the Battle of Normandy, Paris, France: Gallimard Guides, Editions les Nouveaux-Loisirs, 1994.

The Queen Mary, *The Official Pictorial History*, Text by Robert O. Maguglin, Albion Publishing Group, Santa Barbara, CA, 1985, Third Edition 1993.

The Stars and Stripes, Daily Newspaper of U.S. Armed Forces in the European Theater of Operations, 1944–1945 (source of various subjects).

The XX Corps: Its History and Service in World War II, Published by the XX Corps Association, Printed by the Mainichi Publishing Co., Ltd., Osaka, Japan, 1946 (prepared and written by XX Corps personnel).

Thomas, Cameron, *Remembering the Blitz*, National Geographic Magazine, July 1991.

Wikipedia.org (source of various subjects).

Yank, The Army Weekly. Weekly publication by the enlisted men of the U.S. Army, European Editions, 1944–1945 (source of various subjects).

EPILOG

THE READER OF THESE MEMOIRS may be interested in "the rest of the story" regarding several of the characters and the military organizations that are the core of this soldier's war stories and his military service during the three years he served in World War II.

XX Corps, United States Army

The Headquarters of the XX Corps remained in Tutzing, Germany, until the end of 1945. The original members of the Headquarters staff gradually departed for home and eventual discharge, and others were deployed to other military organizations. The duties of the XX Corps personnel involved compiling records and documenting historical information for the archives of the U.S. Army.

The mission of the XX Corps in World War II had been accomplished, and its actions and battles are recorded in history. The Ghost Corps was an exemplary military organization, and its accomplishments of service and victories in battle will forever be its legacy in the European struggle to defeat the tyrants who had tried to conquer the world.

In January 1946, the duties of the XX Corps were turned over to the 9th Infantry Division. A huge farewell parade was held in Tutzing on February 28, which had been its home since June 1945. The deactivation of the XX Corps was completed on March 1, 1946.

Third Army of the United States

The Third Army became the army of occupation of the U.S. Zone in Germany following the surrender of the Nazi Government in May 1945. General Patton retained command of the Third Army following its merger with the Seventh

Army. These two armies became the combined occupational force in southern Germany.

Patton, however, was unhappy with his new duties of overseeing a "paper army" rather than an "action army" of fighting men. He turned over his Third Army to a new commander, Lt. General Lucian K. Truscott, and its headquarters were moved from Bad Tolz to Heidelberg. Truscott relinquished his command due to ill health, and Lt. General Geoffrey Keyes, former commander of the Seventh Army, became the new leader of the Third Army.

On February 15, 1947, the occupational and operational responsibilities of the Third Army were phased out and its role in post-war Germany ended. The Headquarters returned to the United States and moved to Fort McPherson, Georgia. Twenty-six years later, on October 1, 1973, the U.S. Third Army was inactivated.

General Walton H. Walker

On April 27, 1945, eleven days before the end of the war in the ETO, Walton Harris Walker received his third star, giving him the rank of Lieutenant General. Patton was present at the ceremony, where he personally pinned the three stars on Walker, the same stars that Eisenhower had given to Patton when he had been promoted to Lieutenant General.

On May 21, 1945, Walker relinquished command of the XX Corps and returned to the United States for reassignment. In 1946, Walker assumed the command of the Fifth Army, which had its headquarters in Chicago. Three years later, in 1948, Walker was assigned to be the commanding general of the Eighth Army, which was the American Army of Occupation in Japan, whose mission was to enforce the terms of the Japanese surrender.

When the Korean War broke out in 1950, General Douglas MacArthur, the Supreme Allied Commander in Japan, ordered Walker to take his Eighth Army to Korea to fight the North Korean invaders of South Korea. Walker's American Eighth Army, along with the South Korean Army, was engaged in very difficult fighting with the North Korean and Chinese soldiers throughout the year. On December 23, 1950, General Walker was riding in his command jeep on his way to Seoul to participate in a ceremony to present military awards to soldiers. His vehicle was traveling at high speed when it collided with a civilian truck. Walker died from the impact.

Walker's son, Lieutenant Sam S. Walker, who was also serving in Korea, escorted his father's body back to the United States for burial at Arlington National Cemetery on January 2, 1951. Walton Harris Walker was posthumously promoted to a four-star general. In Europe during World War II, Patton gave Walker the nickname of "Bulldog," and the U.S. Army named a newly developed light tank the "M41 Walker Bulldog." Walker received many honors and battle citations during his service and after his death.

General George S. Patton, Jr.

After the war ended on May 8, 1945, Patton indulged in some R&R while he stayed in a palace near Regensburg, Germany, in Bavaria. In June, Patton returned to America for a brief visit to Los Angeles, where he, along with Army Air Forces Lt. Gen. Jimmy Doolittle, was honored with a huge parade through the city. General Doolittle had been the leader of a squadron of sixteen B-25 medium bombers that were launched from the aircraft carrier *USS Hornet* and bombed targets in Japan. This "Doolittle Raid" occurred on April 18, 1942.

After the parade, a huge reception for the two generals took place at the Los Angeles Memorial Coliseum before a crowd of over one hundred thousand people. The next day Patton gave a speech in front of the Burbank City Hall and at the Rose Bowl in Pasadena. This trip turned out to be the last time that Patton was in his native country.

During the summer of 1945, Patton became the military governor of Bavaria, and his duties involved the restoration of civilian governments in the towns and villages. This work included the screening of German civilians to find former Nazi sympathizers and to locate former people with trade skills like bakers and butchers to help re-establish their former businesses. It was also imperative for U.S. Military Government to restore electricity, water supply, and sewage treatment. Patton, however, had little aptitude for this kind of work, and he was very unhappy with this role. He was relieved of his command of the Third Army and his administration of military government on October 7, 1945.

The next day, Patton traveled to the small resort town of Bad Nauheim, north of Frankfurt, to receive his new assignment. He was named the Commander of the U.S. Fifteenth Army, which was a paper command whose assignment was to study, analyze, and chronicle the strategies of battles used in the European Theater of Operations.

Patton went to Paris in October where the French Ministry of War honored him with a special luncheon, and General Charles de Gaulle made a speech comparing him to Napoleon. Several weeks later, Patton traveled to Stockholm, where he gave a speech before the Swedish-American Society and received high honors from the Swedish Army.

On December 7, Patton received orders to go to Paris and make arrangements to travel back home to The States. However, two days later, on Sunday the 9th, Patton decided to go pheasant hunting with Major General Hobart R. "Hap" Gay, Patton's Chief of Staff. Patton, Gay, their driver, and Patton's dog Willie were traveling in their 1938 Cadillac on the autobahn near Mannheim, Germany, about fifty miles south of Frankfurt. An American soldier, who was driving a 2 ½ ton GMC Signal Corps truck, made a sudden turn and collided with the Cadillac, shoving it down an embankment. The collision smashed the Cadillac's radiator and pushed the motor into the dash. Gay and the driver had only minor injuries, but Patton was thrown forward, causing his head to strike a metal partition between the front and backseats. Patton was rushed to a military hospital in Heidelberg, twenty miles away.

He was conscious but in severe traumatic shock. The impact caused a severe cervical spinal cord injury, and he was paralyzed from the neck down. Patton died on December 21, 1945, twelve days after the accident, at the age of sixty. His funeral was held at Christuskirche (Christ Church) in Heidelberg. He was buried at the Luxembourg American cemetery in Hamm. His gravesite is unique because it is placed at the head of this cemetery, and all of its 5,076 graves fan out beyond Patton's grave. These were Patton's beloved boys, and most of them died in the Battle of the Bulge, only a few miles north of this cemetery.

Statue of General George Patton and his dog, Willie, at the Patton Museum in California

Colonel Welborn B. Griffith, Jr.

Colonel Griffith was the G-3, or Operations Officer, of the XX Corps, whose duties included developing the plans of battle for all military units that were attached to the XX Corps. The XX Corps was one of the Corps that was part of General George Patton's Third Army. The XX Corps and the Third Army entered combat on August 1, 1944. Colonel Griffith was my boss, and I had worked for him for eighteen months.

Chapter 15 relates the story of Griffith's search of the Cathedral de Notre Dame de Chartres in the city of Chartres, France, on the morning of August 16, 1944. The American artillery had an order to shell and destroy the cathedral because it was suspected that German soldiers were occupying it and using the twin towers as observation posts. Griffith was disturbed when he heard that this beautiful edifice was about to be destroyed, and he took it upon himself, and without regard for his own safety, to make a reconnaissance of the cathedral to determine if this rumor was true. Upon finding no enemy soldiers there, he immediately informed the artillery battalion to rescind their order to shell it, and thus this beautiful structure was saved from destruction.

Griffith then left the cathedral and went to the village of Lèves, a suburb of Chartres, where he joined a tank crew, and while he was riding on the tank, they encountered a German roadblock and machinegun nest. Griffith was killed by enemy fire. On the day of his death in 1944, while I was back at Corps Headquarters, I did not hear any of the details of how he died. However, in the fall of 2011, while surfing the internet, I found the family of Colonel Griffith, and after meeting in person with his daughter, I learned the details of that fateful day.

I logged onto the web site of *National Review on Line* where I found a letter that was written by the husband of Colonel Griffith's granddaughter, in which he related the story of how the Cathedral of Chartres was saved from destruction through the efforts of the Colonel, and who then was killed several hours later while riding on a tank. This article was an exciting discovery which led me to finding the daughter of the Colonel, Alice Griffith Irving. She was the Colonel's only child, and she was thirteen years old at the time of his death.

I met Alice soon after finding her family on the internet, and for several days, we shared information and memories about her father who was my boss in the army for eighteen months until the day he died. Welborn Barton Griffith Jr. was born on November 10, 1901, in Quanah, Texas. He graduated from West Point Military Academy, Class of 1925. While he was at the Academy, he excelled in various sports, including four years as a tackle on the Army football team. He also participated in boxing, wrestling, lacrosse, and horsemanship. Alice told me the story of his heroic exploits on the last day of his life.

On that fateful day of August 16, 1944, Colonel Griffith and his jeep driver entered the city of Chartres and drove to the Cathedral de Notre Dame de Chartres. He found several soldiers shooting randomly at the cathedral, but there was no returning enemy fire. He questioned the soldiers, and they insisted that there were enemy snipers in the spires of the edifice, so the Colonel walked through the cathedral and found no German soldiers in the nave and side

Chartres Cathedral, Chartres, France

chapels. Next, he decided to climb the many steps of the two steeples and told the American soldiers on the street outside the cathedral, "I'm going up into the top of the spire. I'll ring the bell and put out a flag. If I don't ring the bell after a while, you attack." It was not long when the bell rang, and the American flag waved from the belfry. Griffith climbed down and notified the artillery to rescind their order to destroy the cathedral. He and his driver then headed for the village of Lèves on the outskirts of Chartres.

Alice had a document which was a daily journal of events that were written by a French Catholic priest who was in Chartres on the day the cathedral was saved from destruction. This priest lived at a monastery in a town located about seventeen miles from Chartres. It was his turn to go to Chartres Cathedral to hold masses and perform his usual pastoral acts at the Seminary, hospitals, and at vespers during his appointed stay of eleven days. When he arrived safely in Chartres, he was welcomed by the Monsignor at the Seminary, where he stayed during these days.

The priest described the shelling and the fires during the night of August 15, because the American tanks were now inside the city and their troops were engaged in fierce street fighting with the enemy. Sleep was impossible that night. The priest wrote a long account in his journal on Wednesday, August 16. The following excerpts, translated from French, are from that day's entry in which he describes his eyewitness account of the events at the Cathedral of Chartres.

"I just learned that the cathedral has been hit, at least the 'new' bell tower on the north side.

I saw for myself a passerby carrying away a big piece of sculpture. It's said that the Germans were shooting out of vandalism. According to others, it's the Americans who were told that enemy soldiers were in the bell towers. We see in front of the iron gate of the Prefecture all the Americans, the crowd which is gathering, the flowers that are offered, and the flags that are unfurled.

At this same moment, rapid rifle shots on the Place de la Cathedral, an exchange of machine gun fire which seems to be coming from the small garden in front of the school. We go back inside the cathedral to go down by way of the sacristy to the crypt. But the door that leads down to the crypt is locked, so we are going to stay put and see what happens next.

Suddenly, the gunfire becomes more intense, reverberating a hundred fold in the cathedral, then commotion and men's voices. Some Americans have come in by way of the north door and cross the cathedral toward the south door, rifles in their hands, helmeted and out of breath. This manhunt in a holy place shocks and scares us.

What if the Americans, thinking we are Germans hidden here, start shooting at us without any explanation as soon as they see two heads? What should we do? We can't get out of here. This will certainly be the most difficult moment of our liberation, this quarter hour, between 11:30 and noon that we are spending here. A civilian that came into the cathedral with the Americans explains to us that there are Germans in the bell towers who are shooting from above. The Americans, having found the guardian, forced him to open the doorway which gives access to the towers and they have gone looking for snipers. A while ago, the occupying authority had demanded the keys to the bell towers and had forbidden anyone access.

An American soldier, armed with a carbine, is posted at the corner of the little Rue aux Herbes, and is shooting in the direction of the bell towers. He undoubtedly doesn't know that there are Americans in the gallery and he risks shooting at the first head he sees up there. Having seen us signaling to him, he runs over to the entrance of the south door, and finally understands that there are not just Germans, if there are any, up in the bell towers, but also American soldiers in pursuit of them. After this laborious warning, we return to the Seminary as they have been impatiently awaiting our arrival."

This terse, eyewitness account of the priest who actually was inside Chartres Cathedral on August 16, mentions the American soldier who climbed the bell towers just before noon. Undoubtedly, this American soldier was Colonel Griffith!

After Griffith had sent a message to the artillery group to withdraw the order to destroy it, he and his driver drove their jeep to the village of Lèves, a suburb of Chartres, on the main road to Paris. He encountered a patrol of about fifteen German troops at a roadblock who were holding up the advance of our troops. He returned fire with his M-1 and sped back looking for help. He found a tank from the 7th Armored Division which was patrolling the town and told the sergeant of the tank crew to proceed to the place where he had encountered the enemy.

Colonel Griffith was a big man and wasn't able to squeeze into the tank's turret, so he sat on the back of the tank behind the turret as they drove through the streets of Lèves. He carried a rifle in his right hand and a pistol in his left. During the tank's advance, they were subjected to intense machine gun, rifle, and rocket launcher fire, and the Colonel died instantly from the five bullets that pierced his back. He fell off the tank and laid in the street.

Griffith's body lying on the street in Leves, France (August 1944)

(Photo courtesy of Alice Griffith Irving)

There were eyewitnesses of this ambush who told Alice what they had seen when she met them years later. Two French boys quickly carried his body out of the street and placed it on the sidewalk. The residents covered the body with a blanket, flowers, and an old American flag that a French family had hidden in their home. Then the villagers brought chairs to the shrine and held a vigil through the night until the next morning when American troops picked up his body.

XX Corps staff officers made arrangements for the funeral, and they searched for a mortician and an appropriate casket in the city of Chartres. He was buried in a farm field along with other fallen soldiers, located at Savigny-sur-Braye, about fifty miles southwest of Chartres. His funeral was conducted by the XX Corps Chaplain, and he was buried with full military honors.

Several years following the end of World War II, a French resident of the town of Lèves, Bertrand Papillon, established a small, historical military museum with items going back to the Crusades. Later, he added the story of the American colonel who had saved Chartres Cathedral from destruction. Mr. Papillon was an adolescent in 1944 and had personally witnessed some of these events. As an adult he had collected eyewitness accounts, but he wanted to know more about the American soldier who died on the street in Lèves.

In 1961, a plaque was placed on the wall of a house on the street where Griffith was killed. His dog tags read: "Griffith Welborn." So the French people thought his last name was Welborn. They put these

Original plaque in Leves, France

(Photo courtesy of Alice Griffith Irving)

words on the plaque: "Le Colonel Americain Welburn." They used his given name, but misspelled it.

Bertrand Papillon had a love of history, and he wanted to know more about the American Colonel who had died in the liberation of his village. Inspired by the fiftieth Anniversary of D-Day in 1994, he attempted to find the Colonel's family in the United States, so he wrote a letter which found its way to the National Personnel Records Center in St. Louis. A notice was placed in the military magazine *"U. S. Retired Officer"* in a section called "In Search of." Nell Griffith, the Colonel's widow, who lived in North Carolina at that time, by chance saw her husband's name in the ad that requested information about him. Mr. Papillon had successfully made contact with the Griffith family and thus found a new wealth of information for his museum. A new plaque, with the Colonel's name corrected, was made from stone from the same quarry that had provided stones for Chartres Cathedral.

Corrected plaque in Leves, France
(Photo courtesy of Alice Griffith Irving)

August 16, 1995, was the fifty-first anniversary of the death of Colonel Welborn B. Griffith Jr. Monsieur Papillon and the citizens of Lèves planned a ceremony to dedicate the corrected plaque and place it on the building on the street where he died. Alice and her husband Fred, as well as several members of her family, were invited to the ceremonies as guests of honor. The memorial service was held in the Cathedral de Notre Dame de Chartres. The Griffith family entered through the Portail Royal of the cathedral, which is only opened for dignitaries, heads of state, and for church festivals. The *"Star Spangled Banner"* was played on the great organ for the first time in its 850 year history, and the Dean of the Cathedral, Canon Legaux, made a speech which praised the courage and bravery of Colonel Griffith on that fateful day when he saved the cathedral. The Canon cited this quote from the French statesman and author, André Malraux, "The only tomb worthy of a hero is in the hearts of the living." The Dean said, "That is true today as we keep in our hearts the name of Colonel Welborn Griffith."

Several years later, the village of Lèves established a small park which they dedicated to the memory of Colonel Griffith. It was located at the tip of a hill where he died at the enemy roadblock.

Colonel Welborn Barton Griffith Jr. was posthumously awarded the Distinguished Service Cross by the President of the United States, "for extraordinary heroism in connection with military operations against an armed enemy while serving as Operations Officer (G-3) with Headquarters, XX Corps, in action against enemy forces on August 16, 1944, at Chartres and Lèves, France."

Griffith received another posthumous award, the Silver Star, "for conspicuous gallantry and intrepidity in action against the enemy in World War II. Colonel Griffith's gallant actions and dedicated devotion to duty, without regard for his own life, were in keeping with the highest traditions of military service and reflect great credit upon himself, his unit, and the United States Army."

The Colonel also received these citations: the French Croix de Guerre avec Palm, the Legion of Honor, the Legion of Merit, and the Purple Heart.

I am honored and humbled to have been so closely associated with this hero, who was my boss and mentor from the first day I reported to him as a new army recruit at the Desert Training Center in Camp Young, California, until the day he was killed in action in Chartres, France. The Colonel, who was twenty-two years older than I was, exhibited a gentle manner, and he was very kind to me. He influenced the shaping of my character and instilled in me the virtues of respect, discipline, honesty, duty, and a deep human concern for my fellow soldiers.

Colonel Welborn B. Griffith, Jr.
(Photo courtesy of Alice Griffith Irving)

Joseph M. Messner

I met Joe Messner the day I arrived at Camp Young, California, in the Desert Training Center. I was the new recruit who had been sent there from Fort Sheridan with a group of guys from Wisconsin and Upper Michigan. I was assigned to the G-3 Section of the IV Armored Corps, the predecessor organization of the XX Corps. Joe had arrived several weeks earlier, and he was the draftsman in G-3, whose duties included the drawing of war maps.

Joe and I became very close during the three years that we served together. We were sent on detached service to Fort Leonard Wood to be umpires for the field maneuvers of an infantry division. We slept in a custom-designed double tent that was our home during the XX Corps' sweep across northern France. We shared personal information about our families and each other's thoughts about many subjects.

When the war ended, we were both discharged back to civilian life. Joe went home to Pittsburgh, married his fiancé Mildred, and raised a family. He had an engineering job at one of the large steel mills in Pittsburgh. I enrolled at the University of Wisconsin in Madison and earned two degrees in Business Administration. I met my future wife Eleanore there, and eventually we got married and raised a family. Throughout the following years, Joe and I kept in touch by writing letters to each other, especially at Christmas time, and we continued to share news about our respective families.

In 1991, Eleanore and I planned a motor trip to the East Coast, and we decided to travel through Pittsburgh. Joe and Mildred welcomed us into their home for a wonderful visit. Joe and I reminisced for many hours, recalling precious memories and looking at photos and memorabilia of the three years we spent together at XX Corps Headquarters. We had not seen each other for forty-six years so this was a wonderful reunion of two war buddies.

Several years after this visit with Joe, I received a letter from his daughter informing me that her father had passed away suddenly from a heart attack. I mourned the death of my buddy Joe, who was a great warrior and my dear friend.

Author (left) with Joe Messner (1991)

Index

Edwards Brothers Malloy
Thorofare, NJ USA
May 5, 2014